Getting into Medical School

FOR

A Wiley Brand

by Carleen Eaton, MD

FOR

DUMMIES

A Wiley Brand

Getting into Medical School For Dummies®

Published by
John Wiley & Sons, Inc.
111 River St.
Hoboken, NJ 07030-5774
www.wiley.com

For general information on our other products and services, please contact our Customer Care Department within the U.S. at 877-762-2974, outside the U.S. at 317-572-3993, or fax 317-572-4002.

For technical support, please visit www.wiley.com/techsupport.

Wiley publishes in a variety of print and electronic formats and by print-on-demand. Some material included with standard print versions of this book may not be included in e-books or in print-on-demand. If this book refers to media such as a CD or DVD that is not included in the version you purchased, you may download this material at http://booksupport.wiley.com. For more information about Wiley products, visit www.wiley.com.

Library of Congress Control Number: 2013934915

ISBN 978-1-118-42427-8 (pbk); ISBN 978-1-118-46004-7 (ebk); ISBN 978-1-118-46006-1 (ebk); ISBN 978-1-118-46008-5 (ebk)

Manufactured in the United States of America

10 9 8 7 6 5 4 3 2 1

About the Author

Carleen Eaton, MD, is a graduate of the UCLA School of Medicine and the founder of prehealthadvising.com, an admissions consulting firm specializing in helping applicants to health professions programs. She has used her expertise in admissions and test preparation as well as her experiences as an applicant who received acceptances to top-ranked medical schools to guide hundreds of applicants successfully through the medical school admissions process. She was a guest on a National Public Radio segment discussing medical school interviews and has spoken to groups at colleges and universities about medical school admissions topics such as the personal statement and the medical school application timeline.

Dr. Eaton was an award-winning instructor and medical school admissions consultant at a national test preparation company. During her tenure, she focused on students preparing for the MCAT and other health professions admissions examinations and advised medical school applicants. She has also developed and taught a biology lecture series that is featured at the online educational site Educator.com. Prior to medical school, Dr. Eaton received her bachelor of science in microbiology and molecular genetics from UCLA and did research in the field of infectious diseases at the West Los Angeles VA Medical Center. She currently lives in Southern California with her husband, two daughters, a toy poodle, and a cat.

Dedication

For Matt.

Author's Acknowledgments

Thank you to everyone at Wiley who played a role in taking this book from concept to completion. Senior Acquisitions Editor Tracy Boggier found me at just the right time and worked to make this project possible. Senior Project Editor Georgette Beatty gave me invaluable advice and kept me on track throughout the writing process. Technical Editor Rachel Tolen provided a knowledgeable review of the material, and Copy Editor Megan Knoll helped to put a final polish on my prose. I also appreciate the hard work of Senior Project Editor Chrissy Guthrie, Copy Editor Christy Pingleton, the Composition department, and everyone behind the scenes who contributed to *Getting into Medical School For Dummies*.

Writing this book would have been impossible without the support of my family. My husband, Matt, has always encouraged me through his faith in my ability to accomplish more and better things. He also kept the home front running while I spent every spare moment (and many not-so-spare ones) on my computer. My parents, Tony and Mary Martinich, cheered me on and were always there to lend a hand. My daughters, Madeline and Betsy, made sure that life remained lively during this endeavor and inspire me as I watch them discover their own potential.

Publisher's Acknowledgments

We're proud of this book; please send us your comments at `http://dummies.custhelp.com`. For other comments, please contact our Customer Care Department within the U.S. at 877-762-2974, outside the U.S. at 317-572-3993, or fax 317-572-4002.

Some of the people who helped bring this book to market include the following:

Acquisitions, Editorial, and Vertical Websites

Senior Project Editor: Georgette Beatty

Senior Acquisitions Editor: Tracy Boggier

Copy Editor: Megan Knoll

Assistant Editor: David Lutton

Editorial Program Coordinator: Joe Niesen

Technical Editor: Rachel Tolen

Editorial Manager: Michelle Hacker

Editorial Assistant: Alexa Koschier

Cover Photo: © EricHood/iStockphoto.com

Composition Services

Senior Project Coordinator: Kristie Rees

Layout and Graphics: Carrie A. Cesavice, Jennifer Creasey, Joyce Haughey

Proofreader: Cynthia Fields

Indexer: Christine Karpeles

Special Help
Christina Guthrie, Christine Pingleton

Publishing and Editorial for Consumer Dummies

    Kathleen Nebenhaus, Vice President and Executive Publisher

    David Palmer, Associate Publisher

    Kristin Ferguson-Wagstaffe, Product Development Director

Publishing for Technology Dummies

    Andy Cummings, Vice President and Publisher

Composition Services

    Debbie Stailey, Director of Composition Services

Contents at a Glance

Table of Contents

Introduction

● ●

*G*etting into Medical School For Dummies is a guide for anyone who's considering a medical career, whether you're having your first thoughts about entering medicine or are in the midst of putting together your application package for medical school. In this book, aspiring physicians can find help on everything from making the decision to become a doctor to managing the premedical years and the application process to getting off to a great start in medical school.

The road leading from premedical student to medical student is a long one, but knowing what to expect each step of the way helps you succeed and makes the journey less stressful. Use this book as your road map to lead you through the bumpy parts of the path to achieving your goal of getting into medical school.

Read on to discover what getting accepted to medical school takes and how to approach each step of the application process. You'll also find information about many other topics to help you someday join the rewarding, challenging, and noble profession of medicine.

About This Book

I wrote this book as someone who is an MD and a medical school admissions advisor. I drew both on my experiences as a former applicant to medical school and on a decade of experience (so far) advising students who are striving for admission to medical school. I know what juggling a heavy load of premedical courses, filling out endless application essays, and going through nerve-wracking med school admissions interviews is like, and I keep these experiences in mind with every tip, thought, and bit of guidance I give you.

Getting into Medical School For Dummies also stands out as a resource for future physicians because

   ✔ **It's thorough.** I cover not only nuts-and-bolts topics related to applying to medical school (such as writing a compelling personal statement, obtaining strong letters of recommendation, and nailing the admission interview) but also many other related subjects (such as dual-degree programs, osteopathic [DO] medical schools, paying for your medical education, and preparing for medical school).

✔ **It's clear.** In classic *For Dummies* style, this book is logically structured, organized, and easy to follow. This book helps you understand what you need to do as well as when and how to do it in order to get admitted to med school. (Keep in mind that you don't have to read this book from cover to cover; you can read only what you want and put the book away until you need it again.)

✔ **It's practical.** I focus on giving you hands-on, how-to guidance to help you achieve your goal of admission to medical school. I go far beyond simply describing the application process; I also lead you through each step.

✔ **It's written for applicants from many different backgrounds.** This book is for applicants in any situation, not just traditional applicants. Some applicants plan to go straight from college to medical school; others take time off between the two phases of their education. Many applicants are trying for a seat in medical school for the first time; others are reapplying after unsuccessful initial attempts.

Conventions Used in This Book

To help you get the most out of this book, I use a few standard conventions:

✔ Some of the terms related to the medical school admissions process may be unfamiliar to you. I put new terms in *italics* the first time that I use them so that they stand out, and then I explain the meaning of each term in the context of medical school admissions.

✔ I use **bold** text to highlight keywords in bulleted lists and the action parts of numbered steps.

✔ In some sections I provide you with web addresses so that you can look up resources related to topics discussed in the book; these addresses appear in `monofont`. Certain addresses may have needed to break across two lines of text when this book was printed. If that happened, I haven't put in any extra characters (such as hyphens) to indicate the break. Simply type in the web address exactly as you see it in this book, pretending as though the line break doesn't exist.

What You're Not to Read

As you read this book, you may notice that some of the text is placed in a box with a shaded background. These boxes are called *sidebars* and may include examples or other information that you may find interesting but that isn't essential to the topic at hand. Other bits of text are marked with the Technical Stuff icon. If you skip any of these items, you won't miss out on anything critical and will still be able to easily follow the rest of the text.

Foolish Assumptions

If you're reading this book, I assume that you have an interest in a medical career. Because med students have so many different journeys to the profession, that's about all I can assume with certainty. That said, I'm guessing at least one of the following applies to you:

- ✔ You're still at the very early stages of your exploration of the medical profession.
- ✔ You're already committed to becoming a physician.
- ✔ You're gearing up to apply for medical school soon or are even in the midst of the application process already.

One thing I don't assume is that you're familiar with specific types of programs such as dual-degree programs or osteopathic medical schools, so the chapters focusing on special types of programs begin with a general description to give you the foundation you need before I delve deeper into the topic.

How This Book Is Organized

This book is organized into six parts, which are divided into chapters covering a specific topic or related topics. This structure makes it easy for you to quickly find the information you need. Here's the breakdown.

Part 1: Planning the Premedical Years

This part describes the phases of education and training required to become a physician as well as the pros and cons of the profession. You also get the straight story about what you need to do to be competitive for admission to medical school. In addition, Part I covers other topics relevant to students who are preparing to begin or who have already started their premedical studies. Some examples include picking a major, choosing premedical courses, and making the most of time outside of class through extracurricular activities. This part helps you build your resume as a premedical student so that you're a strong candidate for admission to med school.

Part II: Applying to Medical School

This part is the longest one in the book. It contains seven chapters dedicated to various aspects of the medical school application process:

✔ Chapter 5 provides an overview of the application process, including a timeline to keep you on track throughout the admissions cycle.

✔ Chapter 6 takes on a topic that weighs heavy on the minds of premedical students: the Medical College Admission Test (MCAT). It fills you in on what to expect on the test and how to prepare so that you can achieve a stellar score.

✔ Putting together a strategic list of medical schools is a challenging task, but with the help of the tips in Chapter 7, you'll be set to target schools that are a good fit for you.

✔ Chapters 8, 9, and 10 go into depth about different steps of the application process. Among the topics addressed are crafting your personal statement and other parts of the primary application, asking for letters of recommendation, completing secondary applications, and acing medical school interviews.

✔ Chapter 11 gives you pointers on how to handle any of the three types of responses you may receive from a medical school you've applied to: acceptance, rejection, or placement on the waitlist.

Part III: Osteopathic Medical Schools, Dual-Degree Programs, and More

Many physicians practicing medicine are graduates of osteopathic medical schools. These doctors hold a DO (Doctor of Osteopathic Medicine) rather than an MD. Chapter 12 introduces osteopathic medicine and medical schools as well as discusses the application process for DO schools.

In this part, you also become familiar with dual-degree programs offered by MD and DO schools, including joint baccalaureate-MD/DO programs and programs that combine a medical degree with a master's or PhD.

This part concludes with a chapter describing the option of obtaining a medical degree internationally as well as the issues that path can create, such as obtaining a residency training position and medical licensure in the U.S. as a graduate of an international medical school.

Part IV: Nontraditional Applicants, Reapplicants, and Disadvantaged Applicants

This part focuses on applicants with special circumstances, such as those who are considered nontraditional applicants and applicants who have applied to medical school at least once previously. This part also addresses issues concerning minority applicants and applicants who are socioeconomically disadvantaged or have a disability.

- ✔ Chapter 15 takes on topics relevant to career-changers and other nontraditional applicants.

- ✔ Chapter 16 tackles subjects relevant to reapplicants, such as when to reapply, how to strengthen their application portfolios, and factors to consider when putting together their lists of medical schools.

- ✔ Chapter 17 focuses on minority and socioeconomically disadvantaged applicants as well as applicants with disabilities. Among the topics I address are enrichment programs available for minority and disadvantaged students and the issue of disclosing a disability when applying to medical school.

Part V: You're In! Getting Ready to Go

Part V takes you beyond the admission process by providing you with information about two topics of major importance for soon-to-be medical students. Chapter 18 discusses the cost of attending medical school, helps you plan a budget, and describes the various types of financial aid available to medical students. Chapter 19 provides tips about how to prepare for medical school and how to succeed after you're there.

Part VI: The Part of Tens

The Part of Tens is a tradition in *For Dummies* books; it features information in ten (or so) quick pieces. Chapter 20 describes ten things that you should know about med school, such as where you stand in the hierarchy of medicine and how staying on the good side of the nurses is critical during clinical rotations. In Chapter 21, you find out how to decipher some of the baffling slang that med students and doctors use.

Icons Used in This Book

The symbols you see on some pages of this book are there to make sure you don't miss out on especially important information. I use the following icons:

This icon marks critical information. These are the items that you don't want to overlook if you're determined to secure yourself a seat in medical school.

The information marked with this icon is interesting but not essential to know as you prepare to apply to medical school.

You find this icon in the margin next to text containing a tip to keep in mind as you're building your application portfolio as a premedical student, going through the admissions process, or getting ready to head off to medical school.

Watch out when you see this icon. It warns you about aspects of the application process or other topics presented in this book that may trip you up if you're not careful.

Where to Go from Here

Depending on your situation, you may find it most helpful to head straight for a specific chapter or to start from page one and read the entire book from front to back. (I won't complain if you do!) Either way works because this book is nonlinear, so you don't have to worry about getting lost if you read the chapters out of order.

If you're just starting to consider a medical career and don't know much about the profession or how to become a physician, start with Part I. This part is also the ideal starting point if you haven't yet begun your premedical studies or are currently a premedical student and are looking for help with topics related to the premedical years.

If the application process is looming directly ahead of you and you're pressed for time, consider going right to Part II, where you find a thorough discussion of the admission process and plenty of tips on how to put together a strong application package for medical school. In Chapter 5, I give an overview of the medical school application process so that even if you don't know the first thing about when, where, or how to apply, you'll understand the structure of the application process and timeline by the time you finish the chapter. If you've already started working on your application and are stuck on a particular step, flip to the relevant chapter to find immediate help.

Applicants to osteopathic medical schools, dual-degree programs, or international schools may prefer to start with Part III to get information about the particular type of program they're aiming for before going back and reading other chapters relevant to their situations.

No matter where are on your journey to medical school, I wish you the best of luck!

Part I
Planning the Premedical Years

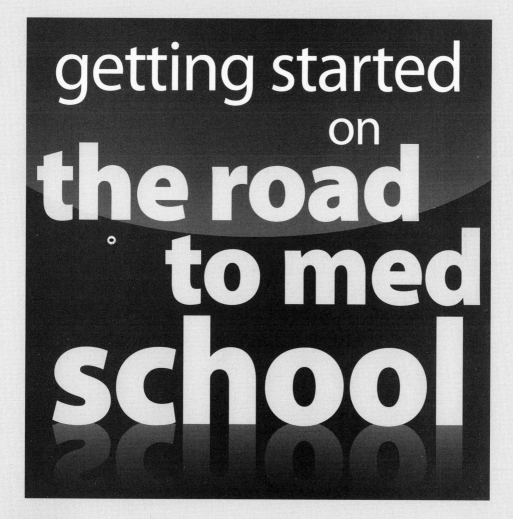

In this part . . .

- ✓ Explore the pros and cons of a career in medicine, check out different practice settings, assess your chances of med school acceptance, and decide whether medicine is right for you.

- ✓ Survey the steps to become a practicing physician: college, medical school, residency, and (for some specialties) fellowship.

- ✓ Go through the premedical years by choosing an undergraduate school, selecting a major, and planning your course work.

- ✓ Discover the importance of taking part in extracurricular activities, such as clinical and research experiences, community service, and clubs and organizations.

Chapter 1

Turning Your Dream of Going to Medical School into a Reality

. . . .

In This Chapter

▶ Considering a career as a physician

▶ Getting an overview of the premedical years and the medical school application process

▶ Investigating osteopathic medical schools and other programs

▶ Looking at issues affecting nontraditional and other applicants with special situations

▶ Gearing up to start medical school

. . . .

*M*edicine is one of the most attractive and competitive professions to enter. However, with perseverance and a strong commitment, you can achieve your goal of becoming a physician as long as you're willing to work hard. To get you started, this chapter gives you the big picture about what becoming a physician entails, surveys the medical school application process, and provides you with tips for getting ready for medical school. The later chapters of this book delve deeper into these topics to help you as you undertake your quest to get into medical school.

So You Want to Be a Doctor: Thinking about Medicine as a Career

Among the many benefits of a career in medicine is the opportunity to be part of a profession that is intellectually satisfying, personally rewarding, and constantly changing. Physicians have a unique opportunity to impact people's lives in a positive way on a daily basis in the context of a job with a high level of responsibility and autonomy. But these advantages come at a price. One of the major drawbacks to a medical career is that it takes at least

11 years of post-secondary education and training to become a full-fledged, practicing physician. The three phases you undergo are

- College (4 years)
- Medical school (4 years)
- Residency (3 years or more depending on specialty)

Some highly specialized fields require an additional year or more of training through a fellowship.

Premedical students traditionally take the courses required for entry into medical school during their undergraduate studies. However, for those who develop an interest in medicine after receiving a bachelor's degree, a post-baccalaureate premedical program offers a route to completing the basic science classes needed to be admitted into medical school.

Admission to medical school is highly competitive. Your academic record and scores on the Medical College Admission Test (MCAT) are typically the most important factors in the admissions process; however, schools also consider many other factors such as your extracurricular experiences, letters of recommendation, personal statement, and interpersonal skills.

Explore the medical profession carefully before you make your decision about whether to pursue a career as a physician. The self-assessment tool in Chapter 2 helps get you thinking about whether the medical profession is a good fit for you.

Mapping Out College and Participating in Extracurricular Activities

During college, you complete your prerequisite coursework for medical school and obtain your bachelor's degree (only in rare cases do students enter medical school without a bachelor's degree). When choosing a college, focus on finding one that's the right fit for you and that offers an academic program you're interested in and opportunities for involvement in activities outside the classroom.

You also need to determine which major to pursue as a premedical student. Medical schools don't require a particular major; as long as you complete the prerequisite coursework, you can choose any major, including one in a discipline outside the sciences. However, even if you major in a nonscience field, taking some upper level science classes is a good idea; doing so enhances your application and helps prepare you for med school.

If you discover your interest in medicine after you've already obtained your bachelor's degree, you can take the coursework needed to enter medical school as a post-baccalaureate student. Post-bac options range from highly structured career-changer programs to taking courses independently through a local college or university. (For a list of required and recommended premedical coursework for both traditional and post-bac applicants, flip to Chapter 3.)

Taking your prerequisites at a four-year institution rather than a community college is strongly recommended. Med schools generally prefer that prereqs be completed at a four-year school, and some programs won't accept ones completed at a community college.

Schools seek students who are not only academically qualified but also well rounded. Demonstrating that you've explored medicine is especially important, so gaining experience in the field of medicine before applying to medical school is essential. Volunteering at a hospital or in an outpatient setting, doing physician shadowing, and participating in research are ways to gain exposure to the medical profession so that the schools (and you) know that you're confident about your career choice. Admissions committees also take into account employment, community service, leadership, and other non-medical experiences when assessing an applicant. Check out Chapter 4 for details on making the most of extracurricular activities.

Assessing the Medical School Application Process

Securing a seat in medical school requires aspiring physicians to go through a very comprehensive admissions process. By completing each aspect of the application early and well, you maximize your chance of ending the cycle with an acceptance in hand.

Looking at the timeline

If you plan to go directly from college to medical school, you apply to medical school at the end of your junior year of college. The three major steps of the application process are

- ✔ Submitting your primary application
- ✔ Completing secondary applications
- ✔ Going to interviews

The American Medical College Application Service (AMCAS) application is the application service used by most allopathic (MD) schools in the United States. Most osteopathic (DO) medical schools use the American Association of Colleges of Osteopathic Medicine Application Service (AACOMAS). Public medical schools in Texas (MD and DO) use the Texas Medical and Dental Schools Application Service (TMDSAS). The AMCAS, AACOMAS, and TMDSAS applications are known as *primary applications*.

AMCAS and AACOMAS applications become available online in May and may be submitted beginning in early June; TMDSAS opens in early May, and applications may be submitted starting then. Admissions to most medical schools are *rolling*, which means that schools evaluate applications as they receive them. That's why submitting your application early in the cycle is extremely important.

In addition to a primary application, most medical schools also require a school-specific *secondary* (supplemental) application. If you submit your primary application in June, most of your secondaries will arrive during the summer. Fill them out and return them to the schools as soon as possible.

Interviews start in August at some schools and are in full force by early fall at most schools. They typically continue through January or early February, although at some programs they run as late as April. Allopathic medical schools begin offering acceptances as early as mid-October for regular applicants. Early decision applicants to AMCAS schools are notified by October 1.

See Chapter 5 for more details about the med school application timeline.

Taking the MCAT

Taking the MCAT is one of the most important and most dreaded parts of applying to medical school. The MCAT consists of three sections: physical sciences, verbal reasoning, and biological sciences. Each section is scored on a scale from 1 to 15 (1 is the lowest), for a total score of 3 to 45. A 31 is typically competitive for allopathic medical schools. (Prior to 2013, the test also included a writing sample, but that has been phased out in the lead-up to the full test revision in 2015.)

The revised MCAT is scheduled to be released in the spring of 2015. As part of the changes to the MCAT, the test is revamping the science and verbal reasoning sections, adding a section testing behavioral science topics, and becoming longer.

The MCAT is a difficult test and requires extensive preparation. Some students find taking a test preparation course to be the most effective way to prepare; others prefer self-study. Either way, you need to set up a study schedule and allow at least three months of time to get ready for the exam — longer if you're splitting your time between studying for your classes and preparing for the MCAT. Chapter 6 has details on test-prep strategies and the current and revised MCAT.

Selecting schools

Compiling a strategic list of medical schools is an essential part of success in the application process. If you overreach, you may find yourself finishing the cycle without a single acceptance. Underestimating yourself may lead to regrets as you wonder "What if?" you had tried for your dream schools.

Aim to compile a targeted list of schools that takes into account school type (public or private), rank, cost, curriculum, size, location, and how likely you are to be admitted. The goal is to put together a list that is a manageable length and gives you a good chance of being admitted *somewhere* but that won't risk selling you short.

Submitting primary applications

Although the three types of primary applications (AMCAS, AACOMAS, TMDSAS) each have a different format and specific requirements, they ask for the much of the same basic information. This includes biographical/background information, colleges attended, coursework, grades, MCAT scores, work experiences, extracurricular activities, honors/awards, and a personal statement. (TMDSAS also has two optional essays.) You only have to fill out a particular primary application once. After your primary is submitted to the application service and has been verified, the information on it will be transmitted to each of the schools that you have designated. Primary applications require a fee that depends on the number of schools to which you're applying.

Writing the personal statement is the most difficult part of completing the primary application for most applicants. Start brainstorming at least two months before you plan to submit your application, and anticipate going through many drafts to perfect it. Chapter 8 provides guidance about writing the personal statement and completing other areas of the primary application.

Obtaining letters of recommendation

Some undergraduate institutions and post-baccalaureate programs have pre-medical committees that write a letter endorsing or evaluating students or alumni who are applying to medical school. The committee usually includes the premedical advisor as well as one or more faculty members. The committee compiles a letter discussing the applicant's candidacy for medical school. The committee letter may include quotations from individual letters of recommendation and/or may have individual letters attached to it.

If your institution doesn't offer a committee letter, don't worry; you simply obtain individual letters from faculty and others to submit as part of your application. Each medical school has its own requirements for individual letters, so check with the schools to make sure you obtain the correct type and number of letters. (See Chapter 9 for more information).

Completing secondary applications

After submitting your primary application, you get a brief break before you move on to the next stage of the admissions process: secondary applications. The simplest secondaries require only that you submit a fee and perhaps fill out a short form. Other secondaries include several short-answer or essay questions that ask you to explain why you've chosen to apply to the school or to elaborate on your experiences and background.

Keeping up with secondaries can be difficult, but submit them as quickly as you can without compromising on the quality. After you fill out a few secondaries, you'll likely find that you have a bank of essays to work from that you can modify for other schools; however, make sure you tailor your answer to the school and question being asked. Check out Chapter 9 for more details on completing secondaries.

Interviewing with schools

Landing a medical school interview is a big accomplishment; you're much closer to being admitted to medical school if you've reached this stage.

At most schools, the interview visit includes touring the medical school; meeting medical students; attending talks by the admissions office, faculty, and/or administrators; and undergoing one to three interviews. Interviewers may be basic science faculty, physicians, or medical students. At some schools, interviews are conducted one-on-one; at others, you interview in front of a panel of two or more interviewers, either by yourself or with another applicant or applicants.

Some schools have switched from traditional interview formats to the *multiple mini-interview* (MMI) format. During an MMI, applicants rotate through a circuit of timed stations. Types of stations include those that require role-playing, teamwork, or analyzing a bioethics case.

Chapter 10 provides tips on getting ready for both traditional and MMI format interviews as well as a list of commonly asked interview questions.

Hearing whether you're in, out, or waitlisted

Months of preparation and waiting culminate with a decision from the admissions committee.

- ✔ If it's a "yes," take care to send in any required forms and/or a deposit to reserve your seat in the class. Students who are in the fortunate position of holding multiple acceptances may decide to go for a *second look* weekend offered by some schools in the spring before making their final decisions.

- ✔ A "no" answer is disappointing, especially if a school is one of your top choices. However, if you receive a negative response, consider contacting the admissions office to see whether you can get feedback about the reason for the rejection. This information may help you during the current cycle or in the next one if you have to reapply.

- ✔ If you're put on the waitlist, don't give up; you still have a chance of being admitted. Keep in touch with the school (unless it discourages that) by sending a letter of update, letter of interest, and/or additional letter of recommendation. This extra information keeps the school apprised of your ongoing activities and desire to attend its program.

Chapter 11 has full details on what to do when you hear back from medical schools.

Considering All Your Options

Attending an osteopathic medical school is another route to becoming a physician. DO schools are similar in many ways to their MD counterparts but have some distinctive attributes as well. International schools also offer an alternative for students seeking to obtain a medical degree.

Some medical schools team up with undergraduate or graduate institutions to offer joint degree programs. By participating in one of these setups, you can receive your bachelor's and medical degree or both a medical and graduate (master's or doctorate) degree as part of an integrated program.

Osteopathic medical schools

You can achieve your goal of practicing medicine by obtaining an allopathic or osteopathic medical degree. Both allopathic and osteopathic medical programs are four years long and include courses in basic science subjects as well as clinical rotations in hospitals and outpatient settings. Graduates of DO schools are eligible for medical licensure throughout the United States after completing medical school and one or more years of residency training as well as passing a series of licensure examinations.

The *osteopathic* philosophy emphasizes a holistic approach to patient care as well as disease prevention and wellness. Osteopathic medical schools traditionally have focused more on primary care than allopathic schools; however, many DOs are found in specialties as well. The major difference between allopathic and osteopathic medical education is that only DO schools include training in osteopathic manipulative medicine (OMM) as part of their curriculum.

The structure of the application process for allopathic and osteopathic medical schools is similar, although they use different primary applications. Many osteopathic medical school applicants apply to MD schools as well. Head to Chapter 12 for more information about osteopathic medical schools.

Dual-degree programs

Dual-degree programs, which I discuss in Chapter 13, combine an MD or DO with another degree. High-school students interested in medicine may apply to joint baccalaureate-MD/DO programs. These programs last six to eight years and lead to both a BA or BS degree and a medical degree. Admission into the medical school affiliated with the program is often provisional, and matriculation into the program's medical school component may require maintaining a minimum grade-point average (GPA) during the undergraduate component and/or taking the MCAT and achieving a certain score.

Students interested in pursuing a career that combines both clinical medicine and research may opt to enter a joint MD-PhD program. These programs usually last seven to eight years and often provide participants with full tuition for medical school as well as a stipend for living expenses. Admission into these programs is very competitive and requires a strong background in research.

International medical schools

Some students choose to obtain their medical degrees outside the United States either because they're unable to gain acceptance to a U.S. medical school or for other reasons, such as ties to a particular country.

Careful research prior to attending an international school is essential, because the quality of education at international institutions varies significantly. International medical graduates (IMGs) must undergo certification by the Educational Commission for Foreign Medical Graduates (ECFMG) in order to apply for residency training programs and to become licensed in the United States. Obtaining a residency position is generally more difficult for IMGs than for graduates of U.S. medical schools. Also note that although some international medical schools are eligible to participate in U.S. federal loan programs, others aren't.

Note: Canadian medical schools are accredited by the same agency as U.S. schools, so graduates of these schools aren't considered IMGs. Canadian medical schools offer medical educations that meets the same standards as those offered by U.S. schools, and, like U.S. schools, they're highly competitive in terms of admission.

I cover international medical schools in detail in Chapter 14.

Taking Care of Special Situations

Med school applicants come from all backgrounds and demographics. Nontraditional applicants, reapplicants, minority and socioeconomically disadvantaged applicants, and applicants with disabilities are among those who may face particular challenges as they work toward achieving their dream of practicing medicine.

Nontraditional applicants

Some future doctors come to the conclusion that they want to pursue a medical career only after they've graduated from college or have pursued another profession. These nontraditional applicants have the typical concerns about getting into medical school, such as whether their grades are high enough or whether they have sufficient clinical experience. However, they also may have additional issues to address: returning to school after years out of the classroom, juggling family and financial responsibilities along with their studies, and fitting in among their mostly younger classmates.

Although nontraditional applicants may have some extra challenges, they also have the advantage of professional and other experiences that may help them stand out to admissions committees because they offer something different. (Flip to Chapter 15 for more about nontraditional applicants.)

Reapplicants

If you're planning to apply to medical school for a second or subsequent time, reevaluate every element of your application to identify and address weaknesses before you forge ahead. Some steps that you may need to take to improve your odds of admission include the following (see Chapter 16 for details):

- ✔ **Strengthening your academic record.** You can accomplish this task through a formal academic record enhancer post-baccalaureate program or by taking courses at a college or university outside of a structured program.
- ✔ **Retaking the MCAT.**
- ✔ **Adding new clinical, research, and community service experiences.**
- ✔ **Applying to a broader range of schools.**

Before you reapply, you should also update your personal statement and secure at least one new letter of recommendation.

If reapplying immediately won't leave you with sufficient time to strengthen your application portfolio, consider waiting a year so that you can ensure that you've got everything in order before trying for admission again.

Minority and disadvantaged applicants and applicants with disabilities

To further diversify the physician workforce, many medical schools and other organizations offer outreach programs, enrichment opportunities, and scholarships for students who are members of groups underrepresented in the medical profession. Minority and socioeconomically disadvantaged students interested in medicine can also find information about resources available to them from premedical advisors, medical school diversity offices, and premedical and medical student organizations.

Advances in technology have opened the doors to medical school wider than ever for individuals with disabilities. However, these applicants often have extra tasks to tend to as they apply to medical school, such as arranging for accommodations on the MCAT, determining whether and when to disclose a disability to programs, and working with schools to address accommodations during their medical education. Chapter 17 addresses these areas as well as topics relevant to minority and disadvantaged applicants.

Heading to Medical School

With the application process behind you, you can get ready to start medical school. One of the top items on your list of things to do is to figure out how you'll pay for medical school. If you're relocating, you also have to tackle logistics such as finding a place to live and what kind of transportation you need in your new city. After the year gets underway, being organized, building a support system, and effectively managing stress help ensure your success as a medical student.

Confronting the cost

The *cost of attendance* (COA) of medical school includes not only tuition but also books, equipment, and other educational expenses, as well as living expenses such as rent, transportation, and food. Use the estimated cost of attendance supplied by your medical school's financial aid office as the basis for crafting a budget for the next four years.

Most medical students need some financial aid to pay for medical school. For many medical students, federal loans are the major source of funding for their medical education. Some medical schools award school-based (institutional) aid to students in the form of grants or scholarships or low-interest loans. Private loans are an option for students who need additional aid.

Some students fund their education through service-based scholarship programs that require a commitment to serve in the armed services or provide care to patients in an underserved area for a certain number of years after the recipient's medical training is complete. Other types of scholarships are awarded based on merit, financial need, or other factors.

Working during the summers before and after your first year of medical school is a means to generate some additional funds, but don't plan to hold a job during the school year. Being a medical student is very much a full-time commitment.

Chapter 18 has the full scoop on paying for medical school.

Getting off to a good start

During the summer just prior to medical school, you may also want to get a head start academically by perusing an anatomy atlas or brushing up on other subjects you study in your first year. However, don't make the summer into a crash course for the first year of medical school. You're about to head into a very demanding academic setting, and going into it refreshed is important as well. You also may be busy over the summer finding a place to live near your med school, packing up, and taking care of all the other details involved with relocating.

Staying organized and formulating a study schedule can help you keep up with the large volume of information you need to master in medical school. Taking breaks to relax, spend time with friends and family, and maintain your physical and emotional health is also important.

Succeeding in medical school is easier with a strong support system in place. Reach out to your classmates to form study groups or organize social events with the people who are going through the experience of being a medical student alongside you. In addition, check with your school's student affairs office to find out what resources your school offers to medical students for academic or other support. Medical school can be stressful, but after you get the hang of it, you may find that the time goes quickly. Before you know it, you'll be a doctor.

Check out Chapter 19 for more tips on starting and succeeding in medical school.

Chapter 2

Considering a Medical Career

In This Chapter
▶ Weighing the benefits and drawbacks of being a physician
▶ Looking at the road to becoming a physician
▶ Exploring practice settings
▶ Checking out the odds of admission
▶ Determining whether a career as a physician is right for you

*F*ew careers match medicine in the length and rigor of training, level of responsibility, rewards offered, and sacrifices required. Because of the unique nature of the profession and the years of preparation entering this career takes, your decision about whether to pursue this route deserves careful consideration. By exploring what becoming a doctor entails, what the job is really like, and what qualities you need to succeed in medicine, you equip yourself to make an informed decision about your future path.

In this chapter, I describe both the positive and negative aspects of being a physician as well as cover each phase of education and training on the road to becoming a practicing doctor. I also give you a glimpse at the settings physicians work in and a look at the statistics you face as an applicant, from the number of candidates you compete against to the grades and test scores you need to have a shot at a spot in medical school. Finally, you can use a self-assessment to help you determine whether a medical career is a good fit for you.

Understanding the Pros and Cons of Entering Medicine

The late nights and long hours that physicians work are notorious; however, a doctor's job also offers the substantial rewards that come from having the ability to alleviate suffering and treat disease. Along with these more obvious aspects of the job are more-subtle benefits and drawbacks that contribute to making medicine a unique and complex profession. In the following sections, I provide an overview of some of the best and worst parts of a medical career to help you get a realistic view of what you're getting into before you decide to embark on the journey from premedical student to practicing physician.

Some experienced physicians say that if you can be happy doing anything other than medicine, you should do that instead. This advice is a caution to aspiring doctors that a physician's life isn't the easiest one. However, if you're sure that medicine is what you truly want to do, and you're prepared to deal with the challenges that come with the territory, get ready to forge ahead.

Evaluating the rewards

The benefits that a career in medicine offers are alluring enough to draw tens of thousands of aspiring physicians to apply to medical school every year. Although some students are attracted to medicine in hopes of prestige, a good salary, or a stable job, the greatest rewards that medicine offers are less tangible than a good paycheck or holding the title of doctor:

- ✔ **Getting the opportunity to make an impact on the lives of others:** As a doctor, you have the ability to help others improve their health and well-being by applying the knowledge and specialized training you possess. Going to work every day knowing that you can make a difference in someone else's life is one of the greatest satisfactions of a medical career.

- ✔ **Being in a position of responsibility:** Although nurses, therapists, and other medical professionals are important members of the healthcare team, in many ways the physician bears the ultimate responsibility for the patient. The physician makes the medical diagnosis, formulates the treatment plan, and oversees the care of the patient. If you're more inclined to lead than to follow, medicine offers the kind of autonomy and responsibility you may be apt to appreciate.

- ✔ **Having a career that's intellectually satisfying:** Practicing medicine requires a vast store of knowledge, and because medical science is constantly advancing, a physician continues to learn throughout his or her career. Medicine can be an ideal field for those who crave challenges and find learning to be a pleasure rather than a chore.

- ✔ **Getting the chance to choose among diverse career paths:** Although clinical practice is the foundation of most physicians' careers, it's far from the only option. Some physicians work in academic settings doing research and teaching, others focus on clinical research or public health, and still others are engaged in health policy or administrative roles.

Assessing the drawbacks and sacrifices

Although focusing on only the positive aspects of a medical career while you gear up to declare yourself a premedical student or apply to medical school may be tempting, take a realistic look at the profession early on. That way, you can determine upfront whether the benefits truly outweigh the drawbacks for you instead of realizing years down the road that a doctor's job isn't quite what you bargained for. Some of the sacrifices required to become a physician and the challenges that come with the work include the following:

- **Spending eight years in school and at least three more in residency:** While you're stuck in school for what seems like forever, you watch your friends get jobs, start families, buy houses, and get on with "grown-up life." Meanwhile, you're still sharing an apartment with a roommate and studying for midterms.

- **Long and irregular work hours:** Residency is infamous for its grueling hours and relentless call schedule. However, for some medical specialties (such as surgery and obstetrics), middle-of-the-night emergencies, weekends on call, and missed family dinners may be a way of life even long after you've become an attending physician.

- **A high-stakes, high-pressure work environment:** Being a physician can be stressful. A doctor's job is one in which the ramifications of an oversight or mistake can be much more serious than in most lines of work. The ability to manage stress is important in medicine, and those who don't have (or at least develop) good coping mechanisms may end up wishing they'd opted for a lower-key profession.

- **Paperwork:** Doctors go into medicine to treat patients, not to spend hours filling out charts and dealing with insurance companies. However, documentation and administrative tasks go with the territory and are a part of the job you may not be fully aware of even if you've shadowed physicians and put in months as a volunteer in a clinic.

Becoming a Physician in a Few Not-So-Easy Steps

Going from premedical student to attending physician is a process that requires more than a decade of studying, memorizing, test-taking, and clinical training. Even receiving your MD or DO (the degree for osteopathic medicine — see Chapter 12) doesn't mean that you're at the end of your training; in fact, an even greater challenge lies ahead: residency. Only after four years of college, four years of medical school, and three or more years of hands-on experiences practicing your craft in a residency program (and potentially a fellowship) are you ready to strike out on your own as an attending physician. In the subsequent sections, I provide an overview of each of the phases of the education and training you need to complete to become a practicing physician.

Starting out: The premedical years

The first step to becoming a doctor is to attend college to complete the prerequisite coursework required for entry to medical school and to attain your bachelor's degree. Medical schools require a series of core science courses that provide the foundation in biology, chemistry, physics, and other disciplines that allow you to dive into a full load of more-advanced science courses in medical school. (Flip to Chapter 3 for a specific list of prerequisite courses.)

However, the four years of your undergraduate career aren't just about preparing academically for medical school. While you're learning organic chemistry and solving physics problems, you're also exploring medicine through physician shadowing and clinical volunteering, as well as participating in activities in areas such as community service, research, and leadership (see Chapter 4 for more about extracurricular activities). The premedical years call on your time management and organization skills to juggle everything you need to accomplish. Then, if all goes well, you move on to the next step: medical school.

Moving closer to your goal: Medical school

After you advance from premedical to medical student, you're immersed in four years of intense academic studies and clinical experiences to equip you with the knowledge and skills you need to pursue a residency to train in your chosen specialty. You can break medical school into two parts: the preclinical years and the clinical years.

The preclinical years

The first two years of medical school, sometimes known as the *preclinical years,* are similar to college in many ways: Learning takes place mostly in the classroom and teaching labs, and you have plenty of studying and test-taking to do. However, unlike in college, your education is much more focused. Gone are the humanities and social science electives; instead, you take courses in subjects such as anatomy, physiology, biochemistry, genetics, neuroscience, and pharmacology. You also complete courses in which you learn to take a patient history and perform a physical examination as well as other skills you need on the medical wards.

At most schools now, students get at least some patient contact in the first two years. This trend toward early clinical exposure is a welcome development for med students eager to get some hands-on experience with patients.

The clinical years

The third and fourth years of medical school, traditionally referred to as the *clinical years,* are when you find yourself truly feeling like a doctor-in-training. During this time, you complete a series of *clinical rotations* (also known as *clerkships*) at hospitals and outpatient facilities in all the major specialties of medicine, including surgery, pediatrics, internal medicine, psychiatry, family medicine, and obstetrics and gynecology. You also have the chance to supplement your required third-year rotations with fourth-year electives to explore additional specialties or more deeply investigate disciplines you're considering pursuing for your career.

As a member of the medical team on the wards and clinics, you follow your own patients under the supervision of the resident and attending physicians. You also participate in *rounds* (where you see patients and discuss the diagnosis and treatment plan with the team), take overnight call, and help with admitting and discharging patients. By the end of medical school, you've acquired the tools you need to head into the next phase of your training as a first-year resident.

Preparing to practice medicine: Residency

Although you earn the title of doctor upon graduation from medical school, residency is where you learn most of the nitty-gritty of patient care. After med school graduation, newly-minted doctors have a brief break before beginning their respective residency programs in July. The first year of residency, commonly called *internship,* is a time of very intense learning. Although interns are supervised by more-senior residents as well as attending physicians, the level of responsibility is much greater for an intern than for a medical student. And despite recent reforms in resident duty hours, the schedule is still grueling. Work weeks are 80 hours per week averaged over four weeks for most specialties, with first-year residents now limited to "only" 16 hours per day on duty. From the second year of residency on, you may be taking overnight call every third or fourth night, spending more than 24 hours straight in the hospital.

With each year of residency, you gain more autonomy; as a senior resident, you have a significant amount of responsibility for the patients on your unit and help to supervise junior residents and medical students. This system of increasing responsibility prepares you for the day when your training is complete and you're ready to practice on your own.

For both residency and fellowship (described in the next section), you receive a stipend that starts around $50,000 for a first-year resident, with modest increases for each year of training — much less than an attending salary but still enough to be considered a real paycheck.

Deciding to go further: Fellowship

Following residency, some physicians opt to continue on to a fellowship in order to enter a field that requires more highly specialized training. For example, if you plan to become a cardiologist, you first do a three-year residency in internal medicine or pediatrics and then go on to subspecialize in cardiology by completing a three-year fellowship, for a total of six years of post-graduate training.

Similar to residency, as a fellow you spend your time in hospitals and outpatient settings, learning your craft through hands-on experiences. However, your training is even more focused on a particular branch of medicine.

Some fellowships, and even some residencies, have a research component to them and are an especially good fit for those who aspire to a career in academia.

Finishing at last: Becoming an attending physician

Eventually, you reach the last day of your training and are ready to go out and practice your specialty as an attending physician. As I discuss in the following section, physicians work in a variety of clinical environments — diagnosing and treating patients, performing surgery, managing chronic conditions, and providing preventive care — as well as in nonclinical roles in research, teaching, and administration.

Although your days of formal training are behind you, you're always learning, even as an attending. In a field advancing as rapidly as medicine, to stop learning means you risk falling behind and being unable to provide the highest quality care to patients. Practicing physicians keep up with changes in their fields by reading medical journals, attending conferences, and taking continuing medical education (CME) courses to meet requirements for licensure renewal.

Becoming Licensed to Practice Medicine

Although you receive your medical degree after graduating from either an allopathic or osteopathic medical school, you need to obtain a medical license in order to practice medicine in the United States. To become licensed, you need to pass a series of licensing examinations as well as complete one or more years of residency (the number of years required varies by state).

The three parts or *steps* of the United States Medical Licensing Examination (USMLE) are

- Step 1, which is usually taken after the second year of medical school.

- Step 2 Clinical Skills (Step 2 CS) and Step 2 Clinical Knowledge (Step 2 CK). Step 2 CS and Step 2 CK are taken separately, typically during the fourth year of medical school.

- Step 3, which is usually completed at the end of the first year of residency.

Note that graduates of DO schools can obtain licensure by passing the Comprehensive Osteopathic Medical Licensing Examination (COMLEX-USA) series rather than the USMLE. See Chapter 12 for more details about licensure for osteopathic physicians.

You can find the specific requirements for medical licensure in your state by checking with the state medical board. A summary of the licensure requirements for each state is provided at the Federation of State Medical Boards (FSMB) site at `www.fsmb.org/usmle_eliinitial.html`.

Surveying Practice Types

One of the decisions you need to make as your residency winds down is the type of practice setting you want to work in. With the days of the solo practitioner waning and a wider variety of healthcare delivery systems in use than ever before, you may be unsure of what exactly your future work environment will look like. In the following sections, I explore the major options available for practice environments.

To get a head start in considering your options, speak with physicians within the specialty you intend to pursue about their practices. Many will be happy to give you an honest assessment of what it's like to be in private solo or group practice, care for patients in a community clinic, balance a career that includes patient care and research, and so on.

Even if you research each practice setting meticulously, finding the setup that works for you may take a couple of tries. If your first job out of residency isn't your last, that's all right; just learn from each experience and keep working toward finding the niche that gives you the best fit.

Private solo and group practices

In a private, solo practice, a single physician owns a practice and works independently with his or her support staff. Although such an arrangement is less common now than in the past, this option is still attractive to doctors who value the autonomy and flexibility of practicing alone. One disadvantage however, is that solo practitioners bear the often time-consuming responsibilities of owning and running a business. Solo practices may be the only option for physicians practicing in remote areas that have few other physicians.

In a group practice, two or more physicians join forces and work together as part of a partnership. As part of a group, physicians benefit from having colleagues on-site to consult with, having someone to share call with and to cover patients when one member is on vacation, and bearing less financial risk. A major drawback of this setup, however, is that decisions must be made by a group, and members may not always agree about how the practice should be managed. Yet if the partners are compatible, a group practice can be an excellent choice because it offers many of the benefits of a private practice while allowing for some shared responsibility as well.

Community clinics

The term *community clinic* usually refers to clinics serving low-income or other disadvantaged populations, such as patients who are uninsured or underinsured. Such clinics may be funded by federal or local governments and/or private donors. This setting is attractive to physicians who are committed to working with needy patients on either a full-time or part-time basis.

Working in a setting with underserved patients can be very gratifying, but it also may come with challenges, such as limited resources, a high turnover in the patient population and/or staff, a heavy workload, and lower compensation than for other practice settings. However, the opportunity to make a positive difference for populations most in need of healthcare can outweigh these potential drawbacks.

Academic institutions

If your ideal career includes a combination of patient care, research, and teaching, then an academic institution (such as a medical school or a hospital that trains residents or fellows) may be the optimal practice setting for you. As a physician in academia, you may spend one part of your workweek performing basic or clinical research, another part seeing patients in your practice, and another part doing rounds with residents and medical students at the hospital. For some doctors, an academic career is weighted more heavily toward research; for others, clinical medicine is the primary focus. Balancing all three facets of medicine — research, patient care, and teaching — can be difficult; for those who manage it, however, the reward is a diverse, dynamic job.

Although holding both an MD and a PhD is becoming increasingly common for academic physicians, you can also pursue this career path with an MD or DO alone supplemented with a strong background in research.

Practicing as a hospitalist and other options

The delivery of healthcare has changed significantly in the past few decades and will likely continue to do so. With these changes have come new practice options for physicians. Among these is the job of *hospitalist,* a physician employed by a hospital and paid a salary to attend to patients who have been admitted for inpatient care. For example, a pediatric hospitalist manages children admitted to the hospital he or she works for but doesn't see patients on an outpatient basis. Hospitalists may work in teaching hospitals or community hospitals.

Other physicians work for health maintenance organizations (HMOs) or integrated health delivery systems as salaried employees instead of working on the traditional fee-for-service basis. Although some physicians feel that these practice models offer less autonomy, other doctors prefer them because they may provide more stability and a better work-life balance. Another advantage that these settings may offer is greater freedom from the administrative tasks required in private practice, allowing the physician to focus on patient care.

Assessing Your Chances of Acceptance to Medical School

The biggest question on the mind of many premedical students is "What are my chances of getting into med school?" I address that burning issue in the following sections by looking at some of the statistics pertaining to medical school admission as well as discussing the factors that schools consider when evaluating applicants.

As you read the next few sections, keep in mind that statistics are just a guide and that your chance of admission can be increased by managing your application strategically in terms of your timing, choice of schools, and your primary application package (see Chapters 5, 7, and 8, respectively, for tips on these areas).

Playing the numbers game: Medical school applicants versus seats in medical schools

With an aging population and a major anticipated increase in the number of insured people in the United States (thanks to the passage of the Patient Protection and Affordable Care Act in 2010), the demand for healthcare is higher than ever and projected to continue to rise. In response to these trends, new medical schools have opened and existing ones expanded the number of seats in their classes in an effort to increase the supply of physicians.

In a 2006 report, the Association of American Medical Colleges (AAMC) called for an increase of 30 percent in total medical school enrollment. An October 2012 press release states that schools are on track to meet that goal by 2016. The number of spots in osteopathic medical schools has been expanding as well, with an increase in enrollment of over 4 percent between the 2010–2011 and 2011–2012 academic years alone, according to a 2012 report by the American Association of Colleges of Osteopathic Medicine (AACOM).

This growth is good news for aspiring physicians; however, the increase in the number of places available in medical school classes has been accompanied by an increase in the number of applicants to both allopathic and osteopathic medical schools. (*Allopathic* physicians are holders of an MD; *Osteopathic* physicians have a DO degree.) To understand what all this information means to you, check out the graph in Figure 2-1 illustrating the number of applicants versus the number of seats in medical schools for the entering class of 2012.

With nearly 15,000 applicants for about 5,300 places in osteopathic schools and slightly over 45,000 applicants for about 19,500 seats in allopathic schools, there are almost three applicants for every DO spot and two to three for every MD spot. (Technically, the number for MD spots is closer to 2.3, but who wants to be treated by three-tenths of a doctor?) However, as you evaluate these numbers, note that some applicants apply to both allopathic and osteopathic schools, so the total number of unique applicants is less than the number of DO and MD applicants combined.

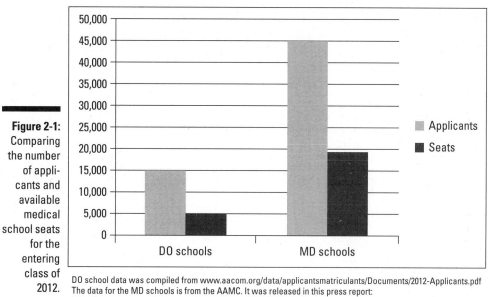

DO school data was compiled from www.aacom.org/data/applicantsmatriculants/Documents/2012-Applicants.pdf
The data for the MD schools is from the AAMC. It was released in this press report:
https://www.aamc.org/newsroom/newsreleases/310002/121023.html.

Illustration by Wiley, Composition Services Graphics

Gauging grades and test scores: GPA and the MCAT

The most important factors in determining your chances of admission
to med school are your grade-point average (GPA) and Medical College
Admission Test (MCAT) score. Even an applicant with amazing extracurricular experiences and outstanding letters of recommendation is likely to
be denied admission if she can't demonstrate the academic potential for
medical school. As I describe in Chapter 6, many schools do an initial assessment based on your GPA and MCAT score that determines whether your file
advances to the next stage of review or is denied. Even if you make it all the
way to the interview stage (discussed in Chapter 10), MCAT score and GPA
are often still important determinants of the committee's final decision.

Table 2-1 shows you the mean GPA and MCAT scores for *matriculants* (entering students) to MD and DO schools so you know what to aim for as you
tackle your classes and prepare for the MCAT.

Table 2-1	Mean GPA and MCAT Scores for 2011 Matriculants	
Type of Program	*Mean GPA*	*Mean MCAT Score*
DO	3.48	26.5
MD	3.67	31.1

Source: Data pertaining to DO programs compiled from the 2013 Osteopathic College Information Book at http://www.aacom.org/resources/bookstore/cib/Documents/2013cib/2013cib-p12-13.pdf. Data pertaining to MD students compiled from Table 17 "MCAT Scores and GPAs for Applicants and Matriculants to U.S. Medical Schools, 2000-2011" at https://www.aamc.org/data/facts/applicantmatriculant/.

As Table 2-1 illustrates, the MCAT scores for matriculants to allopathic schools is considerably higher than for osteopathic schools. This gap is one of the biggest differences between admission to DO and MD schools and makes osteopathic medical schools an option worth investigating for applicants for whom the MCAT is a weakness but who have an otherwise strong application package. (See Chapter 12 for details about applying to DO schools).

For any school, allopathic or osteopathic, having a lower-than-average MCAT score or GPA certainly doesn't guarantee you won't be admitted, nor do great numbers ensure you're in. However, your chances of admission are greater if you have high grades and a good MCAT score, so excelling academically is the best way to give yourself an advantage in a very competitive process.

An excellent resource for statistics about applicants and matriculants to medical school are the AAMC FACTS tables at www.aamc.org/data/facts/.

Looking beyond the numbers

Getting admitted to medical school requires more than a great GPA and stellar MCAT score. Although having strong academic credentials is important and even necessary for securing a spot in medical school, admissions committees assess many other factors of an application as well:

✔ **Extracurriculars:** Clinical experience, research, community service, leadership, and other activities are part of the package you have to offer and are vital to the application.

✔ **Strong personal character:** Maturity, compassion, professionalism, and good interpersonal skills are qualities that schools seek in applicants. Because these personal characteristics can't be quantified through grades and standardized tests, letters of recommendation and the interview are also critical components of the admissions process.

✔ **Intangibles:** Your background, obstacles you've overcome, your ability to contribute to the diversity of the class, and other intangible factors come into play when a committee considers your application.

The admissions process isn't simply about the percentile you achieved on the MCAT or the number of *A*s you've earned; it's also about what you have to offer as an individual.

Deciding Whether Medicine Is Right for You

Making the decision to pursue a career as a physician takes a lot of time, research, and introspection. Before starting your journey to medicine, read about the profession, talk to physicians, volunteer in hospitals and clinics, and think carefully about what you want from a career and why you're interested in becoming a physician. If you determine that medicine is the best choice for you, get ready to put in a lot of hard work and many years to achieve your goal. But also know that you're entering a very rewarding, challenging, and honorable profession.

The following questionnaire can help get you thinking about your motivations to pursue a medical career, your expectations about the field, and whether your personal qualities and interests make you a good fit for the profession.

Unlike the quizzes in your premed classes, this one has no good or bad grade. The goal is simply to help you focus on why you're interested in medicine, consider how thoroughly you've explored the field, and understand what characteristics are important for a physician to have.

1. Making an impact on the lives of others is important to me. __ **yes** __ **no**

2. Family expectations are a strong motivating factor for my interest in medicine. __ **yes** __ **no**

3. I enjoy the study of science and its applications. __ **yes** __ **no**

4. Ongoing learning and being challenged are high priorities for me in a career. __ **yes** __ **no**

5. I connect well with others and have good communication skills. __ **yes** __ **no**

6. Medicine is appealing primarily because it offers a stable career and high salary. __ **yes** __ **no**

7. I adapt to new situations well and have developed tools to cope with stress. __ **yes** __ **no**

8. I work effectively in environments requiring teamwork. __ **yes** __ **no**

9. I have spent time in clinical settings and would enjoy working in such environments. __ **yes** __ **no**

10. I'm energetic and possess a high level of stamina. __ **yes** __ **no**

11. I've spent a significant amount of time researching medicine as a career, speaking with physicians about their jobs, and observing physicians at work. __ **yes** __ **no**

12. I'm compassionate toward people who are facing difficulties. __ **yes** __ **no**

13. The prestige associated with being a physician is a major reason for my desire to enter medicine. __ **yes** __ **no**

14. I understand the amount of education and training that becoming a physician entails. __ **yes** __ **no**

15. I'm comfortable with responsibility and able to make difficult decisions when necessary. __ **yes** __ **no**

After you've taken the self-assessment, consider the following:

✔ A "yes" response to Questions 1, 3 through 5, 7 through 12, 14, and 15 indicates that you've explored what a career in medicine entails and believe that you have some of the qualities that are important for a future physician. Keep in mind, however, that some of the characteristics you need to function effectively as a doctor are ones you hone during medical school and residency, so if you answered "no" to questions regarding particular qualities, don't feel like you're precluded from being a good fit for medicine.

✔ A "yes" response to Questions 2, 6, and/or 13 suggests that you may be becoming a physician for reasons that won't sustain you throughout your career. Although doctors as a whole are well compensated, a good salary and job stability alone aren't necessarily enough to make the extended training and demands of a physician's job worthwhile. If parental pressure or a desire for prestige is your main reason for entering a medical career, you may also find yourself disappointed in the long run. You're the one who will be doing this job day in and day out, and if it's not one you love, you may be dissatisfied no matter how much validation you receive from family, friends, and society.

The decision about which career to choose is a weighty one, so take your time in making it. If you aren't sure that medicine is right for you, keep investigating this field as well as other professions that interest you. Taking an extra year or two to confirm your choice is much better than ending up on a track to a career that isn't the best fit.

Chapter 3

Mapping Out Your College Years

* *

In This Chapter

▶ Recognizing the importance of the premedical years

▶ Picking a college and selecting a major

▶ Understanding the prerequisites for med school

▶ Investigating study abroad and post-baccalaureate programs

* *

Getting into medical school begins long before you fill out your application or even take the Medical College Admission Test (MCAT). Your choice of college, major, and classes are all important when it comes to securing a spot in med school. To make the best decisions amid a seemingly endless array of options, you need to understand both the purpose of the premedical years and the impact that they have on your application. As a premedical student, your goals are to build the academic foundation you need for med school and demonstrate to prospective schools that you'll make a great med student. By planning early and strategically, you can make the most of your college years and give yourself the best chance at making it into med school.

In this chapter, you discover how to select a college and major as well as which courses you need to enter medical school. I also introduce premedical post-baccalaureate programs, a valuable option for those who are making the switch to premedicine toward the end of their college years or after graduation.

Understanding the Role of the Premedical Years

The words *premedical student* conjure images of a harried individual, pale from long hours in the library, rushing from lab to lecture with a bulging backpack, haunted by the thought that his *A* in physics may slip to an *A–* if he stops studying for even a moment. Although being a premedical student is no easy task, it's not quite akin to this caricature, either. To be competitive for med school, you need to take rigorous classes and do well in them, but these years are also a time to explore your interests both inside and outside academia. This approach is good not only for you but also for your application because schools want well-rounded students who are able to relate to patients from all walks of life. By making wise decisions about your college and course of study, you can both prove yourself academically and pursue your interests outside of the classroom.

Building a foundation for medical school

In medical school, you're immersed in anatomy, histology, biochemistry, and neuroscience, among many other challenging subjects. To be ready for the torrent of information you face, you need a strong academic background. The premedical courses are designed to give you the basic information that you need to succeed in your med school classes. Med schools therefore require prerequisite courses, most of which are in the sciences (I list these classes in the later section "Planning Your Premedical Course Work"). By doing well in your undergraduate courses, you show the med schools that you're ready to excel as a student in their program.

When you enter college, plan to not only complete your prerequisite courses for med school but also obtain a bachelor's degree. Although some medical schools only require students to have a specific number of undergraduate units (such as 90) for admission to medical school, in reality, starting medical school without having earned a bachelor's degree is very rare.

No matter how great your extracurriculars are, admission to med school will be out of reach if you don't take the right courses and do well in them. Your premed years are, therefore, a time to gain the information you need to start med school and the grades that will get you in the door in the first place.

Exploring your interests

College is a time to do more than just make the grades and complete the classes you need to move on to the next step. It's also your chance to take classes in art history or anthropology, study abroad, try a new sport, or take advantage of whatever else may interest you. With the time crunch you face in med school and residency, college may be the last opportunity you have for many years to try new things "just because." In addition, developing your interests can help you when admissions time comes because med schools seek students who can add to the diversity of their class in some way, including through their unique talents, hobbies, and experiences.

As you're trying different fields, you may find that you expand your interests within medicine as well. A political science class may be your first step to an exploration of global medicine. A Spanish course may help you bridge the language barrier with some of your future patients. So if something intrigues you, try it. It may just lead you to your niche in the field of medicine.

Choosing an Undergraduate School

Selecting an undergraduate school is a daunting task for any high school senior, but as a premedical student, you face an added layer of complexity. Not only do you need to find a school that can give you a good education, that makes you feel comfortable, and that's located somewhere you want to spend four years of your life, but you also have to think about how your choice of college will affect your application. Does the school provide the resources and support to give you your best chances of admission to med school? Is the "best" school necessarily the ideal one for you to attend? In the following sections, I discuss factors to weigh in making this important decision.

As you make your decision about what school to attend, investigate whether it offers programs of interest to you outside the premedical track. You may discover after a semester or two that the premedical path isn't right for you, and finding your new niche will be easier if you're at a school that provides other options that are a good fit you.

Recognizing that where you go matters

When it comes to med school admissions, just about everything matters: where you go, the classes you take, how you do in those classes, and what you do with your time outside of school. Because med school is incredibly demanding, schools look for evidence that a student can succeed in a very rigorous academic setting. Attending a more selective undergraduate college may put you at an advantage in obtaining admission to med school. In fact, a person with a 3.6 GPA from a highly selective undergraduate school may be better off than someone with a 3.9 from a school that is less well regarded. Keep in mind though, that a school's name can only help to a certain degree. The applicant with a 3.0 from an Ivy League school is in a worse position than a peer with a 3.7 from a less selective school.

Attending a prestigious college provides an advantage in admissions, but that fact doesn't mean that you can't get into med school if you don't attend a top-tier undergraduate school. Med students and physicians come from a vast range of schools: large and small, public and private. The simple rule is to attend the most competitive undergraduate school that accepts you; however, if you know that you're more suited to being "a big fish in a little pond" and that it will be very difficult for you to maintain a strong grade-point average (GPA) at a more competitive school, then you may be better off attending the school that you're most likely to excel at, even if it's less well known.

Make sure the college you choose to attend is accredited; medical schools specify that prerequisite course work must be taken at an accredited institution. (See the later section "Reading the fine print: Policies for AP credit and community college courses" for more information about restrictions on prerequisite course work.)

The MCAT serves as a common yardstick that allows schools to compare applicants from different schools and with various majors. A great MCAT score demonstrates to med schools that you're ready to tackle their curriculum, even if you didn't attend a college with a dazzling reputation. (See Chapter 6 for information on how to succeed on the MCAT.)

A big discrepancy between your GPA and MCAT score may be a red flag to med schools. If you have a 3.9 GPA but can't break a 30 on the MCAT, it may indicate either that your school practices grade inflation or that the content of its courses is lacking. Therefore, don't just look at the name of the school; consider also the strength and rigor of its core science courses so that you'll be prepared to succeed on the MCAT.

Comparing major research institutions and small liberal arts colleges

One applicant I worked with had a strong GPA from a highly-ranked public university and had taken full advantage of the outstanding research and clinical opportunities available at his school. He scored a 33 on the MCAT and was solidly positioned for admission to med school when he found himself in a dilemma: The huge lecture courses his school favored meant minimal contact with his professors, creating a major obstacle to gaining letters of recommendation.

This applicant's situation illustrates some of the advantages and drawbacks of attending a large research institution. These schools often provide a rigorous science curriculum, ample research opportunities, and the chance to be taught by professors who are leaders in their fields. If the university also has a medical school, then possibilities for volunteering or physician shadowing are convenient and abundant. The downside is that the large, competitive environment can be impersonal and competition can be intense. Classes, especially lower-division courses, are usually taught in large lecture halls that may hold hundreds of students, with smaller lab or discussion sections run by graduate students. Mentorship, guidance, and letters of recommendation are more difficult to obtain in such a setting.

Some students are concerned that they may be lost in the crowd at a large public school. However, participating in a smaller educational program, such as an honors program, can make a big school feel smaller than it actually is.

By contrast, a small, liberal arts college encourages students to attain a broader-based education and typically offers smaller classes. All sections of a course, including labs, may be taught by a professor. Opportunities for research and volunteering may be more limited, but the positions that do exist may be easier to obtain and allow for more autonomy because these schools have fewer premedical students competing for the same experiences. The overall environment is also typically more personal and supportive.

These two types of institutions represent the extremes in undergraduate education, and between them lies almost every size and type of school. To choose the right fit for you, assess how you learn best, whether you thrive on competition or prefer collaboration, and whether you're comfortable asserting yourself to get what you need or require an environment that offers easier access to opportunities.

Like private schools, public schools vary widely in terms of size, focus, and quality of education, so you should consider each one individually. However, a public school in your state of residence may be the least expensive option, a factor that's especially important if you need to finance both your college and medical school through loans. Therefore, keep cost in mind as you consider colleges. (In Chapter 18 you find out about the costs of med school and how to pay for them.)

Finding a school with strong support for premeds

Navigating through the premedical years is a lot easier and less stressful if you have guidance. Attending a school where advising, academic support, mentors, and peer groups are available as you decide on everything from class schedules to the best place to volunteer smooths the way for you to succeed. Some schools offer virtually no help for premedical students, whereas others have very knowledgeable and accessible premedical advising offices to assist students through each step of the application process.

To find out whether a college has resources in place for premeds, ask the following questions:

- ✔ Does the school have a premedical advisor or advising office?
- ✔ What services are offered by the premedical advisor/advising office?
- ✔ Is there a premedical club? How active is it?
- ✔ What academic support services are available, especially for core science classes?
- ✔ How large is the premedical community at the school?

Lack of a premedical advisor doesn't have to be a deal breaker. If you find a school that otherwise fits your needs but has weak or no advising, you may decide to attend anyway; you'll just need to be proactive in building your own support network. Seek out a professor, an academic advisor, a physician, or another mentor who's knowledgeable about medical school admissions to guide you along the way. For example, the advisor for a department that may include a significant number of premedical students (such as biology) may have experience in issues relevant to premedicine even if she isn't officially a prehealth advisor. If your school has a premedical club, consider joining it; the club may have a faculty advisor who serves as a resource for members of the group. Upperclassmen who are premeds may also have tips about where to find advising if your school doesn't have a designated premedical advisor.

Looking at location

Whether you attend school near home or across the country, in a city, suburb, or rural setting is not just a matter of cost and convenience; it also impacts the opportunities you'll have as a premedical student. For example, large urban areas have a higher density of hospitals, physicians' offices, and clinics for you to volunteer or shadow in. However, a college set in a rural area can offer you the chance to gain exposure to rural medicine, an experience that's less common among premeds and, therefore, may help to set you apart in the application process. Particular locations may have unique opportunities; for example, a college located in Washington, D.C., may offer easier access to internships in the area of health policy.

Opportunities extend beyond the walls of your university, so don't limit your college visit to the campus tour — take a look at the surrounding community to see what it has to offer you as an aspiring physician.

Selecting a Major

Although specific premedical courses are requirements for entering medical school, no specific major is required. As long as you take the necessary prerequisite courses and meet other requirements specified by medical schools, you're eligible to apply. (I tell you more about the prereqs in the later section "Planning Your Premedical Course Work.") In fact, you don't even have to be a science major. Majoring in history, economics, psychology, or any other area is perfectly acceptable. In the following sections, you find out about the advantages and challenges of science and nonscience majors for a premed student.

Going the traditional route: Science majors

Choosing a science major has the significant advantage of allowing you to fulfill requirements for your major at the same time that you complete the required course work for med school. In addition, a science major will take you far beyond the core science courses into upper-division science classes, which some med schools encourage.

If you've always been a "science person," then choosing a science major allows you to focus on your interest and minimize the number of humanities and social sciences classes you have to take. Within the sciences, you should choose whichever field intrigues you the most: biology, biochemistry, neuroscience, molecular biology, or any other area of study. Also, your upper-division science courses provide a smaller setting than the lower-division ones, thereby giving you a better opportunity to establish a relationship with your professors, which could lead to a research position or letter of recommendation.

Choose the area of science that you're most interested in studying for your major instead of picking a field because you think it will "sound better" to the admissions committee. "Molecular genetics" may have a more exotic ring to it than "biology," but if biology is what you prefer and are most likely to excel in, declare yourself a bio major. Also be aware that scheduling classes for more-specialized science majors can be complex because many courses may need to be taken in a particular sequence.

Taking a different path: Nonscience majors

In a sea of biology majors, the rare history, music, or French major stands out. When med schools say they want diversity in their student body, they don't just mean racial or ethnic diversity; they're also looking for people who can bring a different perspective to the practice of medicine. So if you prefer reading great works of literature to manipulating mathematical equations or debating philosophy over studying biochemical pathways, then delve into whatever you most enjoy. Fitting in the science classes along with the requirements for your major takes some extra planning, but it's well worth it for the chance to have greater breadth in your education and to develop your skills in other areas.

Although a wide array of majors can prepare you for medical school, selecting one that's intended to prepare you for a specific alternate profession such as teaching or nursing is typically unadvisable. Generally, a liberal arts degree is more flexible and provides you with a broader education than a major designed to train you for a specific profession other than physician.

If you do select a nonscience major, be aware that although your unique background may give you an edge in admissions, the lack of upper-division science course work may be a drawback on your application. Therefore, take at least a few science courses beyond the required ones. This strategy is especially important if you have a poor grade in a science course; a *C* has a greater negative impact on the science GPA of a nonscience major than it does on the GPA of someone with many more science credits.

Beginning in 2015, the MCAT will include a section that tests content from social sciences such as psychology and sociology, reflecting an increasing emphasis by medical schools on the importance in medicine of a broad-based education and an understanding of areas outside the hard sciences. (Check out Chapter 6 for information about the MCAT.)

Planning Your Premedical Course Work

As you plot out the four years of your undergraduate career, you need to make sure that you meet the core requirements for medical school. You should also try to include additional science classes to make you a more competitive applicant. I give you the scoop in the following sections.

Here are a few general pointers for planning your schedule:

- ✔ **Seek help from your advisor when you first enroll in college to determine the appropriate level of math and science courses for you to take.** Colleges may use placement exams as well as assess your high-school record to ensure you start with math and sciences courses that fit with your background. Being in the right classes helps you avoid getting in over your head your first semester as a premedical student.

- ✔ **Make sure you spread out your science courses.** Overloading yourself with too many tough courses at one time makes for a rough semester and can potentially damage your GPA. Many students actually find the intro courses to be more difficult than more-advanced ones; at some colleges, intro courses are designed to weed out less capable students, so don't underestimate the difficulty of an intro class in a subject like chemistry or biology.

- ✔ **Schedule classes relevant to the MCAT to be completed before you take the test.** Although you don't have to have all your prerequisites completed by the time you submit your applications to med school, neglecting to take them before the MCAT can jeopardize your score. (See Chapter 6 to get the scoop on the topics tested on the MCAT.)

The essentials: Familiarizing yourself with the prerequisites for medical school

Although the exact prerequisites vary from school to school, the majority of medical schools require those shown in Table 3-1. One semester of calculus and one semester of statistics satisfy the mathematics requirement for most medical schools.

Table 3-1	Prerequisite Course Work for Medical School
Course	*Number of Semesters*
General Biology with Laboratory	Two
General Chemistry with Laboratory	Two
Organic Chemistry with Laboratory	Two
Physics with Laboratory	Two
College Mathematics	One or two
English	Two

Biochemistry is also required by 15 allopathic medical schools as well as some osteopathic schools; even if your med school doesn't require it, taking biochemistry can help you prepare for the MCAT as well as for medical school. A few schools require anatomy or other specific science courses. In addition, numerous schools specify a certain number of humanities and/or social science credits. Therefore, checking with each school you plan to apply to about its requirements early in your college career is essential. This tactic ensures that you can complete all needed course work before matriculating into med school. (Flip to Chapter 7 for more about choosing medical schools.)

Most med schools don't accept online course work to fulfill prerequisites. Others accept online course work on a case-by-case basis.

Reading the fine print: Policies about AP credit and community college courses

You breezed through high school chemistry, got a 5 on the AP exam, and were thrilled when your college gave you the go-ahead to skip general chemistry and go straight into organic chemistry. Three years later, as you're preparing to apply to med school, you make an unwelcome discovery: None of your dream med schools accept AP credits for prerequisite course work.

To avoid this nightmarish scenario, I recommend that you take the prerequisite courses in college instead of trying to use AP credit for them. If a student chooses to use AP credit to pass out of a prerequisite, she may need to take one or more upper-division courses in the same subject in order to fulfill a medical school's requirements. Students who attempt to use AP credit to fulfill the prerequisite course work in a subject and don't take upper-level courses in that discipline may run into trouble at application time. Every school sets its own policies regarding AP credits, so check with the schools you're considering to make sure you know what your options are.

Understandably, only a rare premed student would willingly pass up general chemistry to take physical chemistry, for example, so many students who can pass out of a lower-division science course opt to take it instead. However, biology is the one subject where passing out of the lower-level course and going straight to an upper-level one may be possible (although you should confer with your academic advisor first). Keep in mind that the MCAT tests the material from the core sciences courses, and taking those in college — even if you covered the material in high school — provides a great refresher of this information before the big test.

The policies for medical schools regarding prerequisite course work taken at a community college vary. Some schools accept community college credits for prereqs without restriction; others only consider community college courses for which a student was given transfer credit by a four-year institution; still others evaluate these courses on a case-by-case basis; and a small number of medical schools don't accept community college courses to fulfill prerequisites at all. Note that accepting these classes is not the same as actually encouraging them. In fact, med schools generally recommend that applicants take basic science courses at a four-year institution. The perception, accurate or not, is that the level of rigor at a community college is not the same as that of a four-year institution.

If you're attending community college prior to transferring to a university, focus on your general education requirements and save as many science classes for after the transfer as you can. If you do end up taking most or all of your prereqs at a community college, plan to take some upper-division science classes at a four-year institution. Doing well in those will demonstrate to med schools that you have the foundation you need as a med student. Rocking the MCAT doesn't hurt either.

Going above and beyond: Courses that are recommended but not required

As I discuss in the earlier section "Taking a different path: Nonscience majors," taking science classes beyond the bare minimum is highly recommended. By taking extra science courses, you give the med schools more evidence that you can excel in their program; plus, the extra courses further reinforce your science knowledge for the MCAT. But which ones should you take? To answer this question, here's a list of courses to choose from that medical schools advise students to take, although they may not be required for admission (biochemistry tops the list because it's most important, but the others are simply listed in alphabetical order):

- ✔ Biochemistry
- ✔ Anatomy
- ✔ Cell biology
- ✔ Developmental biology
- ✔ Ethics
- ✔ Foreign language (Spanish is especially useful in medicine)
- ✔ Genetics
- ✔ Immunology
- ✔ Microbiology
- ✔ Molecular biology
- ✔ Physiology
- ✔ Psychology
- ✔ Sociology

 If you're taking the MCAT in 2015 or after, taking both psychology and sociology is necessary. The revised MCAT includes a new section called "Psychological, Social, and Biological Foundations of Behavior." Behavioral science courses give you the background you need to tackle the questions on this part of the test. (See Chapter 6 for more about the revised MCAT.)

Studying Abroad

 As with anything else, studying abroad takes a bit of extra planning and forethought for a premed student, but spending a semester away also offers rewards for students personally and as future applicants. Studying abroad gives you a great opportunity to immerse yourself in another culture, perfect a foreign language, and experience a different educational and social environment. Many premedical students participate in study abroad programs, but to ensure that you get the most out of your time overseas without disrupting your application to med school, do the following:

- ✔ **Check with your school's Overseas Study Office early in college to research programs and learn about their timing so that you can plan your premedical course work.**

✔ **Participate in a study abroad program sponsored by a U.S. institution and verify that the courses, credits, and grades will appear on the transcript of the sponsoring U.S. school.** You want to ensure that you receive credit for these courses on the Association of American Medical Colleges (AMCAS) or American Association of Colleges of Osteopathic Medicine Application Service (AACOMAS) application (see Chapter 8 for details about these applications).

✔ **Don't go abroad during the time that you're taking the MCAT, submitting applications, and interviewing.** During the summer and fall of the application cycle, you're busy filling out primary and secondary applications, and in the fall through winter, if all goes well, you'll be on the interview trail. (Check out Chapter 5 for the application timeline.)

✔ **Take your prequisite course work for medical school in the United States and use your time abroad to study language, culture, and other areas that interest you.**

✔ **Arrange for a clinical experience while you're abroad, if possible.** By doing some physician shadowing or volunteering in a hospital or clinic in another country, you can discover how medicine is practiced outside the United States and continue to enhance your application, even while you're away.

Perusing Premedical Post-Baccalaureate Programs

If you decide before or early in college that medicine is the field for you, you can take the needed courses as an undergrad and set off for med school straight out of college. But what if you're a theater major who decides during your last year of college that medicine is your calling? With Physics for Poets as the only science class on your transcript and just two semesters to go, how do you ever reach your new goal? Or what if you've spent years in the workforce as a bond trader, ballet dancer, or graphic designer before deciding on med school? Then what do you do?

The answer: Take your prereqs as a post-baccalaureate student. Premedical post-bacs for career changers range from highly structured programs with a set curriculum and extensive support services to do-it-yourself options in which students take courses independently. In the following sections, I discuss the pros and cons of each option to help you determine which type of post-bac education best fits your needs.

Note: Post-bac programs for students who have a science background but need to improve their academic credentials are different than the post-bacs I discuss here, which are often referred to as *career changer programs.* See Chapter 16 for a discussion of academic record enhancer post-bacs.

No matter what type of post-bac program you choose for your science pre-reqs, the best way to assure your success at application time is to do well in those courses and to master the knowledge you need to score well on the MCAT (see Chapter 6 for details).

Considering formal post-bac programs

Formal post-bac programs offer several major advantages:

- ✔ A set curriculum with a guarantee of obtaining needed classes.

- ✔ A peer group of students aiming for medical school.

- ✔ Premedical advising, MCAT preparation, and help with applications to medical school (the specific resources offered vary from program to program).

- ✔ Linkages or affiliation with particular medical schools, allowing for application and acceptance to a medical school during the post-bac program while prerequisite courses are still in progress. This setup avoids the *gap year* that a post-bac student would otherwise have by applying at the end of the program. (It's found only at the more selective post-bac programs.)

Although the benefits are significant, these programs have drawbacks as well:

- ✔ **They're expensive.** Tuition tops $40,000 for some 15-month programs.

- ✔ **They may lack flexibility.** Many of these programs require a full-time commitment. If you need to work full time or have other responsibilities, a less structured program may be a better fit.

- ✔ **Admission is competitive.** The application process usually includes an assessment of your GPA; your SAT, ACT, or GRE scores; letters of recommendation; and a personal statement. Although the application process isn't as grueling as the one for med school, top post-bac programs, such as those with numerous linkages, are highly selective.

- ✔ **They're really stringent about previous prereqs.** You may be ineligible for these programs if you've already taken some of the medical school prerequisites.

A great resource for finding post-bac programs is The American Association of Medical Colleges searchable database at `services.aamc.org/postbac`. Using this tool, you can generate a list of programs based on institution, program type, or location. To find career changer programs, select "Career-changers" under "Special Program Focus."

Taking post-bac courses independently

If time constraints, money, or other factors prevent you from taking part in a structured program, you can still obtain the courses you need to apply to med school. By taking classes through a university extension, an open university, or other avenues that colleges offer for non-degree-seeking students, you can put together your own post-bac.

Some benefits of this route are as follows:

- ✔ **Lower cost:** A do-it-yourself post-bac is usually far cheaper than a formal program, especially if you complete your course work at a state school.

- ✔ **Greater flexibility:** You can make your own schedule based on your preferences regarding when to take courses, how many classes to take at a time, and which courses to take together.

- ✔ **Local classes:** You can take classes at any four-year college or university in your area that's available to you, and you don't have to worry about relocating to attend a program. (As discussed earlier in this chapter, taking prerequisite courses at a community college is not recommended.)

Like structured programs, DIY post-bacs have drawbacks:

- ✔ **Lack of availability of classes:** Non-degree students have the lowest enrollment priority at most schools, making it difficult to obtain classes. University extension classes are usually easier to get into than the courses offered to regularly enrolled students at a college, but they're typically more expensive and may have very limited offerings in the sciences.

   If you can't get the classes you need, the "greater flexibility" benefit noted in the preceding list is purely theoretical. Instead, you may find yourself scrambling to enroll in any course you can find, even if it's at an inconvenient time or means you have to take the classes in a different sequence than you prefer.

- ✔ **Limited or no advising:** Without being part of a regular program, you may not have access to a premedical advisor, leaving it up to you to map out your classes and stay on track with the application process.

- ✔ **No linkages to medical schools:** Affiliations with med schools are a valuable aspect of some formal post-bacs. As an independent student, you don't have access to these connections.

- ✔ **Limited or no financial aid:** If you aren't part of a program that leads to a degree, you may not be eligible for financial aid or may have only limited financial aid options available to you.

Chapter 4

Making the Most of Extracurricular Activities

A great GPA and strong Medical College Admission Test (MCAT) score can get you past the first cut for med school admissions, but what will the schools think when they dig deeper into your application? That all you did was study for four solid years? Or that you're a well-rounded individual who adds something unique to their programs and understands that medicine is about more than memorizing diagnoses and medications?

Acing the courses you need to apply to med school is only one facet of being a premed student. To develop into a truly competitive applicant, you need to leave the lecture hall behind and venture into physicians' offices, hospitals, research labs, community service organizations, and student groups. This chapter guides you in selecting extracurricular activities, getting the most out of your experiences, and managing your time so that you can balance your academic commitments with your life outside the classroom.

Understanding the Role of Extracurricular Activities in Admissions

As I describe in Chapter 2, most medical schools receive thousands of applications each year, so the initial screening is often based on applicants' numbers. If a candidate's GPA and MCAT scores are above the threshold a school sets as a cutoff, the application moves to the next stage of the process. At that point, other elements of the application, such as extracurricular activities, the personal statement (see Chapter 8), and letters of recommendation (see Chapter 9) are scrutinized to determine whether the applicant receives an interview offer. (Note that some schools do a holistic review of all applications from the outset, which includes reading the personal statement and assessing other elements of the application package such as extracurricular activities; however, GPA and MCAT are still important factors even if the entire application is assessed initially.)

Although a high GPA and strong MCAT score are necessary to landing an interview, they aren't enough to get you an interview on their own. Even an applicant with a 3.86 GPA and a 35 MCAT may be passed over if his application is little more than a string of *A*s and a day or two of shadowing. Conversely, an applicant with a 3.5 GPA and an MCAT of 30 whose activities demonstrate that he's an engaged and enthusiastic individual who is committed to a career in medicine, dedicated to service to others, and has well-developed interests may end up across the table from an interviewer. Year after year, I see some applicants with slightly lower numbers (although not too low!) beat out their seemingly more competitive counterparts because of their achievements outside of academia.

In the following sections, I explain the importance of both medical and non-medical activities outside the classroom in ensuring a well-rounded application.

Demonstrating familiarity with the medical field

The only way to truly know whether you want to be in medicine is to come as close as you can to actually trying it. Achieving that means immersing yourself in clinical settings — observing physicians, volunteering in hospitals, helping out in clinics, and interacting with patients. The time to find out that distinctive hospital smell sends you heading for the door or that you find patient care tedious is before you apply to med school, not after you're in the gross anatomy lab, wishing you had chosen a nice, clean cubicle job. Med schools are aware that healthcare is like no other field, and it's important to them that students make their decision to apply based on reality, not a glamorized version of medicine. Only by getting in the trenches can you discover whether medicine is right for you.

Clinical volunteering and shadowing are both important experiences and serve slightly different functions. (I discuss both options in more detail later in this chapter.)

- ✔ *Volunteering* allows you to experience a clinical environment as a participant. Although your responsibilities may be limited, interacting with patients by delivering meals or entertaining pediatric patients in the playroom allows you to find out whether you're comfortable around individuals who are ill and whether you derive satisfaction from helping them. However, because most volunteer positions involve interaction primarily with nurses and medical support staff, they don't provide much opportunity to learn about the day-to-day duties of a doctor.

✔ When you *shadow* a physician, you almost exclusively observe, rather than participate in, patient care, but you get a firsthand view of a physician's responsibilities to help you determine whether you'd thrive in that role.

Showing that you have a life outside the library

Medicine is a highly social profession. Doctors interact with patients, patients' family members, colleagues, nurses, and other members of the healthcare team. The skills you need to perform a physician's job, therefore, extend far beyond intelligence and diligence; a doctor must be able to communicate effectively, teach, lead a team, and function in many different, challenging environments. The interpersonal skills and qualities required of a successful physician are most effectively developed and practiced outside the classroom. The part-time job you held in the library, the three different intramural sports you played, and your position as choreographer of your school's dance team all contribute to developing the qualities you offer as a medical student and future physician.

Medical schools want students who have the ability to connect well with patients, not just memorize information. As someone with outside interests, you show the committee that you won't become one of those physicians who's utterly brilliant but whose bedside manner leaves patients cold. At the same time, you bring something different to the student body than just your grades when you have a background in art, spent the summer as a white-water rafting guide, or served as a resident assistant mentoring the freshmen on your floor.

Gaining Clinical Experience

Convincing an admissions committee that you truly want to be a physician is an impossible task if you haven't set foot in a doctor's office or hospital other than as a patient. Therefore, clinical experience is the most important of your extracurricular activities. *Clinical experience* can take place in any setting where patients are cared for: primary care clinics, hospitals, specialty practices, or hospice. Clinical activities can also take place outside the United States. Participating in a medical mission or other overseas experience provides exposure to healthcare in other countries and is an opportunity to contribute to care in an area with severely limited resources.

No matter what settings you choose, start gaining experience early in your premedical career so that you have time to explore multiple environments and pursue at least one experience for a year or more.

Keep a log of your clinical experiences, including the activity, location, date, and number of hours worked. You'll be glad you did when it comes time to fill out your application to med school. Also, jot down notes about interesting experiences you have, observations you make, lessons you learn, or memorable interactions with patients. These bits are invaluable as you write your personal statement and descriptions of activities. (See Chapter 8 to find out how to effectively weave your experiences into your personal statement.)

Volunteering in clinical settings

By working in a clinical setting, you test and develop your comfort in working with patients, confirm that medicine is the right fit for you, and start to discover your particular interests within the profession. However, volunteering in a clinical environment isn't quite as simple as showing up at your local hospital, offering your services, and being sent off on an assignment within the world of medicine. If your university has a large number of premedical students, area clinics and hospitals may actually have a surplus of volunteers, leading to long wait lists and/or a competitive application process for spots. Attending volunteer orientation, obtaining a TB test, and completing training on the Health Insurance Portability and Accountability Act (HIPAA) are just a few of the numerous other steps you need to take before you can actually set foot in the hospital as a volunteer, adding additional time to the process. Therefore, setting up clinical experiences requires organization and often persistence.

To secure a volunteer position and ensure a meaningful and productive experience during your tenure as a volunteer, keep these suggestions in mind:

- ✓ **Don't limit your search for volunteer spots to teaching hospitals.** *Teaching hospitals* (hospitals affiliated with medical schools and/or that train resident physicians and fellows) are only one environment in which to explore medicine. *Community hospitals,* which are usually smaller than teaching hospitals and focus on serving the medical needs of community members, are also excellent places to gain experience. Because they may have a fewer volunteers, community hospitals may offer greater flexibility in the tasks that you're allowed to perform and more opportunity for patient contact.

- ✓ **Gain experience in both inpatient and outpatient settings.** The environment, approach to patient care, and types of cases you see at a hospital are very different from those in an outpatient clinic or practice. To obtain a comprehensive view of medicine, you must spend time in both environments.

✔ **Check out low-cost or free clinics for opportunities to volunteer.**
Community clinics often rely on volunteers because they have only
limited resources and paid staff. By working in this setting, you not only
gain clinical experience but also participate in community service. At
the same time, you have the chance to learn about the needs of medically underserved patients.

✔ **Be enthusiastic and proactive.** You get out of your experiences as much
as you put into them. If you complete your assigned tasks, ask the nursing staff or your supervisor what else you can do to help. Be willing to
do any task, no matter how mundane it seems. Stock the nurses' station
with supplies? Sure! Organize files? You're on it! As you prove yourself
with smaller duties, you'll be gradually entrusted with greater responsibility and more contact with patients. Conscientious performance as
a volunteer can even lead to a paid entry-level position such as medical
assistant or *phlebotomist* (technician who draws blood). Note, however,
that a training course and certification may be necessary for these jobs.

✔ **Make connections with the physicians you meet.** Although you may
encounter physicians only briefly and intermittently while volunteering,
introduce yourself as a premedical student and express interest in the
physician's work or specialty. You may begin a relationship that leads to
the opportunity to observe the physician during slow times during your
shift or on a separate occasion in his practice.

Shadowing physicians

As a hospital volunteer, most of your day is spent with nurses, patients, and
support staff, so although you gain valuable experience in a clinical setting
and find out about the roles of various members of the medical team, you don't
get much exposure to medicine from a doctor's perspective as a volunteer.
The best way to understand what a doctor's job entails is to observe or
shadow a physician through his or her workday. Watching a physician diagnose patients, develop treatment plans, perform surgery, and even complete
less glamorous duties such as charting or dealing with difficult patients gives
you a glimpse of what being a doctor is really like. Thus, shadowing is an
essential part of your premedical resume.

To line up shadowing experiences, try the following pointers:

✔ **Contact every physician you know and even those you don't.** Your
own family physician, doctors you've met through volunteering, your
roommate's family friend, or any other physician you have even a slim
connection with can get you an in.

✔ **Look up physicians in your area and e-mail or call their offices.**
Explain that you're a premedical student interested in observing the
physician and give a brief summary of your background.

> ✔ **Be persistent.** Doctors are busy and may not respond right away, but most are happy to help out an aspiring physician. One applicant I worked with sent letters to 40 physicians, hoping to line up at least a few days of shadowing. By the end of the year, he had shadowed close to 20 physicians in fields from obstetrics to geriatrics, all without having had a single contact person in medicine to start with.

Your role during a physician shadowing experience is that of an active observer. Between patients or at the end of the day, ask pertinent questions about what you saw, such as why particular tests were ordered or what diagnosis the physician was considering given a set of symptoms. If you'll be returning for a second shadowing visit, read up on what you saw during the first visit and return with a few questions ready.

Dress and act professionally whenever you shadow a physician, and demonstrate consideration for patients and respect their rights to privacy.

Doing international medical missions

Along with taking part in clinical activities in the United States, many premedical students participate in medical missions as part of teams of doctors, nurses, and other healthcare professionals going abroad to provide care in developing countries. Trips are typically one to two weeks long and are an opportunity to not only learn more about medicine and the impact of poverty on health but also experience another country and culture. If you participate in one of these trips, expect to put in long hours and work very hard while you're there. However, you can also expect the satisfaction of helping populations that have very limited access to medical care as well as the chance to step outside your comfort zone.

If you're interested in going on a medical mission, check to see whether your university offers opportunities for undergraduate students to volunteer abroad in a medical setting. (Your premedical advisor is a good resource for finding out about these experiences.) Your campus may also have a student group that works with an outside organization that coordinates service trips; examples of such organizations include Global Brigades and Volunteers for Definitive and Intercultural Adventures (VIDA). If you don't find such a group, consider starting one. Founding a group not only allows you to participate in a mission but also demonstrates leadership and initiative.

During a medical mission trip, you shouldn't undertake responsibilities such as diagnosing or treating patients or perform procedures for which you haven't been trained or that you wouldn't be allowed to do in the United States. Besides the ethical issues that these actions raise, the perception of using patients in developing countries for "practice" isn't looked on favorably by medical schools. If you aren't comfortable doing something, then you probably shouldn't be doing it. Before you go a trip, search the Association of American Medical Colleges (AAMC) website `www.aamc.org` for guidelines about participating in patient care abroad as a premedical student.

A mission trip isn't a substitute for long-term volunteering in your community. Although it may not be as exciting as an overseas adventure, the month-in-and-month-out volunteering you do in the hospital down the street or clinic across town carries more weight in demonstrating your commitment to medicine than a week or two abroad does.

Delving into Research

Clinical experience is essential to becoming a competitive med school applicant, but what about research? Do you have to have research on your application to be seriously considered for medical school? Does it have to be lab research? Do med schools even consider clinical research?

Questions about whether to do research and how much/what kind to do are some of the most common ones applicants ask me. In the following sections, I clarify the role of research in the application process, help you decide whether you should participate, and discuss the various options for research involvement.

Deciding whether to do research

Some applicants are eager to conduct research and may even aspire to a career in academic medicine. For this group, the decision isn't whether they should do research but rather when and where. For most students, though, the question is "Should I do research?" These students envision a career in clinical medicine and often aren't sure whether they'll like research or how critical doing research prior to med school really is. Even if you aren't a physician-scientist in the making, research can be beneficial to your application, especially if you're interested in med schools that are more research-focused (a category that includes many top-tier programs).

Along with the opportunity to enhance your application, reasons to participate in research include the following:

- ✔ **Developing an understanding of how advancements are made in medicine:** This knowledge allows you to better assess new findings and therapies as a clinician in the future.

- ✔ **Discovering firsthand whether you're interested in research:** Attending lab sections that are part of lecture courses are much different from taking part in investigation with a team as a part of a research lab; therefore, you shouldn't use lab sections as the sole means of evaluating your affinity for research.

✔ **Getting a chance to be published or to present your work:** Your work may result in poster presentations, an abstract, or even an article in a peer-reviewed journal. All these achievements are excellent to have on your application.

✔ **Building relationships:** Doing research lets you to work more closely with a faculty member than you would in class, allowing for mentorship and potentially a letter of recommendation from someone who knows you and your work well. (Flip to Chapter 9 for basics on letters of recommendation.)

✔ **Developing skills that are transferable to a medical career:** The ability to weigh evidence, think critically, and analyze data is important in both research and in the practice of medicine.

Here are a couple of reasons not to do research:

✔ **You have absolutely no interest in it and can't imagine liking it no matter how hard you try.** Or, you actually did try it and know that it isn't for you.

✔ **You're too deeply involved in other medicine-related activities to fit it into your schedule.** Don't try to cram in research if taking on a research project means that your grades will suffer or you won't be able to dedicate yourself sufficiently to other activities that are more meaningful to you. (In the section "Fitting It All In" later in this chapter, I talk about how to prioritize activities and manage your time as a premed student.)

Doing basic or clinical research

Basic research takes place in a laboratory setting and involves conducting experiments to answer a question. As a student doing basic or *wet lab* research, you first learn laboratory procedures and techniques and may start out by assisting a graduate student or post-doctoral fellow with his work. Later, you may advance to having your own project or work independently on one area of a larger project. Experiments need to be conducted rigorously and meticulously and may take many repetitions, so they require a detail-oriented approach. The day-to-day work involved can be tedious, and you may invest a huge amount of time to produce only small results. However, doing research is often intellectually stimulating and offers the potential to contribute to the store of scientific knowledge.

Clinical research focuses on the study of the diagnosis, treatment, or prevention of medical conditions or on other aspects of patient care. It often involves human participants; for example, a *clinical trial* is a specific type of clinical research that studies the safety and efficacy of a medication, procedure, or therapy on humans. Undergraduate students working on a clinical trial may be responsible for helping recruit participants or gather or analyze data. Working on a clinical trial or participating in another type of clinical research appeals to students who prefer a setting that involves patient contact.

Clinical research usually offers less opportunity for autonomy than basic research does and is generally less desirable on a med school application than basic research is. However, if basic research doesn't fit your interests, assisting with clinical trials is a good option.

Setting up a research experience

Finding a lab or clinical study to participate in takes initiative, just as arranging for a clinical experience does. Here are some guidelines:

✔ For basic research opportunities, start your search by approaching one of your current or former professors who studies an area of interest to you. Attend office hours or contact the professor to set up a meeting with him about volunteering in his lab. If he doesn't take undergraduate students in the lab, ask whether he knows of a colleague who may be able to provide a research opportunity for you.

In addition, check with the advisor for the department that you're interested in volunteering in and with your premedical advisor. Even if the first or fifth attempt doesn't work out, you'll eventually find a lab eager to have a willing volunteer to help.

✔ To find a clinical research experience, contact physicians affiliated with an academic institution. If you're shadowing a doctor at a teaching hospital, ask whether he or a colleague does clinical research. If your university doesn't have a medical school affiliated with it, contact medical schools or teaching hospitals nearby.

After you've obtained a research position, continue your work there for at least two semesters. Because you aren't in the lab full time, you may take weeks or months to become familiar with the work the team is doing, learn the techniques needed, and begin doing productive work. In addition, check with your university about receiving credit for your research experiences; many schools offer credit for research students perform with the university's faculty.

Summer Undergraduate Research Programs (SURFs), *Summer Internship Programs* (SIPs), and *Research Experiences for Undergraduates* (REUs) are eight-to-ten-week summer research experiences hosted by academic institutions throughout the country. (Institutions use different names for these programs, but the terms I list are among the more common ones.) During that time, participants work full time on a research project and receive a stipend (and often free housing). Selection for these programs is highly competitive, so previous research experience (in addition to good grades and strong letters of recommendation) can give you an edge when you apply even if experience isn't required. The following resources provide more information:

✔ See the AAMC list of summer internship programs at `www.aamc.org/members/great/61052/great_summerlinks.html`

✔ You can find the National Science Foundation REU sites at `www.nsf.gov/crssprgm/reu/reu_search.cfm`

Giving Back: Taking Part in Community Service

Medicine is a profession centered on service to others. Therefore, medical schools look for evidence that an applicant is committed to serving other people. However, simply stating "I want to help people" on your personal statement or in the interview isn't particularly convincing evidence of your altruistic nature. The best way to demonstrate that you get satisfaction through service is to be involved with your community.

Sometimes community service and clinical experiences overlap: Volunteering to deliver meals to homebound seniors with Alzheimer's disease brings you into contact with individuals suffering from chronic illness but also provides a much-needed service. However, many community service activities lie outside the clinical realm. Opportunities to become involved through both on- and off-campus organizations are endless: passing out groceries at a food bank, tutoring kids at a homeless shelter, and helping to build homes for families during an alternative spring break are a few examples of ways to give back.

Seek out projects that take advantage of your skills and talents. If you've been taking dance lessons since you were five and are eager to share your love of hip-hop and jazz, then volunteer to teach dance to kids at an after-school program serving low-income families. If your friends constantly compliment you on what a great listener you are, sign up for shifts at a crisis hotline.

Although there is no "right" community service activity to choose, especially seek out those that allow you to interact directly with clients. Doing so allows you to develop important physician skills, such as being a good listener and providing comfort to individuals in need. To find community service opportunities, contact your school's community outreach office (community engagement office). Also check to see whether your institution maintains an online database of community service positions.

Joining Clubs and Organizations

Joining a club or other organization allows you to participate in an area of interest within a structured setting and meet others who share your passion. Clubs geared toward students aiming for careers in the health professions provide valuable opportunities to explore medicine, network with health professionals, and discover ways to get involved in a clinical environment. In addition, groups unrelated to medicine (such as student government, sports teams, or a community orchestra) give you the chance to pursue a new or existing hobby. In addition to providing a break from your studies, cultivating interests outside medicine gives you the opportunity to show that you're a well-rounded applicant who brings more to the med school class than the ability to memorize biochemical pathways.

Being part of a premedical club

Premedical clubs vary from a handful of loosely-organized students to a large, well-established organization that features guest speakers from different specialties in medicine, has workshops on completing the application, and sponsors opportunities to volunteer at health fairs or other events. No matter what the size or structure, a premedical club gives you a tribe of like-minded peers to go through the trials and tribulations of the premedical years with. Through involvement in a premed club, you build a network of premed students, physicians, and advisors that helps you navigate the premedical years more smoothly and less stressfully.

Some competitiveness is inevitable when a group of premeds are together because eventually, those of you applying the same year will be trying for the same spots. However, you also find a spirit of collaboration as you work toward a shared goal. Club members farther along the premed path often share their wisdom gained from going through the application process and give tips about where to volunteer or who to shadow. As the years pass, you may become a mentor for new members or hold a leadership position in the group. Both teaching and learning are part of medicine, and within a premedical club you can try them both.

Exploring other clubs and interest groups

From photography to judo, you can find a club for any interest. You can even list hobbies you've participated in informally on your primary application; however, by participating in a club or group, you can more easily document your involvement and discover opportunities that you may otherwise miss. If you enjoy playing pick-up games of basketball, check out your school's intramural team; if you have a passion for archeology, turn off the *Indiana Jones* movies and join the archeology club. Like to run? Team up with a group of athletes who train together, and try to take it to the next level by entering a race. With a group of peers for inspiration, you'll likely do more with whatever endeavor you choose than if you go it alone.

Although most universities have an extensive array of clubs, you may need to go out into the broader community to find what you're looking for. Whether it's joining a community theater group or an organic gardening club, you'll be able to more deeply explore and demonstrate your interests with the resources of an established organization at your disposal.

Having Paid Employment as a Premedical Student

To help pay for your expenses during college, you may need to work during the summers, during the school year, or both. Applicants who work often worry that their job as a restaurant server or retail salesperson doesn't contribute to their application and puts them at a disadvantage because it takes up time that other premeds are spending doing research or volunteering. Some applicants even ask me whether they should include jobs unrelated to medicine or research on their application at all, thinking that such experience is irrelevant.

I advise applicants to put any jobs that they have held during college on their applications and to understand that committee members know that working develops time management, interpersonal and communication skills, and an understanding of how the real world works. These advantages may offset a shorter list of club memberships and shadowing experiences when the application is reviewed. Medical schools also take economic disadvantage into account when evaluating applications and realize that holding a job may impact your ability to earn the highest grades you're capable of. By including your paid employment on your application, you make schools aware of this additional demand on your time.

If you're fortunate enough to find a paid position in a medically-related setting, you have the opportunity to earn money while also adding to your clinical or research resume. Such positions include research associate, clinic assistant, phlebotomist, nurse assistant, or ER scribe. However, work of any type provides a different perspective and set of life experiences than someone who hasn't done paid work will have. Because schools look for diversity when putting together a class, having significant work experience (medical or otherwise) can set you apart as well as prove to the committee that you can multitask and withstand the time demands of med school. Juggling a job with premed classes and outside activities is challenging but not impossible. (Hit the following section for tips on managing your time.)

Fitting It All In

You may be wondering how you're supposed to volunteer in a hospital, shadow physicians, do research, participate in community service, and cultivate a hobby or two all while taking a full load of classes and maintaining a great GPA. The fact is you don't have to do everything; instead, you should pick a few areas to tackle and invest yourself fully in them. Med schools seek to put together a diverse class; that is, they want the class as a whole to include students from an array of backgrounds and with different interests. What they don't expect is that a single individual is going to encompass the entire range of possibilities for a premed student. To succeed as a premed student, choose your activities wisely, prioritize, strategize, and manage your time effectively.

By understanding how schools evaluate applicants' extracurricular activities and the importance of balancing variety with depth of involvement, you can determine which activities to participate in, when to do them, and for how long. In the following sections I cover what is and isn't important when it comes to activities. I also discuss tips for accomplishing what you need to without sacrificing every minute of your spare time and living on four hours of sleep per night.

Prioritizing and organizing

Your priorities as a premed should be as follows: academics first, everything else second. If your activities outside of class are interfering with your grades, cut back on them. I'm not saying that you have to get a 4.0 and that you should sacrifice everything else to attain that goal, but to have a realistic shot at med school, you need to make the grades. (Flip to Chapter 2 for insight into the numbers you need to be competitive.)

After grades, clinical experience is the most important item on the application. If you have time for only a couple of activities outside of school, make sure that at least one of them is clinical. Research and community service are close seconds after clinical experience. However, if you volunteer in a hospital during the school year in addition to being involved in a research project, for example, you may not have time to do community service as well. That's perfectly okay; you just need to make choices and stagger your activities. By limiting the number of activities you participate in at one time, you make sure your involvement in the activities you do select can be meaningful.

If your school is located in a small college town or other area where finding clinical experiences to participate in may be difficult, consider focusing on community service activities during the school year and devoting summer and other breaks to gaining clinical experience when you return to your hometown.

To manage your time effectively and choose among options for extracurriculars you should

✓ **Develop a written schedule for each semester.** Block out time for classes, labs, studying, volunteering, and every other commitment you have. Make sure that your schedule is realistic: If the schedule doesn't look doable in writing, it definitely won't be achievable in real life, where things like eating and sleeping are also competing for your time.

✔ **Learn to say "no."** One activity tends to lead to another. If you're a member of a club, for example, you'll inevitably be asked to help plan events, be on committees, or take on a leadership role. Don't be afraid to turn something down if you can't handle it at the moment. The same goes for friends asking for favors or pressuring you to go out when you really need to study.

✔ **Leave yourself some leisure time.** Everybody needs time to recharge. Getting into medical school doesn't require devoting every second of your life to improving your application. Your time will be even tighter in med school and especially in residency, so now is the time to develop the tools to lead a balanced life.

Balancing depth with breadth

Spending 3 months each volunteering in 4 different hospitals doesn't equate to 12 months spent in a single setting. Sticking with one position for an extended period is better than dabbling in several places because the former shows a sense of commitment and demonstrates genuine interest in an activity. Staying in one place also allows you to gain insights that can only be developed over time and provides opportunities to acquire additional responsibilities and leadership within a role. Of course, if you sign up for a volunteer activity, accept a job, or join a club that turns out to be a poor fit, you don't have to stick with it, but too much jumping around makes you appear unfocused. Schools like to see that an applicant has progressed within a couple of well-developed areas of involvement.

At the same time, don't limit your participation to one area only. Consider how your application will be perceived as a whole. Do you sound like someone who is genuinely interested in medicine, has meaningful interests, and demonstrates growth within the activities you've undertaken? If the answer is "no" to any part of this question, go back and determine what's lacking, either in the range of activities or the level of involvement.

Pick your activities with your interests in mind instead of trying to read the mind of the committee for each decision you make. You're most likely to continue with and build on an activity you're truly interested in. Note that you write about each activity on your primary application instead of just listing it. If you're truly engaged in an endeavor and learn from it, your enthusiasm will come through on your application and during your interview. (You can read about the primary application and interview phases in Chapters 8 and 10, respectively.)

Part II
Applying to Medical School

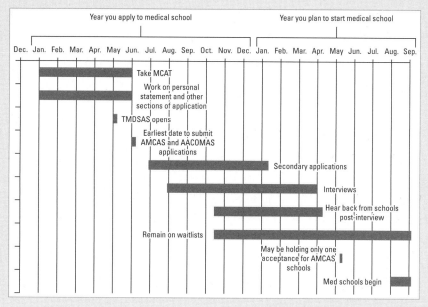

Illustration by Wiley, Composition Services Graphics

web extras

Understand the impact of letters of recommendation on your primary application in an article at www.dummies.com/extras/gettingintomedicalschool.

In this part . . .

✔ Understand the medical school application timeline so you can figure out when to take the MCAT, submit primary and secondary applications, request letters of recommendation, and more.

✔ Prepare for the MCAT with information on registration, test sections, study tips, and more.

✔ Select the best medical schools to apply to based on your needs and wants.

✔ Complete primary applications, including the personal statement, the work and activities section, and the information on course work.

✔ Secure great letters of recommendation from the best evaluators you have.

✔ Take care of secondary applications with more writing and the right timing.

✔ Get ready for interviews and handle decisions from schools whether you're in, out, or waitlisted.

Chapter 5

Surveying the Application Process

*W*hen you're looking to secure a spot in medical school, timing matters. A lot. The admission process to medical school is not only complex but also very long — nearly a full year, not counting your preparation before applying — and the chances of acceptance depend in part on when you submit your application.

Applying to med school is a multistep process, beginning with submitting your primary application, continuing with secondary applications, and concluding with interviews. To maximize your chances of admission, you need to understand how the application process works and when the optimal time to undertake each step is. A superb applicant who applies late in the cycle may find herself settling for a safety school, and a borderline-competitive applicant with a late application may end up without any offers of admission at all. Although applying early doesn't guarantee acceptance, it does increase your chance of admission.

In addition, timing is an aspect of the process you have control over. You can't change the *C* you received in organic chemistry to an *A* or magically add a couple of points to your MCAT score, but you can familiarize yourself with the application process, make a solid timeline, and stick to it, ensuring that you give yourself the greatest chance of success in this competitive process.

In this chapter, I describe the three main steps required to apply to medical school and the options you have for timing your application. I also discuss how a rolling admissions process works and how to use this system to your advantage. I guide you through the application timeline, from the start of the academic year in which you apply up until the day you matriculate into med school. Finally, I talk about early decision programs and utilizing your school's premedical advising office.

Getting Familiar with the Three Major Steps of the Admissions Process

Your application to medical school begins when you submit one or more types of *primary applications* through a centralized application service. Centralized application services allow you to submit one application to multiple schools. After completing the primary, you have a brief break before you're back to filling out forms for the next step of the application process — the secondary stage. Each individual school has its own supplemental *secondary application,* which you submit directly to the school. Finally, with the paperwork behind you, you get to the exciting part: interviews. At that point, you visit the schools that invite you and have a chance to prove yourself in person.

These three steps — primary application, secondary application, and interview — are the main elements of the admissions process. In the following sections, you get an overview of each so that you have the framework to understand the details about completing your application. (For the full scoop on these stages, see Chapter 8 on primary applications, Chapter 9 on secondary applications, and Chapter 10 on interviews.)

First up: The primary application

A primary application is a comprehensive document that includes your background information, academic record, test scores, employment and extracurricular activities, and personal statement. You submit this application along with copies of your official transcripts to an application service. ***Note:*** Application services function only as clearinghouses for information; they don't evaluate applications or make admissions decisions. The services process applications and verify that the coursework listed on your application matches your transcripts before transmitting a copy of your application to each school that you've designated. Each application service charges a fee based on the number of schools you are applying to. Many applicants need to submit only one primary application, although others may need to use two or three application services depending on where they're applying.

The three centralized application services are the following (see Chapter 8 for details):

- ✔ American Medical College Application Service (AMCAS), used by most allopathic medical schools

- ✔ American Association of Colleges of Osteopathic Medicine Application Service (AACOMAS), used by most osteopathic medical schools

- ✔ Texas Medical and Dental Schools Application Service (TMDSAS), used by public medical schools in Texas (both allopathic and osteopathic)

You can submit primary applications as early as May (for TMDSAS) or in June (for the other services). See the later section "Being Conscious of the Application Timeline" to make sure you're on top of the timing for each step.

Next in line: The secondary application

In addition to a primary application, medical schools require a secondary (supplemental) application. A secondary typically consists of three elements:

- A fee ranging from $35 to $200 (separate from the fee paid the application service for the primary application)
- Letters of recommendation (see Chapter 9 for details on these letters)
- Several short-answer or essay questions

The simplest secondaries require only a fee and letters of recommendation; the most complex include a list of essay questions that may take more than five pages to answer.

Many schools send secondary applications to all applicants; however, a fraction of schools, particularly public schools and some of the more selective private schools, only send secondaries to applicants who have passed through a screening process, usually based on GPA and MCAT scores.

Expect to receive a wave of secondaries as soon as the schools receive your primary application following coursework verification by the application service — anywhere from two days to six weeks after you submit to the service. (The shorter wait times occur very early and very late in the cycle.) After an initial rush of secondaries, the remainder will trickle in over the coming weeks and months. As a result, the secondary phase can last three or more months, which means that you may have completed your interviews at some schools while still waiting for secondaries at others.

Taken alone, a single secondary — even a long one — is easier to complete than the primary application. However, the secondaries for the 15, 20, or more schools you may apply to taken together may take weeks or months to finish. As I discuss in Chapter 7, determining how many secondaries you can complete in a timely manner is one consideration in making your list of schools. Submitting your primary application early won't help you if you lose your advantage at the secondary stage because you're overwhelmed with applications.

Time to talk: The interview

When a school has received all elements of your application (primary application, MCAT scores, secondary application and fee, and letters of recommendation), your file is complete and ready for review by the committee. Based on your credentials, the school may decide to offer you an interview, decline to interview you, or place your application on hold for consideration at a later date. A *pre-interview hold* may occur if the committee wants to evaluate more of the application pool before making a final decision about whether to offer you an interview. If you receive an interview, it means you're in the top 10 to 25 percent of applicants (depending on the school).

The interview is an opportunity for schools to learn about your personality and communication skills as well as to find out more about your background, interest in medicine, and reasons for applying to their schools. It's also your chance to see the schools, meet some of the faculty and med students, ask questions, and consider whether each program is somewhere you'll be happy at for four years. (For details about what to expect on interview day and how to ace the interview, head to Chapter 10.)

Timing Your Application

Timing your application to med school is more than just deciding the week or month that you'll apply. Before you can do that, you first need to determine the year that you'll be applying. Going straight from college to med school with only a summer break in between was once the norm, but in recent years about half of those applying have taken a year or more off after college (known as a *gap year*).

Whether you go straight through or take some time to work, travel, or volunteer before continuing your education depends on whether you need an extra year to strengthen your credentials as well as whether you're mentally and financially ready for four more years of school. By understanding your options, you equip yourself to make the best choice for your circumstances.

Entering medical school immediately after college

The traditional path to medicine consists of spending four years as a premedical student, graduating from college in the spring, and then heading off to medical school a few months later in the fall. Because the application process takes approximately one year to complete from when the admissions cycle opens, going immediately from college to med school means that you submit your application the summer between your junior and senior years of college. (The entire process, beginning when you start researching schools, obtaining letters of recommendation, writing your personal statement, and taking care of other items before the admissions cycle opens, takes longer than one year.)

Entering med school directly following college is best for applicants who

✔ **Want to finish their medical education as quickly as possible:** College, med school, and residency combined take 11 to 16 years to complete — longer if you decide to do a fellowship. Therefore, going straight through is the best route if you're eager to finish and become an attending physician. (You can shave off an additional year or two from the total by attending a six- or seven-year combined BS-MD program as I discuss in Chapter 13).

✔ **Don't have a good plan for how to spend a gap year:** When you take time off before medical school, programs want to see that you use the time productively. Doing a little MCAT studying and spending the rest of your time hanging out with friends and perfecting your video game skills will leave the committee wondering how motivated you really are.

✔ **May have a difficult time returning to school after taking a break:** Some premedical students fear losing their momentum if they spend a year away from their studies. When you're in school, the studying and test-taking mode is second nature, and going back to spending evenings and weekends getting ready for the next test after a year of freedom can be a tough adjustment (as can returning to a student income and lifestyle).

Taking a gap year

Because you submit your application at the end of your junior year if you plan to go straight from college to medical school, you need to have a strong GPA, solid clinical and extracurricular activities (see Chapter 4), and letters of recommendation (see Chapter 9) by the end of your third year of college. This schedule is achievable if you decide before or early in college to become a physician, but if you make the decision to pursue a career in medicine later on, you may need some extra time to get clinical experience and strengthen your overall application. Enter the gap year.

For some applicants, a gap or *glide* year is part of the plan from the outset, and it's a period of time they look forward to. For others, a gap between college and med school is the result of being rejected on the first try, necessitating another round of applications and an unexpected extra year of time. Whether you take a gap year out of choice or necessity, use it wisely; it's an opportunity to enhance your application. Some good ways to spend a gap year include the following:

✔ **Working in a job related to clinical medicine, research, or health policy:** A paid position in any area relevant to medicine gives you valuable experience, is an asset to your application, and helps you save up for medical school.

✔ **Participating in a long-term volunteer experience:** During a gap year, you have the time to invest more deeply in volunteering than you may have been able to while attending school. Volunteering can be the primary activity you do during your year off, especially if you participate in an organized program that offers full-time, substantial volunteer experiences. If you're working in a nonclinical job, use volunteering as a way to stay involved in clinical and community service activities on a part-time basis.

AmeriCorps, sometimes known as "the domestic Peace Corps," is a network of programs offering one-year volunteer opportunities in various fields, including healthcare. The program provides a stipend to cover living expenses and an education award that volunteers can use to pay back loans or for future schooling. You can find information at www.americorps.gov.

✔ **Improving your academic record:** If your academic record is weak, consider enrolling in a post-baccalaureate program designed for students aiming to improve their academic standing. Some of these programs offer undergraduate-level coursework while others, called *special master's programs* (SMPs), lead to a graduate degree. (I describe the different types of post-bac programs in detail in Chapter 16.) This option doesn't give you a break from school, but it can improve your GPA and increase your chances of admission if your grades are subpar.

Taking some time during your gap year to travel (in addition to doing activities that will strengthen your application) is fine too, but consult the later section "Being Conscious of the Application Timeline" to determine when you can take off without disrupting the application process.

Understanding Rolling Admissions

To understand the impact of timing on your application, you need to be familiar with rolling admissions, the system used by most U.S. medical schools. With *rolling admissions,* schools don't wait until the application deadline to begin reviewing applications. Instead, an applicant's file is reviewed as soon as it's complete. The result is that some applicants have submitted their primary and secondary applications, been interviewed, and actually received offers of acceptance before others have even completed the primary application. Early applicants fill spots in the class, making snagging one of the few remaining places more difficult for later applicants who are still competing against a large applicant pool. A committee that is aware that many spots are already filled may be more selective in offering interviews later in the cycle.

A few schools begin sending out interview invitations in July, and by mid-September, most schools have begun scheduling interviews. Because offers of admission may be extended as early as October at some MD schools, and even earlier by some DO schools, you should select the earliest interview date you're offered. This strategy allows you to be considered for a position in the class while all the spots are still available.

Applying early and possibly receiving at least one offer of admission in the fall also means you know for sure that you'll be attending med school the next year and won't have to deal with the time or stress of making contingency plans.

Even though doing every step in the application cycle as early as possible is actually less difficult than achieving As in science classes or a 33 on the MCAT, many applicants who prepare meticulously for every assignment and test in school don't put the same effort into the application process and end up submitting their materials far later than is optimal. (One applicant contacted me in late September seeking advice about his primary application, which he planned to submit before his top choice school's October 15 deadline. If that applicant wanted the best chance of being admitted, he really should've been paying attention to the *earliest* submission date.)

However, even a primary application submitted promptly the day the cycle opens doesn't benefit you if you then fall behind during another step. Too often, applicants who get their primary application done in June don't keep up with secondaries and instead sit on them for weeks or even months. Others dawdle on getting letters of recommendation or wait to take the MCAT until mid-summer (or later!), which results in their files being marked incomplete until the rest of the items arrive. By using the timeline in the next section as a guide, you'll be aware of when to do each step to ensure that you're one of the first applicants to be evaluated, not one of the last.

Although submitting your application early in the cycle is ideal, don't compromise on the quality by sending it if it isn't ready. If holding off until later in the cycle will allow you to submit a stronger application, doing so may be to your advantage; however, don't delay past August 1 if you can possibly avoid it.

Being Conscious of the Application Timeline

To stay on top of the application process, you need to start working on application-related tasks in the beginning of the academic year that you plan to apply.

✔ If you want to enter medical school directly after college, you need to start doing preliminary work for your application in the beginning of your junior year in order to be ready to submit your primary application in June of your junior year. The application cycle continues through that summer and most of your senior year of college. Put another way, if you want to start med school in the fall of 2015, the timeline in this section starts for you in September 2013 and concludes in August or September 2015 when you matriculate into medical school.

✔ If you're taking a gap year, then the events described in the section "Junior year of college" take place during your senior year, and the timeline events in the section "Senior year of college" occur during your gap year.

Although you can complete certain tasks during a range of dates, you should plan to complete each at the earliest possible date.

Figure 5-1 summarizes the major events in the medical school application timeline. Note that this timeline is geared toward getting everything done on the early side, but you should tailor it to fit your circumstances. Some items may be completed later and still be within school deadlines. Every applicant's real timeline is different!

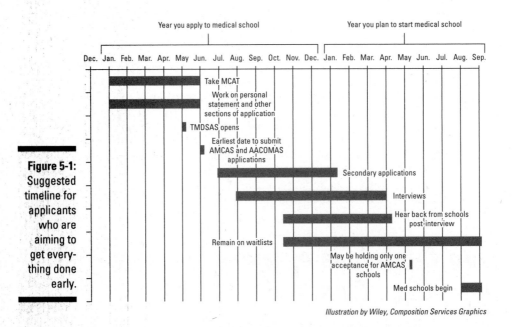

Figure 5-1:
Suggested timeline for applicants who are aiming to get everything done early.

Illustration by Wiley, Composition Services Graphics

Junior year of college

Your junior year is a busy one as you prepare for the MCAT, line up letters of recommendation, compile your list of schools, write your personal statement, and complete the many other items required to apply to med school. Try to take care of as much as you can during the academic year so you're ready to submit your application when the cycle opens (in May for TMDSAS and in June for AMCAS and AACOMAS schools). Remember, however, that the exact order and timing of application events varies from applicant to applicant and school to school.

September to December

Early in your junior year, take stock of your application portfolio and course work and begin researching medical schools. You may also be starting your MCAT preparation and perhaps even registering for the test this semester. Set up a meeting with your premedical advisor for guidance at the start of the semester and keep up your contact with him or her throughout the year.

- **Determine which required and recommended courses you still need to complete before the MCAT and prior to beginning medical school.** Plan your class schedule for the remaining semesters.

- **Assess your application portfolio for weaknesses.** Address those weaknesses by adding or continuing clinical, community service, leadership, and research activities. Chapter 4 has details.

- **Meet with your prehealth advisor to find out whether your school offers a committee letter for recommendations and how to obtain one.** A premedical *committee letter* is a letter of recommendation written by a committee typically composed of your school's prehealth advisor and one or more faculty members (see Chapter 9 for more info). In addition to determining whether your school offers a committee letter, find out what resources your advising office provides for application help, as described later in this chapter.

- **Begin considering possible sources of recommendations.** That's whom you want to ask for individual letters of recommendation (if your school doesn't offer a committee letter) or to contribute to your committee letter per your school's policy.

- **Become familiar with the application process.** Visit the websites for each of the primary application services you're using to find out how each application works. (No time is too early to start this step or to begin checking out the schools!)

- **Gather information about medical schools.** The Medical School Admission Requirements (MSAR) Online database, available for paid subscription through the AAMC site at `www.aamc.org`, is an excellent resource. For information about DO schools, you can download the most recent *Osteopathic Medical College Information Book* online at the AACOM site: `www.aacom.org`. In addition, visit the sites for individual schools and attend open houses or information sessions held by medical schools.

✔ **Register and study for the MCAT if you plan to take the test in January.** Register online at `www.aamc.org/students/applying/mcat/` at least two months prior to your planned test date. Test-takers planning for a spring test date can also get a head start on test preparation by beginning to study for the MCAT in the early fall. Chapter 6 offers tips on tackling the MCAT.

January to March

As the second semester of your junior year gets underway, you may be getting ready to take the MCAT in January or be preparing for a spring test date. It's also time to move forward with some of the writing for the primary application — especially the personal statement — and to ask for letters of recommendation if you haven't already obtained those. Summer positions in clinical and research settings fill up quickly, so work on nailing down your plans for summer break well in advance.

✔ **Consider taking the MCAT in January if you feel prepared; otherwise, register for and prepare for a spring test date.**

✔ **Continue clinical, community service, leadership, and research activities.**

✔ **Begin writing your personal statement and descriptions of work and activities for primary applications.** Chapter 8 can help.

✔ **Develop a list of schools (to be finalized after MCAT scores are received); check out Chapter 7 for guidance.**

✔ **Request letters of recommendation from faculty, physicians, and other evaluators individually or obtain a committee letter per your undergraduate institution's protocol.**

✔ **Arrange for summer plans, such as working in a clinical or research setting or taking classes.**

April

During this month, you keep going with your MCAT preparation if you're planning to take the test in the spring or summer. You should also keep making progress on your primary application.

✔ **Continue to prepare for the MCAT.** Take the MCAT by the end of May if at all possible (and no later than early summer unless you absolutely need more study time in order to achieve a good score) so that you have scores submitted to your schools of choice early in the cycle.

✔ **Continue working on your personal statement and other areas of the primary application.**

May

TMDSAS opens in May, so the admission cycle gets underway this month for applicants to public medical schools in Texas. AMCAS and AACOMAS become available online in May, so you can start filling in your applications for these services in order to be ready to hit "submit" in June.

✔ **Take the MCAT if you haven't already done so.**

✔ **Begin submitting TMDSAS materials.** Primary applications and supporting materials (transcripts and letters of recommendation) may be submitted at this time.

✔ **Start filling out AMCAS and AACOMAS applications.** Supporting materials may be submitted after the application is available online in May; however, you may need to wait until late May or June to receive spring grades before submitting transcripts. *Note:* AACOMAS doesn't accept letters of recommendation. Letters should be sent directly to DO schools during the secondary application process.

June

June is a big month for medical school applicants, because it's when both AMCAS and AACOMAS begin accepting applications. Submit the primary this month and get started with your summer activities such as classes, clinical experiences, or research.

✔ **Submit AMCAS and AACOMAS applications.** AMCAS and AACOMAS open in early June. Submit primary applications as early in the cycle as possible.

✔ **Begin doing paid or volunteer summer work in a clinical, research, or community service setting and/or taking summer courses.**

July

If you submit your primary application in June, by July you're into the secondary stage of the application process. A small number of schools begin extending interview offers this month.

✔ **Receive secondary applications.** Aim to submit secondary applications within one week of receipt. (Check out Chapter 9 for help with secondary applications.)

✔ **Earliest schools begin extending interview invitations.** (Flip to Chapter 10 for the scoop on handling interviews.)

✔ **Prepare for interviews, including purchasing interview attire.**

✔ **Retake the MCAT this month or in August if your initial score was low and you've had sufficient time to prepare again.**

August

Secondary applications are still arriving and interview invitations start to pick up in August. You may even go on your first interview this month.

- ✔ **TMDSAS and ACMAS Early Decision Program (EDP) deadline is August 1.** AACOMAS schools EDP dates vary by individual school. I cover EDPs in detail later in this chapter.

- ✔ **Continue to receive and complete secondaries.**

- ✔ **Many schools begin extending interview invitations by late August, and some schools begin conducting interviews at the end of August.**

Senior year of college

The end is finally in sight. In the fall of your senior year, you finish up the last of your secondaries and hit the interview trail. You may receive an acceptance as early as the fall, but if not, don't worry; the cycle still has months to go.

During the second semester of the academic year, you have to get serious about choosing a school if you have multiple acceptances. If you're wait-listed, you keep in contact with the schools you're on waitlists for by sending update letters and/or letters of interest. If all goes well, you spend the summer after you graduate getting ready to head off to medical school.

September

This month, you head deeper into interview season, although you may still also be filling out the last few secondaries that trickle in.

- ✔ **Interviews are underway at most medical schools.**

- ✔ **Complete remaining secondary applications.** A few schools that screen applications prior to sending a secondary may send secondaries later in the cycle, but an early applicant will have received the vast majority of secondaries by September.

- ✔ **Continue with clinical, volunteering, research, and leadership experiences during senior year.**

October

Mid-October is when some schools that use the AMCAS application send out their first batch of acceptances, so you may hear some good news then.

- ✔ **Interviews continue.**

- ✔ **AMCAS schools notify EDP applicants of decisions by October 1.**

> ✔ **Earliest acceptances for regular (non-EDP) AMCAS applicants are offered on October 15.** Other schools begin offering acceptances later in the fall or winter.

> ✔ **TMDSAS schools begin offering acceptances to nonresident, dual-degree, and other special program applicants.**

November to February

Interviews continue in full swing at through the fall and partway into the winter. TMDSAS schools start extending offers to in-state applications during this period as well.

> ✔ **TMDSAS schools begin extending offers of acceptance to Texas residents in mid-November.**

> ✔ **Interviews continue through late January or February at most schools, and as late as March or April at others.**

March to April

Interview season comes to an end by spring, but the admissions process isn't over yet. Schools are still making decisions about applicants they've interviewed. If you find out that you've been waitlisted, keep up contact with the school.

> ✔ **Interview season ends.**

> ✔ **Schools continue to send out notifications of acceptance, rejection, or placement on waitlists.** Chapter 11 has details on what to do when you hear back.

> ✔ **Update schools you've been waitlisted at with new activities and achievements.** The exact timing of updates depends on when you were waitlisted and when you have new information to provide the schools.

May to June

For AMCAS applicants, mid-May marks the time when they must whittle the number of seats they're holding down to one. As a result, this month can bring good news for those on the waitlist as spaces open up that need to be filled. You also graduate from college, so take some time to celebrate!

> ✔ **Decide which school you will continue to hold your place at if you've been accepted to more than one school.** Applicants may hold acceptances at multiple AMCAS schools until May 15. By May 15, applicants have to choose from the schools they've been accepted to, although they may remain on waitlists for other schools. (You're not committed to that school though; if you get brought up off a waitlist at a school higher on your list, you can withdraw from the spot you're holding.)

Waitlists begin to move primarily after May 15, when applicants holding multiple acceptances relinquish their extra places.

✓ **Graduate from college.** Congratulations!

July to September

Now that you're free from your premedical studies, focus on getting ready for medical school and keeping in touch with schools you're waitlisted at and still interested in attending. But don't make the summer all about work; take some time to enjoy yourself before you embark on your first year of med school.

✓ **Remain on waitlists for schools you continue to be interested in and update those schools and/or send a letter of interest.**

✓ **Prepare to start medical school, including relocating if necessary.** Flip to Chapter 19 for tips about getting ready for medical school.

✓ **Do something fun before starting med school!**

✓ **Begin medical school.**

Considering Early Decision Programs

Applying through an *early decision program* (EDP) may allow an applicant to secure a spot in medical school early in the application cycle. However, applying EDP is only a good option for a small number of applicants because for most, the risks are likely to outweigh the potential benefits. Applicants who are applying through EDP may initially apply to only one medical school in the United States. For AMCAS schools, the EDP deadline is August 1. By that date, an applicant must submit her AMCAS application to the selected EDP school. The school has until October 1 to notify an EDP applicant if she has been accepted or rejected. If accepted, the applicant must attend that school. If rejected from the school, she may apply to other schools. *Note:* The EDP deadline for TMDSAS is also August 1. EDP dates for AACOMAS schools vary.

For the vast majority of applicants, applying during the regular cycle is the best strategy. The problem the EDP process presents for your admissions strategy is that if you're rejected, you have to start applying to other schools after October 1 — very late in the normal admissions cycle. As I discuss in the earlier section "Understanding Rolling Admissions," you maximize your chance of admission by applying early in the cycle, which means completing your primary in June, submitting secondaries during July and August, and interviewing in the fall. By the time a rejected EDP applicant gets into the regular applicant pool, she's months behind the ideal timetable, placing her at a severe disadvantage.

Therefore, only applicants in very specific circumstances should consider EDP. Applying EDP may be an appropriate choice if

- ✔ You're a very strong applicant for the EDP at the school you're interested in applying to.

- ✔ You meet or exceed the school's published EDP eligibility criteria, minimum MCAT score, and GPA and have researched the general profile of the applicant the schools seeks. Contact the admissions office if necessary to see whether it can offer guidance about whether you'd be a good fit for the school's EDP.

- ✔ You have a compelling reason to attend a particular school.

For example, you may benefit from applying via an EDP if you're deeply rooted in an area — you own a home and have a spouse with a job and/ or children who attend school where you currently live. You can't easily relocate and may therefore have a strong preference for a local school. If you're extremely competitive for admission through the EDP at your school of choice, then the benefits of having an assured place in that school early in the cycle may outweigh the risk of potentially being rejected and having to apply to other schools late in the cycle.

For the typical applicant, however, the goal is to maximize the chance of admission to *a* medical school versus getting into a particular medical school. You usually achieve the best odds of getting admitted somewhere by applying to a broad range of schools early in the regular cycle.

Not all schools offer EDP. Approximately 60 percent of allopathic schools and only a small number of osteopathic schools have EDPs. Therefore, check with the school you're interested in to make sure that it has an EDP if you're considering this option.

Getting Help from a Premedical Advisor

You don't need to go it alone when you're applying to medical school. Most colleges have a *premedical* or *prehealth advisor* to help students applying to med school or other health professions programs. Premedical advisors may offer help with everything from setting up your schedule to practicing for the interview, and they can be a very valuable resource. In the following sections, I explain how to use your school's advising office and what to do if your school doesn't have one.

Using your premedical advising office effectively

If you're a premedical student just entering college, one of the first things you should find out is whether your school has a prehealth or premedical advising office and what services it offers. In fact, the level of support given to premedical students may even be a factor in which college you select (as Chapter 3 explains). If your undergraduate career is well underway and you haven't visited the premedical or prehealth advising office yet, do so immediately.

The amount and type of help advisors offer vary widely from school to school. Some walk advisees through each step of their premedical career from course selection and lining up shadowing experiences to proofreading application materials, while others primarily point premeds to resources to explore on their own. Any help that you can get to make the application process go more smoothly is important, so don't overlook this opportunity to get assistance from someone who has likely helped many students from your school through the admissions process. Some of the areas that a premedical advisor can help you with include the following:

- ✔ **Planning your course schedule:** Figuring out which courses at a particular college best fulfill the prerequisites for medical school and prepare you for the MCAT isn't always obvious (Chapter 3 includes a list of prerequisite classes). A prehealth advisor familiar with the course offerings at your institution can help you select the best classes and plan the order and timing of courses given your academic background and major. Make sure you seek guidance about your schedule from the academic advisor from the department you are majoring in as well. He or she is essential in helping you to make sure that you fulfill the requirements for a degree in your major.

- ✔ **Assessing the strengths and weaknesses of your application portfolio:** Seeking your advisor's feedback about your overall application allows you to address weaknesses in your application while you still have time and to emphasize your strengths when presenting your candidacy.

- ✔ **Finding opportunities for clinical and research experiences:** Prehealth advisors may maintain a list of hospitals and clinics that take student volunteers as well as programs for students to do summer research, volunteering, shadowing, and international medical missions. Chapter 4 has details on these extracurriculars.

- ✔ **Offering forums about admissions topics:** Topics covered during these sessions can range from preparing for the MCAT to writing your personal statement and selecting schools.

✔ **Obtaining a committee letter or individual letters of recommendation:** Some schools offer a committee letter in lieu of individual letters of recommendation, an option you should take if available. (Many schools prefer and even require that you use a committee letter if your school offers one.) The process of obtaining the letter is coordinated through a school's premed advisor or office. If you're obtaining individual letters, your advisor can assist you in selecting evaluators.

✔ **Providing critical feedback on your application and personal statement.** Your premedical advisor can help you ensure that your personal statement effectively conveys your reasons for pursing a medical career and lets the committee get to know you better as an applicant. She can also give you pointers about your activities descriptions and check to make sure that your application is clear and complete.

✔ **Selecting medical schools:** Premed advisors often have records of which medical schools applicants from their institutions have been accepted to and can use this information to help you make a strategic list of schools.

✔ **Preparing for the interview:** Some prehealth offices offer mock interviews for applicants. The opportunity to practice prior to the real thing allows you to perfect your performance and take the edge off your nerves.

Finding a premedical advisor if your school doesn't have one

Don't worry; you don't have to miss out if your school doesn't have a premed advisor or if you've already graduated. Graduates of schools that have premedical advising can check with their alma maters to see whether advising services are available to alumni. Many schools at least allow alumni to take advantage of limited services, such as sponsorship for a committee letter.

 If your school doesn't offer advising to alumni (or at all), contact the National Association of Advisors for the Health Professions (NAAHP) at www.naahp.org to be put in contact with a health professions advisor who has volunteered to assist students who otherwise don't have access to an advisor.

You may also find a professor or physician who can act as your mentor. In seeking a mentor, look for someone who has a strong understanding of the admissions process — ideally, someone with previous experience as a premedical advisor or admissions committee member.

Finding someone who knows how admissions works is important because well-meaning but inaccurate advice can cause major problems when application time comes. Therefore, you may need to pick and choose the type of help you receive from each individual. For example, a particular science professor at your school may be able to guide you to find research opportunities but know little about specific course requirements for medical school. A physician you shadow may have served as an interviewer for a medical school and can help you practice for the interview but may not be in a position to guide you in selecting schools.

Finally, private admissions counseling services are available to supplement the help offered by a college prehealth advisor or as an option for those who don't have access to a prehealth advisor. Some private advisors are former college prehealth advisors, while others are physicians with experience in admissions or advising. The background, range of services, and cost vary greatly among such services, so if you plan to use a private admissions advisor, check out a potential advisor's credentials and experience to find one who is a good fit for your needs.

Chapter 6

Tackling the MCAT

*I*n addition to completing the prerequisite course work I describe in Chapter 3, applying to medical school means you need to take the *Medical College Admission Test* (MCAT), a standardized examination that tests both science knowledge and critical-thinking skills. The MCAT is one of the most important factors in admissions, so doing well on this test is essential in ensuring that you have a good chance of getting into medical school. A great MCAT score can catapult you from being a contender for mid-tier schools to having a shot at the top ones, while a low score can be an insurmountable barrier, even if you have otherwise-solid credentials. Therefore, you need to approach the test with the same level of planning and preparation you invest in your course work and clinical experiences.

To excel on the MCAT, you first have to know what you're facing and prepare a plan of attack. To help you get ready for what is arguably biggest challenge you face as a premedical student, this chapter familiarizes you with how the test is organized and what it covers before guiding you through the options for preparing. I also discuss what your scores mean and how schools evaluate them, as well as how to decide whether to retake the test. You also find out how to handle your application if the admissions cycle opens before you've received your test score. Finally, you discover what you can expect to see on the MCAT starting in spring 2015, when a new version of the test is released.

Beginning with a Few MCAT Basics

To be accepted to medical school, you need to do well on the grueling rite of passage for premedical students known as the MCAT. This test demands not only excellent mastery of the basic sciences and sharp critical-thinking skills but also stamina — the test takes more than four hours to complete, not counting breaks and the pretest tutorial. (It's more than six hours for the new MCAT.) This computer-based, multiple-choice examination includes topics in both the physical and biological sciences as well as a section on Verbal Reasoning. (See the later section "Looking to 2015: Major Changes Are Coming to the MCAT" for a look at content tested on the updated MCAT.)

The MCAT is offered eight months out of the year but on only a few days in a given month, so registering early is important to help ensure that you take the MCAT at the optimal time and location for you. After the test, you have a month of waiting before your scores are released. In the following sections, I give you the rundown of essentials such as registration for the test, the length and structure of the test, and interpreting your test score.

Registering for the test

The MCAT is offered one to seven times in each of January, March, April, May, June, July, August, and September. (The total number of testing dates in a year is approximately 25.) For some dates, the test is offered in either the morning or the afternoon, and for others it's offered both times of day.

Registration takes place online through the MCAT Scheduling and Registration System at `services.aamc.org/20/mcat/`. The Association of American Medical Colleges (AAMC) recommends registering at least 60 days in advance of the date that you want. The regular registration fee for the MCAT is $270, with an additional fee of $75 for late registration, rescheduling your test, or switching test centers.

Test-takers may apply for the Fee Assistance Program (FAP). The MCAT registration fee for those approved for the FAP is $100. You must receive approval for the FAP prior to registering to receive the reduced fee. Check out the AAMC site at `www.aamc.org/students/applying/fap` for information about the FAP.

Test-takers who need accommodations can apply for them prior to testing. However, don't delay your registration while waiting to hear whether your request for accommodations has been approved. You can hold your seat at a testing center while you await a decision regarding accommodations. Flip to Chapter 17 for more information on accommodations.

Getting an overview of the test's length and structure

Until spring 2015, when the new MCAT is scheduled to be released, the MCAT includes three scored sections: Physical Sciences, Verbal Reasoning, and Biological Sciences. For the transitional years of 2013 and 2014, test-takers have the option of also taking a fourth, unscored trial section. If you opt to take the trial section, expect to see content from behavioral sciences and biochemistry, both of which will be tested on the 2015 MCAT. The trial section is administered after the scored portions of the exam are complete, and participation is voluntary. Table 6-1 shows the breakdown of the 2013–2014 MCAT by section.

Table 6-1	MCAT 2013–2014 Sections and Length
Section	*Time*
Physical Sciences (52 questions)	70 minutes
Verbal Reasoning (40 questions)	60 minutes
Biological Sciences (52 questions)	70 minutes
Optional trial section (32 questions)	45 minutes

Before beginning the first section, you have the chance to take an optional tutorial to become familiar with the computer. An optional ten-minute break is allowed after each section. Following the test, you have five minutes to decide whether you want to void your test, and then you have the choice to complete a survey before leaving. (You can read about the making the decision to void the test in "Considering the option of voiding your exam" later in this chapter.) Total testing time is over four hours if you take only the three scored sections and over five hours if you include the trial section.

Prior to 2013, the MCAT also included a writing sample. However, this section, which schools put very little weight on for admissions, has been eliminated in advance of other changes to the test.

Interpreting your test score

Approximately one month after you take the MCAT, your scores become available online through the MCAT Testing History System (MCAT THx) at services.aamc.org/mcatthx. A score report includes a numerical, scaled score for each scored section (Physical Sciences, Verbal Reasoning, and Biological Sciences); a composite score; and the percentiles for each of these.

The scaled score for each section ranges from 1 (lowest score) to 15 (highest score), for a total score of 3 to 45. The scaled score is derived from a raw score based on the number of questions you answered correctly on the test.

Now for the question you're really wondering about: What's a good score?

According to the AAMC, the mean total MCAT score for tests administered in 2012 was approximately 25. For 2012 matriculants to U.S. allopathic (MD) medical schools, the mean was slightly above 31. Statistics from the American Association of Colleges of Osteopathic Medicine (AACOM) show that for 2011 matriculants to osteopathic (DO) schools, the mean score was over 26. A score of 30 is competitive for admission to an allopathic school if you have an otherwise-strong application, although an applicant with a score in this range should typically focus on lower-tier schools (see Chapter 7 for tips on crafting your list of schools). A score in the 31 to 32 range puts you in a much more comfortable position and is generally competitive for admission. With a score below a 30, admission to an MD school can be more difficult unless you have special circumstances. Breaking into the ranks of the top-tier schools usually takes a score of 34 or 35.

Understanding the Importance of the MCAT in Admissions

The MCAT is extremely important in admissions — far more important than the SAT is in college admissions. Together with GPA, it's one of the biggest factors (if not the single biggest) in determining your chances of acceptance. Given the choice between a relatively low GPA with a stellar MCAT and a poor MCAT with a top GPA, I'd take the first. A great MCAT alone won't get you into med school, but a poor one will severely diminish your chance of admission. And because some schools use MCAT scores to filter out applications without fully reviewing them, a low MCAT score may mean that the nonnumerical elements of your application, such as your personal statement (see Chapter 8), extracurricular activities (Chapter 4), and letters of recommendation (Chapter 9), don't get due consideration. In the following sections, I discuss some of the reasons why schools place so much emphasis on the MCAT and the ways in which schools use the MCAT to evaluate applicants.

Recognizing why schools stress the MCAT in admissions

Some students feel that putting so much weight on a single test is unfair; they believe their grades are a better representation of their potential than the

MCAT is. As you face the MCAT, it may help to know that schools emphasize the MCAT in admissions for specific reasons:

- ✔ **Gauging future success:** For example, studies show performance on the MCAT helps predict the chance of passing the medical licensure examinations.

- ✔ **Evaluating academic readiness:** In addition, the MCAT and GPA help schools assess an applicant's readiness for the incredibly intense academic load in medical school. Of course, being a great physician takes more than textbook knowledge, but grades and MCAT scores give schools a means to determine who is likely to succeed academically.

- ✔ **Providing an objective measure:** As I note in Chapter 3, the MCAT provides a common measure with which med schools can compare students from different undergraduate programs. The rigor of courses and grading varies widely from college to college: A 3.6 at a very selective research university with notoriously difficult science courses may be equivalent to a 3.9 at a school with a weaker science program or more lenient grading. The MCAT helps ensure that students who went to schools with more-rigorous grading policies won't be at a disadvantage to peers who hail from institutions with grade inflation.

Discovering how schools use the MCAT in admissions

Although most medical schools send a secondary application to every applicant who submits a primary application, some programs first weed out applicants based on GPA and MCAT scores. After you get past the secondary stage, the MCAT is essential in determining whether you're offered an interview and ultimately whether you're admitted. It's by no means the only factor schools consider, but without at least a solid score, your application may not even get a serious look because some schools do a full review of only those applications that contain an MCAT above a certain threshold. (See Chapter 9 for more about secondary applications.)

At all stages, MCAT screening may involve evaluating MCAT and GPA separately or in combination, such as by using a formula that gives a particular weight to each factor. A school may require an absolute minimum each for an applicant's GPA and MCAT score but beyond that allow for a higher GPA to compensate for a weaker MCAT or vice versa.

Along with considering the composite MCAT score, many schools also have established minimum scores for each section, such as an 8 or a 9. If you meet the minimum for each section but one section score is relatively weak, good scores in the other two sections may offset the lower score. However, your best bet is to do well in all areas. The goal is to have an evenly distributed score, not obvious strengths coupled with a glaring weakness. Aim for double digits in each section because although a school's cutoff for initial consideration may be slightly lower, a 10 is generally the lowest desirable section score.

A common scenario for uneven scores is strong science scores combined with a lower Verbal Reasoning score. Schools take the Verbal Reasoning section just as seriously as the others, so don't neglect this section to focus exclusively on the sciences when you study. (For more study tips, head to the later section "Preparing for the MCAT.")

When it comes to admissions, exceptions exist. Schools don't look only at numbers, and factors such as coming from socioeconomic disadvantage, being a member of a group that is underrepresented in medicine, or having extraordinary outside accomplishments or life experiences can help you overcome a low MCAT score. Schools want a diverse mix of students and therefore admit some students whose numbers lie outside the typical range if the admissions committee believes that the student will make a valuable contribution to the class and to the profession of medicine.

Checking Out What's on the MCAT

The MCAT currently contains 144 questions, most of which are passage based. A small number of questions in the science sections are *discrete questions* independent of a passage. The MCAT science sections cover topics taught in the basic science courses required for entry into medical school: general biology, physics, general chemistry, and organic chemistry. If you're taking the test anytime up through January 2015, check out the following sections to find out more about each part of the test. If you're aiming for a test date in spring 2015 or thereafter, refer to the later section "Looking to 2015: Major Changes Are Coming to the MCAT" for the scoop on the new MCAT.

Physical Sciences

The first section you'll encounter on the MCAT is Physical Sciences. This 70-minute section encompasses content from both physics and general (inorganic) chemistry. Because most of the questions are passage based, you have to apply concepts and formulas you've learned previously to new situations. For example, a series of chemistry experiments may be described, followed by questions that require you to extract information from the passage and to use your knowledge of kinetics and other topics to answer. Therefore, in addition to content review, your preparation should include plenty of practice with passage-based questions to get you used to this type of testing format.

Here are a few facts to familiarize you with this part of the test:

- ✔ The section includes 7 passages with 4 to 7 questions per passage as well as 13 discrete questions, for a total of 52 questions.

- ✔ The information tested is based on content covered during two semesters of physics and two semesters of general chemistry.

- ✔ Examples of topics tested include stoichiometry, thermodynamics, acids and bases, Newtonian mechanics, fluids and solids, and electromagnetism.

Verbal Reasoning

Following the Physical Sciences section, you switch gears completely as you head into the Verbal Reasoning section. Verbal Reasoning is fundamentally different from the science sections because it doesn't require any knowledge of outside content. For the Verbal Reasoning section, any information you need to answer the questions can be found in the passage (whereas the science passage may require you to recall and apply, say, Coulomb's law).

Having the information right in the passages doesn't mean that this section is easy, though. In fact, many test-takers find this section to be the most challenging one of the examination because it lies outside of the realm of science, where premeds are typically most comfortable. If you're a humanities or social sciences major, you may find yourself more at ease with this section because of the extensive amount of critical reading you've had to do for your college courses.

Essential information about the Verbal Reasoning section includes the following points:

- ✔ The section is shorter than the science sections: 60 minutes for 7 passages, with 5 to 7 questions per passage, for a total of 40 questions. This part of the test contains no discrete questions.

- ✔ The passages discuss subjects within the disciplines of the humanities, natural sciences, and social sciences. No specific course work in these areas is required; however, it does help to have taken humanities and social science courses.

- ✔ Questions focus on details within the passage as well as more global aspects of the passage such as tone or theme. You must be able not only to understand the passage but also to interpret and apply the information you read.

Biological Sciences

The Biological Sciences section of the MCAT is the last scored section of the test and is allotted 70 minutes, the same amount of time as the Physical Sciences section. This section tests biology and organic chemistry topics, and the emphasis is on passage-based questions. Again, memorization alone doesn't lead to a stellar score; in addition to using your science knowledge, you must apply your critical-thinking skills to assess the information in the passage to respond to the questions posed.

Here are some basics about the Biological Sciences section:

✔ The section includes 7 passages with 4 to 7 questions per passage as well as 13 discrete questions, totaling 52 questions.

✔ The information tested is based on content covered during two semesters of general biology and two semesters of organic chemistry.

✔ Examples of topics tested are molecular biology, genetics, organ systems, nomenclature, stereochemistry, and reaction mechanisms.

Although the science content tested on the MCAT is based on topics covered in lower-division science courses, taking upper-division classes in disciplines such as molecular biology, genetics, and physiology reinforces topics that appear on the test. Therefore, if you have room in your class schedule prior to the MCAT, consider taking some additional relevant biology courses beyond the minimum. (See Chapter 3 for a list of required and recommended prerequisite course work.)

Trial section

If you take the MCAT in 2013 or 2014, you have the option to complete an unscored trial section after you've completed the scored sections of the test. The 45-minute trial section consists of 32 questions. The questions you receive cover either biological and physical sciences topics (including biochemistry) or biology, psychology, and sociology topics (subjects found on the Psychological, Social, and Biological Foundations of Behavior section that appears on the new MCAT). Participation is voluntary, so the decision to take this section (or not) is yours.

Preparing for the MCAT

After you decide when you'll be taking the MCAT, you need to develop a plan of attack. (See Chapter 5 for tips about when to take the test.) To do so, you have to sift through the numerous options for preparation — from highly structured classroom courses to independent study — to formulate a plan that works best for you. Keep in mind that you don't have to stick to one approach or set of materials; mix and match techniques to find the optimal combination if needed.

In the following sections, I describe the different options for preparation as well as provide you with study tips and guidance about creating a plan to help you succeed on what is likely to be one of the most important tests in your life. Good MCAT results vastly improve your odds of admission, so although taking the test may be one of the most difficult parts of your pre-medical career, the rewards for mastering it are great.

Examining specific prep approaches

If the thought of studying for the MCAT is so overwhelming you find your eyes glazing over, never fear. You have several study options at your disposal that you can tailor to your specific needs. So wipe away the glaze and read on about how review courses, choose-your-own-adventure plans, and/or tutors can help you nail the MCAT.

Although getting ideas about preparation methods from peers may help familiarize you with what's out there, what works for someone else may be less than ideal for you. A friend who got a 38 may swear by self-study and insist that a prep course is a waste of money, but if you know that you need a structured environment to stay on task, thank him for his advice and then go sign up for a course. By using your knowledge of your learning style and study habits to personalize your preparation, you'll perform as well as possible when test day comes.

Taking a review course

Many premedical students take an MCAT review course offered by a test preparation company. Such courses may take place in a classroom setting or be administered online and usually meet from one to three times a week for a period of two to six months. Other students enroll in intense boot camp-type experiences during spring or summer break as part of their study plan.

Test preparation courses are often comprehensive and include books, diagnostic tests, sets of practice questions, and full-length tests along with the lessons. Some of the advantages to taking an MCAT preparation course are

✓ **They're highly structured.** If you tend to procrastinate, a course with specific meeting times and assignments each week may help you to stay on top of your studying. Unlike a college class, though, you aren't working toward a grade, so you still may be tempted to skip classes or not complete assignments. Having a set plan to follow (and knowing that you've paid for the class) can help keep you accountable even when your motivation wanes.

✔ **They provide access to an instructor.** Whether the instructor is in the classroom with you or the class is offered live online, you have someone to turn to for your questions about the material. This way, if you're stuck on a concept you can get help, saving time and allowing you to move forward with your studies.

✔ **They offer a peer group.** If you take a classroom course, you meet other students who are preparing to take the test at a similar time as you are. Forming a study group with some of these students may help ensure you get your homework done and gives you someone to bounce ideas off of or go to for a pep talk when you need one.

Now for the cons:

✔ **Cost can be an issue.** At the larger test prep companies, courses may run in the $1,500 to $2,000 range. Cost can be one of the biggest drawbacks to taking a class, so if your finances are tight but you're organized and disciplined, going it alone (see the following section) may be a better option. *Tip:* Some colleges and universities offer lower-cost noncredit MCAT prep courses. Check with your premed advisor about these options.

✔ **The course may not be tailored to your needs.** Structured courses may spend roughly equal time on all the science subjects. But if you're a biology major who has biology topics down cold but struggles with physics, you may prefer to cut back on the time you spend on biology and instead invest it where you need extra practice. With a course, you lose some flexibility, although you can make up for that to some degree outside of classroom hours when you're reviewing on your own.

✔ **The quality of the teaching can vary.** Even if a course has great study guides and practice questions, you may not get much out of it if the instructor doesn't teach effectively or isn't engaging. Many test prep companies require instructors to have taken the test and scored in a particular percentile to teach, and the companies provide further training on how to teach the material. Still, the quality of courses and their instructors varies. Sometimes instructors may even be undergraduates with little teaching experience. Make sure you check into a course closely and preferably sit on a class given by the instructor you'll have before you choose a course.

Studying independently

Although many test-takers prepare through a course, self-studying for the MCAT and achieving an outstanding score is entirely possible. However, if you decide to take this path, you need to approach your studies with the same level of commitment that you have for a job, class, or volunteer experience. You also need

✔ A complete set of study materials

✔ A detailed, written schedule

✔ Plenty of self-discipline

For help with the first two, see the later sections "Choosing study materials" and "Making a study schedule." For the third, do an honest self-assessment. If you don't think you have what it takes to study on your own, that's okay; simply select a different approach.

Choosing to study on your own doesn't mean that you're resigned to toiling away alone for the next three or more months. Look for a group of like-minded students and create your own course, dedicating certain days to group study and others to self-study or taking practice tests. If you're having difficulty with a particular subject but don't want to take a full course, consider hiring a tutor to help you get over that hurdle (see the next section). As I mention earlier in this chapter, it's all about finding what works for you and drawing from any resources you need to get the job done. If you realize a few weeks into your plan that you're falling behind or need more support, you can always sign up for a class, but don't wait too long before you make a change so that you ensure you have plenty of time to prepare properly.

Using a tutor

A good tutor provides the expertise of an instructor in the classroom but offers flexibility and individualized attention that's impossible to achieve in a group setting. However, because one-on-one instruction is costly, most people use this option only for a limited number of hours as a supplement to a course or self-study rather than as a major component of preparation.

Ideally, the tutor you work with is not only an expert in his subject but also very familiar with the MCAT. MCAT tutors affiliated with test preparation companies are usually instructors for an MCAT course and therefore have knowledge of their subject and understand how the test works. However, fees for such tutors can run $175 to $200 per hour.

The MCAT tends to focus on some concepts within a discipline more than others, and the mostly passage-based format of the test requires a different approach than preparing for a typical college exam. Although an organic chemistry tutor with no exposure to the MCAT may do a great job of explaining reaction mechanisms, he may not be able to guide you on how to most effectively approach Biological Sciences passages overall or improve your timing. If you need help mastering particular concepts, though, a tutor (such as a graduate student in that subject area) who isn't necessarily versed in the MCAT may still be a good choice and is usually less expensive than one who is also an expert on the test.

To make the best use of your time with any tutor, study thoroughly between each session and jot down topics or questions you're stumped on to cover during meetings.

Choosing study materials

When it comes to study materials, books intended for MCAT review, rather than your textbooks, should be your primary sources for test preparation. Review books focus on the most important concepts for the test instead of providing an in-depth discussion of every topic within a subject area the way textbooks do. Use your textbooks to clarify material in the review books as needed or to dig deeper into a topic if doing so helps you master a concept better. If you haven't taken a particular subject in a long time, you may need to refer to your textbook more frequently. If a class is fresh in your mind, though, you can do the vast majority of your studying from review books.

Along with reading and reviewing content, you should do plenty of practice questions, passages, and tests. If you're taking a course, the materials you need to study are usually included. However, if you plan to study on your own, you should to obtain the following:

- ✔ **A set of books that, taken together, covers content from physics, general chemistry, biology, and organic chemistry.**

- ✔ **A book that focuses on Verbal Reasoning.**

- ✔ **Additional practice questions.** Content-focused books often contain practice questions, but you should do many practice questions and passages before you take the test. You can purchase additional sets of questions and tests through various sources in printed versions and CD-ROMs or via online access.

- ✔ **The AAMC practice MCAT exams.** These tests contain retired questions from previous exams and are therefore the closest you can come to taking the real thing before test day. You can purchase them online through the AAMC (www.aamc.org). AAMC practice tests are probably the single most valuable resource because they're created by the same folks who create the MCAT.

You may find that an organic chemistry book from one series explains material very clearly but that you prefer the physics and Verbal Reasoning books from a different one. You don't have to stick with a single series; instead put together the set of materials that you'll learn from the most easily and effectively.

Because the test is administered on computer, much of your practicing should take place on computer as well, especially as you get closer to test day. Working from a computer screen is different from reading and answering questions from printed material, so by practicing on a computer, you simulate test day as closely as possible.

Making a study schedule

When formulating a study schedule, keep in mind that getting ready for the MCAT is a marathon, not a sprint, shaped by your schedule, your starting point, and your target score. A typical length of preparation is around three or four months, with a lot of variation. Many students put in 300 to 500 hours, though again, each case is unique.

If you're taking the MCAT in April and are a full-time student, you'll have to spread out your studying over a longer period of time because you'll be dividing your time between studying for your courses and MCAT prep (although you may find some overlap between the two tasks if you're taking courses that cover subjects tested on the MCAT). However, if you plan to take the MCAT in the summer, you may be able to clear out your schedule and study for a shorter, more-intense period of time. If your foundation in the sciences is weak, you're shaky in Verbal Reasoning, or you really need to rock the MCAT because you're aiming for a top-tier school, allot yourself extra time.

I'm often asked by students what the total number of hours they should study is, but so many factors are involved that's it's impossible to say exactly. The number of hours you devote to studying should be the number it takes you to master the material and to hit your target score consistently on practice tests.

When formulating a study schedule, begin by assessing how many hours you can realistically study each week. Take into account school, work, extracurricular activities, and leisure time. If things don't look like they're adding up, either cut back on some of your activities or rethink your test date. If you're in school full time or working full time, you may only be able to put in 10 hours to 15 hours a week of MCAT studying many weeks but then ramp up the time during school breaks or vacation time from work and in the month leading up to the test. Here are some tips to consider as you compile a schedule:

- ✔ **Plan to take a full-length practice exam at the outset of your preparation.** Taking a full-length test allows you to understand the type of exam for which you are preparing.

- ✔ **Begin with your weakest areas.** If you're a whiz at physics but have a tough time with organic chemistry, invest more time in organic chemistry early on. This strategy allows you to build the foundation you need in all areas to tackle the material in the context of MCAT passages and questions.

- ✔ **Don't neglect Verbal Reasoning.** Putting Verbal Reasoning off in favor of concentrating on the sciences can be tempting, but as I discuss in the earlier section "Understanding the Importance of the MCAT in Admissions," every part of the test is important.

✔ **Be detailed but flexible.** As you proceed, you may find that you need to spend more time one area and less in another than you'd originally budgeted or that you absorb more information if you study in shorter blocks more frequently. Always have a plan, but be willing to adjust it as you go.

✔ **Include some time off.** At least one MCAT-free day a week helps keep you more focused when you're studying and gives you something to look forward to when the grind starts getting to you.

Figure 6-1 shows a sample study schedule that gives you a snapshot of what a typical week may look like for a student who's studying around 20 hours per week. Test-takers who are in school full time may study for less than this amount each week, while those who are studying in the summer or are in the weeks leading up to the exam may put in even more time weekly. Note how the schedule includes both content review and practice questions and tests.

Preparing for the science sections

The Physical Sciences and Biological Sciences sections test topics that will be familiar to you from your basic sciences classes; however, your preparation for these sections should still start with content review of physics, general chemistry, organic chemistry, and biology. If it has been a year or more since you took a class on any of these topics, you may be rustier on the basics than you realize, so allow extra time for those areas.

If you haven't completed all your prerequisites, I strongly recommend that you hold off on taking the test until you finish them. Studying for the MCAT is difficult enough; trying to prepare for the test before you've had the appropriate course work puts you at a major disadvantage and is a generally bad idea.

Because the MCAT tests not only science knowledge but also critical-thinking and problem-solving skills, you must incorporate abundant practice into your studying to do well on the test. Even in the first few weeks of studying, you should do some practice questions so that you start internalizing the way in which the MCAT tests material. The passage-based format is likely to be very different from the format used on tests you've taken in school. As time passes, you should shift away from content review, spending more time on practice questions and tests and less on reading and memorizing. By the few weeks before the test, your early study pattern will have reversed as you focus primarily on practicing while only brushing up periodically on content.

Don't give in to the temptation to keep pushing back doing practice passages until you're "ready." By diving in and doing questions early on, you reinforce your basic science knowledge through active learning. After you do a set of questions, take the time to review your responses. Incorrect answers help you identify your areas of weakness so that you know where to invest your time reviewing or what types of problems trip you up.

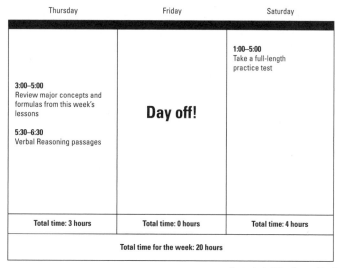

Sunday	Monday	Tuesday	Wednesday
1:00–2:30 Physics content review: work, energy, and power			
3:00–4:00 Do physics practice questions and review answers	**3:00–4:00** General chemistry content review: thermodynamics	**3:00–4:30** Biology content review: respiratory system	**3:00–4:30** Organic chemistry content review: aldehydes and ketones
4:00–4:30 Review physical sciences flashcards	**5:00–6:00** Do chemistry practice questions and review answers	**5:00–6:00** Do biology practice questions and review answers	**5:00–6:00** Do organic chemistry practice questions and review answers
5:00–6:00 Verbal Reasoning passages	**6:30–7:00** Verbal Reasoning passages	**6:30–7:00** Verbal Reasoning passages	**6:30–7:00** Verbal Reasoning passages
Total time: 4 hours	**Total time: 3 hours**	**Total time: 3 hours**	**Total time: 3 hours**

Thursday	Friday	Saturday
		1:00–5:00 Take a full-length practice test
3:00–5:00 Review major concepts and formulas from this week's lessons **5:30–6:30** Verbal Reasoning passages	**Day off!**	
Total time: 3 hours	**Total time: 0 hours**	**Total time: 4 hours**
Total time for the week: 20 hours		

Figure 6-1:
A sample study schedule.

Illustration by Wiley, Composition Services Graphics

Mastering the Verbal Reasoning section

The relatively fuzzy nature of Verbal Reasoning compared with the more cut-and-dried hard sciences makes it the least favorite section for many premeds. However, "least favorite" shouldn't equate with "least studied." Schedule time to prepare for this section of the test right along with the others. Besides underestimating the difficulty of this section, some students don't dedicate much time to it because of the mistaken belief that improving in Verbal Reasoning is impossible. Although bringing up a weak verbal score is generally more difficult than raising a lagging science score, it can be done through practice. Even a point or two of improvement can be important, especially if the difference is between an 8 and a 10, for example.

Because the Verbal Reasoning section doesn't require outside knowledge, your approach to studying for this section will be much different from the one for the sciences. This part of the test isn't about what you already know; it's about what you learn and understand from what you read and how you apply that information to the questions. Verbal Reasoning isn't a straightforward reading comprehension test; along with understanding what you've read, you must be able to analyze and interpret the information.

If you expect Verbal Reasoning to be a challenge for you and you're not in the habit of reading anything other than your textbooks on a regular basis, make reading a new part of your routine. Six months or even a year before the test, begin reading material such as newspapers, journals, or articles about the humanities, social sciences, or natural sciences on a daily basis so that you become comfortable with the type of material found in Verbal Reasoning passages. Reading nonfiction books works well too. Although the Verbal Reasoning passages are only about 500 words, reading material of any length may help you improve your reading speed and comprehension. The material you select should be written on an intelligent level but not be targeted to an audience of experts in the field. By broadening the scope of your reading, you'll be able to shift out of science mode and into Verbal Reasoning more easily when the time comes. One great way to achieve this goal is to schedule at least one humanities "reading" course during the semester before you take the MCAT.

When your MCAT study schedule kicks in, plan to do Verbal Reasoning practice passages on a regular basis. Dedicate at least part of your study time several days a week to Verbal Reasoning. Also, make sure that you do much of your practice under timed conditions. Too often, the reason for a low score is poor time management, resulting in a test-taker having to guess the answers for questions related to the last passage or two. To find tips on timing for all areas of the test, see the next section.

Perfecting your timing

Many test-takers who fare poorly express that they would've done well "if only I had more time." To hone your timing, practice it with the same rigor that you apply to learning the structures of the cell or understanding oxidation reactions. Although the science sections and Verbal Reasoning section are different in many ways, time management is critical for both.

✔ For each of the two science sections, you have 70 minutes in which to complete 52 questions, of which 13 questions are discrete questions. After allowing 10 to 13 minutes to complete the discrete questions, you'll have approximately 8 minutes on average to spend on each of the 7 passages, including answering the associated questions.

> ✔ For the Verbal Reasoning section, you're allocated 60 minutes to complete 7 passages, which works out to just over 8.5 minutes per passage on average.

Some passages take more time than this average and others less because passages vary both in their level of difficulty and the number of questions that accompany them. By timing yourself doing several passages in a row, you can determine how long you take per passage on average. If you're running long, aim to trim off some time each week until you get to where you need to be. No matter how good your science knowledge or verbal skills are, if you work too slowly you'll get a mediocre score at best.

If you're having difficulty with timing for the science sections, determine whether the source of the problem lies in the content, the passages, or the questions. Is a lack of knowledge of the material slowing you down? Are you getting bogged down while reading the passage or failing to use the most efficient method to solve a problem? When you've determined what the issue is, you can focus on correcting it.

The MCAT doesn't penalize you for guessing, so if you're running out of time, quickly select answers for all remaining questions. If you have time to skim the questions and make an educated guess, do so, but otherwise, put a random answer.

Surviving Test Day

The hundreds of hours spent studying and endless days spent doing practice questions all lead up to one thing: test day. No matter how well you do on practice tests, what counts is how you perform on the actual test. By familiarizing yourself with what to expect on test day and understanding how to manage the stress that accompanies any high-stakes situation, you'll be in the best position to perform well when it counts. Your MCAT preparation shouldn't be limited to studying the material for the test; it should also include preparation for the testing experience. Entering the test center doesn't have to be a walk into the unknown; in the following sections, you get a closer look at what test day is like and how to handle the option to void your score, plus tips for minimizing test-day anxiety.

Walking through the testing experience

Because the test is computer based and takes place in a testing center, it's not the same experience as the hundreds of tests you've taken in classrooms during your academic career. So that you aren't seeing the test center for the first time on test day, plan a visit to the testing site prior to the day of the MCAT. Visiting the test center also helps ensure you won't get lost and arrive frazzled or even late. Make sure you find out where parking is as well; the less uncertainty you have to deal with on the actual day of the test, the less stressed you'll be.

On test day, plan to arrive at the test center at least a half hour prior to your scheduled time. After you enter the center, you go through a check-in process that includes verifying your identification and taking a digital fingerprint. You can also expect the following:

✔ To leave snacks, drinks, and everything else in an assigned locker, with the exception of your identification and a set of approved earplugs (if you choose to bring them).

✔ That you'll be entering the testing room at a slightly different time than other test-takers. Test-takers are brought into the room one at a time and assigned a computer. After being escorted to his assigned computer, a test-taker may begin. Instead of a human proctor, your computer keeps track of the time for each section and signals when you may take a break. As a result of this system, other test-takers will be starting, taking breaks and finishing at different times than you.

✔ To show ID and sign in if you leave the test room and then return.

REMEMBER Because there are specific rules and policies about everything from what type of identification is valid to how to report problems that occur during testing, carefully reading the information provided prior to the test is essential.

WARNING! One thing you can't count on is that the testing center will necessarily be the ideal temperature. You may find yourself in a room with the heat up too high or the air conditioning blowing right on you, so wear layers. Be aware, though, that items of clothing you aren't wearing must go in your locker, so you'll have to wait for a break to take off a jacket or sweater if you need to.

After you're brought into the test room and assigned a seat, the action begins with an optional tutorial on how to use the computer followed by the examinee agreement before the test starts. (See the earlier section "Getting an overview of the test's length and structure" for the order and length of the sections). After the test, you have to decide whether you want to void the exam (as I discuss later in the chapter), and then you're on to the last item, an optional survey. When that's done and you've checked out, you can leave knowing that you're free to enjoy your time from now on without nagging thoughts of "I should be studying!"

Dealing with test-day anxiety

If the mere mention of MCAT starts your heart racing and induces a fight-or-flight response, it's time for some stress-relieving techniques. The less anxious you are during the test preparation period, and especially during the days prior to the test, the easier entering the test in a calm frame of mind will be. Doing the following will make your life leading up to the test more pleasant and help you walk into the test more relaxed (or at least as relaxed as a person can be about the MCAT):

- ✔ **Exercise.** If you have an exercise routine, keep it up during your MCAT preparation period. If you don't usually exercise, start. Even a short walk each day will benefit you physically and mentally.

- ✔ **Get sufficient sleep.** Sleep deprivation can be anxiety inducing; especially in the two weeks before the test, being on a regular sleep schedule and getting enough rest each night are important.

- ✔ **Maintain your friendships with people outside the premedical world.** Your premedical friends can be a good source of support, but spending time with friends whose overriding focus isn't getting into medical school will help you keep things in perspective.

- ✔ **Remind yourself that you're ready for the test.** Letting worries about the one practice test or round of flashcards you didn't get to to dominate your thoughts is easy. Instead of dwelling on what you didn't do, focus on all the hours of studying you did complete, the thousands of questions you've answered, and the practice test you aced. Reinforcing the positive will put you in a better frame of mind than obsessing about the negative.

Know that if it comes down to it, you can retake. Although the goal is to take the MCAT once and get a great score, keeping in mind that if you absolutely have to retake you can takes away some of that "the fate of my future rests on a single day" feeling that taking the test can produce. The later section "Retaking the MCAT" gives you the information you need to know about giving the MCAT another try.

Considering the option of voiding your exam

After you've completed the test, you have the option to void your exam. If you void your exam, you won't receive a score for it. You have only five minutes to make a decision before you get the default option: Your exam will be scored. With only a few minutes to think and exhaustion and stress potentially hampering your decision-making abilities, you aren't in the ideal frame of mind to make a choice. Therefore, instead of facing this question cold for the first time on test day, start considering scenarios under which you would or wouldn't void the test before you even set foot in the test center.

If you've gotten to the point where you've actually taken the test, you've presumably worked very hard to prepare. Voiding means retaking at a later date, and taking the MCAT isn't an experience anyone wants to repeat. Also, retaking may mean a delay in having your application considered complete by the schools or even require waiting an extra year to apply. For these reasons, voiding isn't something to do on a whim or because of a vague intuition that things didn't go well. I've talked to a test-taker who walked out of the exam thinking things went fine only to receive a 25 and another who was full of self-doubt but ended up with a score in the mid-30s. Gauging how you did on the MCAT is very difficult, so unless you have a specific reason to think that you didn't do well (such as having guessed on numerous questions), you probably shouldn't void.

Extenuating circumstances such as illness may also be a reason to void. If you're gripped with stomach cramps or a searing migraine halfway through the exam and can barely concentrate due to the discomfort, voiding makes sense. One applicant I spoke with ended up taking the test on only two hours of sleep after a combination of noisy neighbors, insomnia, and early-morning construction robbed him of needed rest. By the end of the test, he knew that he was performing far below his potential and decided to void and retake on a day he would (hopefully) be more rested. The decision to void or not ultimately needs to be made on the spot, but by at least going into the test having some idea of the circumstances under which you may opt to void, you have a head start on knowing what to do when the question pops up on the screen.

Although the option to void the exam exists, you shouldn't plan to take the test unless you're ready, and when you do take it, go in with the mindset that this is it, not "I can always void the test if I don't like the way things go." Voiding should only be seen as a last resort so that you're fully committed to your exam preparation.

Retaking the MCAT

When you receive your scores about a month after you take the test, you need to decide to stick with what you have or try again. If your scores on the MCAT clearly aren't competitive for admission, consider taking the test again. Taking the test twice isn't unusual, and a good score on the second attempt still puts you in a strong position for potential acceptance.

Try to avoid taking the test more than twice because schools are less likely to take a high score as seriously if it took three tries to achieve. Even if a school primarily considers the highest score or most recent score, the committee may also take into account your entire testing history, and it may view taking the test multiple times, especially more than twice, negatively. (If you've taken the MCAT more than once, you can't choose which scores the schools see; they receive every score for tests taken from 2003 onward.)

Although the prospect of taking the MCAT again isn't one you're bound to savor, the extra effort pays off at admissions time if your score improves. If you opt to retest, you need to choose the optimal time to take the test and reevaluate your preparation strategy to increase your odds for success for the retake. In the following sections, I give you guidance about how to make the decision whether to retest as well as pointers about when to retake and how to prepare.

Deciding whether you should retake the test

I can't really give you a hard-and-fast cutoff to use to determine whether you should retake, but generally speaking, if your total score is below a 30 or your score on any section is less than a 9, consider trying again. However, some applicants with higher scores than these may decide to retake, while others with lower scores may not depending on their specific situations and goals. For example, an applicant with a 32 who is aiming for a top-tier school and strongly believes that he can do better may decide to take the test again, while an applicant with a 28 who is primarily interested in osteopathic schools may be satisfied with her score.

When making your decision, realize that retaking brings with it both the potential for an increase in score and the possibility of a drop, so trying again always comes with some risk. For statistics about score changes achieved by MCAT retesters, check out the out the AAMC site at www.aamc.org. Of course, statistics don't tell the story behind the numbers or predict the chances an individual test-taker will improve or decrease their score. To help you evaluate your particular situation, here are some questions to ask:

- ✔ Did I dedicate sufficient time to preparing for the test last time?

- ✔ Was my MCAT score similar to my scores from AAMC practice exams?

- ✔ Do I believe that a different approach to preparation than the one I used would have been more effective?

- ✔ Did a factor such as illness, family commitments, or a heavy class load in the months prior to the test interfere with my preparation or performance?

- ✔ Is my application portfolio, including my current MCAT score, competitive for admission to medical school?

- ✔ Is being admitted to a particular medical school or tier of schools important to me? Are my scores competitive for that school/tier?

- ✔ And, most important: Am I willing to invest the time and effort that it will take to prepare for the MCAT again?

If you believe that your current score won't allow you to reach your goals in terms of admissions, can identify factors that impeded your ability to reach your target score, and are willing to prepare for the MCAT again, retaking the test may be a good choice.

Note that many medical schools don't accept scores that are greater than three years old. So if you're a nontraditional applicant who's decided to delay applying for several years after you take the MCAT, check with the school you plan to apply to so that you can verify whether your score is still valid or whether you have no choice but to retake. Chapter 17 has more information for nontraditional applicants.

Timing your next try

After you decide to retake, your next task is to choose a test date. If you originally took the MCAT by the end of May of the year in which you plan to apply, you have time to put in two months of preparation and still retake the test by the end of July, which, although not optimal, isn't extremely late. With a July test date, the schools receive your scores in August. Although submitting your primary application and MCAT scores by the end of June is ideal, applying later in the cycle but with a higher score is usually worth the trade-off. (For strategies on minimizing the impact of later scores, see the later section "Applying to Medical School Before You Receive Your MCAT Score.")

Two months is the minimum amount of time you should allow before taking the test again. If you think you need more time, don't rush to retake. The stakes are higher with a second try, and retaking before you're ready may result in the same score, or worse, a lower one. If you won't be able to prepare sufficiently to take the test again in time for the current cycle, you have to decide between applying with your current score and delaying your application until the next admissions cycle. If your scores in one or more of the science sections were very low, that indicates a potentially significant deficit in your content knowledge. In that case, wait at least six months to retake and take more science courses or repeat the ones you did poorly in to strengthen your knowledge base before attempting the MCAT again.

Note: You can only hold one seat for the MCAT at a time; therefore, you must wait until after you have taken the MCAT before you register for another test date. For example, if you plan to take the test in March, with a back-up plan of retesting in June, you must wait until after you take the test in March to reserve a seat for a June test date. You can't take the test more than three times in a calendar year.

Preparing the second time around

Before formulating a new study plan, review every element of your preparation from the previous attempt to determine what went right, what didn't, and how you can prepare more effectively this time. For example, if your plan was to do 400 hours of reading, reviewing, question-answering, and test-taking but in reality you didn't break 200 hours, consider ways you can ensure that you stick to your schedule, such as by forming a study group or taking a course. Or perhaps you took a preparation course but ended up missing half of the classes and slacking on the homework because a research project you had that semester was taking up so much of your time. Before you retake, make sure you can cut back on outside commitments for several months so that you can focus on getting ready for the test.

If you put in the hours but didn't see the expected results, doing more of the same isn't the answer, so change your approach. If you studied independently and now realize that you skimmed over certain topics without grasping them thoroughly, take a course, enlist the help of a friend who is strong in that subject as a study partner, or hire a tutor to meet with you each week. If you took a course that did a great job of preparing you for the science sections but wasn't as helpful to you for Verbal Reasoning, seek out a class that focuses on Verbal Reasoning or additional materials to use to practice extensively on your own. Being willing to try something different may help you get the extra two, three, or more points you need to hit your target score. (Flip to the earlier section "Examining specific prep approaches" for details on various study options.)

Applying to Medical School Before You Receive Your MCAT Score

Following the ideal application timeline of taking the MCAT by May so that you have your scores in June by the time you submit the primary application isn't always possible. If a busy spring semester means you need the summer to study or a low score on a spring attempt necessitates a retake, the application cycle may open with your scores still pending. Applying later in the cycle places you at a disadvantage in admissions, though, so look at the options if you find yourself facing a wait for your MCAT scores. The three major strategies for this situation are as follows:

- ✔ Wait until you receive your MCAT scores to submit your primary application.

✔ Formulate a complete list of schools and submit your primary application, and possibly secondary applications, to all those schools early in the cycle, even if your scores won't be available by then.

✔ Submit your primary application to only one or a few schools before you receive your scores and then add schools after you know your scores.

The following sections provide a look at the implications of each strategy. (See Chapter 8 for the basics of primary applications; check out Chapter 9 for more about secondary applications.)

The option that's best for you depends on the exact timing of your MCAT, your confidence that you'll ultimately apply in a given cycle, and your comfort with submitting applications to schools before you know your score. With good planning, you can avoid any of the following scenarios and have your application and scores submitted early. However, if unforeseen circumstances skew your schedule, consider your choices carefully so that you can select the route that most strongly positions you for admission.

Waiting for your scores before you send your application

By waiting for your scores before submitting your primary application, you have a much better idea of the strength of your candidacy before you select schools. Because the MCAT is such a critical factor in admission, knowing your scores means you can more accurately target your list to schools you have a realistic chance of admission to. You also won't risk wasting time and money applying to schools out of your reach. Plus, if you receive your retake scores and discover they're still too low to be competitive, you can take the MCAT once more and apply the next cycle instead without having wasted resources sending in applications for the current cycle.

A major disadvantage of waiting for your scores prior to applying is that you may be applying later in the cycle. If your scores come in June or even July, this delay isn't a major issue; however, if you take an August test, you won't receive your scores until September, which is very late to submit a primary application and may decrease your chances of admission. (For a discussion of how application timing can affect the chance of admissions, check out Chapter 5.)

Sending your application to your entire list before you have your score

Submitting your primary application to a full complement of schools before you receive your scores minimizes the delay caused by a later MCAT test date. Your MCAT score may be available by the time the application service verifies your application and forwards it to the schools, and even if it's not, you can start completing secondaries as you await your score.

However, this strategy has some risks:

- ✔ **Becoming a reapplicant:** The primary concern is that if you receive lower scores than expected, you may end up opting to apply during the next cycle rather than the current one, which means you've spent time and money on the application needlessly. Another issue is that when you do apply the next year, some schools may view you as a reapplicant. (Some schools consider any applicant who has submitted a primary as an applicant; any subsequent application is therefore a reapplication.) Schools may evaluate reapplicants more stringently, expecting them not only to have competitive overall application packages but also to have significantly improved their candidacies from the last cycle. (Chapter 16 reveals the details about reapplying to medical school).

- ✔ **Complicating school list selection:** Another challenge you face if you decide to apply before you receive your scores is that you have to make an educated guess about which schools to apply to. One way to address this issue is to over-apply — select a broad range of schools on the primary and then decide which secondaries to complete after you receive your scores. Or you can go ahead and complete the secondaries as you receive them to keep the process moving forward, knowing that you may not turn out to be competitive for some schools and may end up withdrawing your application later. A drawback to applying broadly, even just for the primary stage of the application, is that it can get very expensive, potentially depleting resources available for secondary applications and traveling to interviews.

  Keep in mind that you're not stuck with the list of schools you select initially; if your scores are higher or lower than expected, you can always add higher- or lower-tier schools based on the new information you have. You'll be applying the add-on schools later than the initial batch, but after your primary has been verified, adding schools is fast; schools usually receive your primary within days, versus the weeks that initial verification can take.

Applying to a few schools without your scores and then adding more

Applying to only one or a few schools initially while awaiting your MCAT scores is a middle ground between the two approaches in the preceding sections. By designating at least one school on your primary application, you get the verification process underway. That way, you can add schools very quickly as described in the preceding section when you receive your scores. This strategy allows you to get ahead in the process without spending a lot of money on schools you end up not being qualified for (or being overqualified for if you ace the MCAT).

One drawback to this approach is that you have to wait until you receive your MCAT scores to complete secondaries for all but the few schools you applied to initially. With a late-summer MCAT date, you may be better off applying more broadly upfront.

Looking to 2015: Major Changes Are Coming to the MCAT

Students planning to take the MCAT in spring 2015 or thereafter will be taking a test that has significant differences from the previous version. Although the new test is still a computer-based, multiple-choice examination, it includes revamped science sections, an added behavioral sciences section, and an increased length, among other changes.

If you're planning to take the new MCAT in the first year or two after its release, you may be concerned about what to expect as well as how to prepare. After all, you're not facing the same tried-and-true version as your peers who are even slightly ahead of you on the premedical path did. The best way to ease your anxiety is to become familiar with the changes early so that you can make sure you've got the content knowledge and the skills you need to get a great score. In the following sections, I give you an overview of the structure and content of the 2015 MCAT as well as tips about which prerequisite classes to take and how to prepare for the exam so that you're ready when test day arrives.

The new MCAT will be administered starting in spring 2015. Those taking the test in January 2015 take the old MCAT.

Familiarizing yourself with the changes

One of the biggest changes to the MCAT is the addition of a new section — Psychological, Social, and Biological Foundations of Behavior — that tests concepts in the behavioral sciences. The previous iteration of the MCAT only tested content in the biological and physical sciences; however, the new test also requires knowledge of disciplines such as sociology and psychology. The addition of this section brings the total number of scored sections to four. (As discussed in the earlier section "Getting an overview of the test's length and structure," the writing sample was eliminated starting with the 2013 MCAT. For the transitional years of 2013 and 2014, the MCAT has only three scored sections.)

The two science sections are changing as well, with the new names for these sections reflecting an emphasis on the application of science concepts in the context of living systems. The Physical Sciences section becomes "Chemical and Physical Foundations of Biological Systems," and the Biological Sciences section becomes "Biological and Biochemical Foundations of Living Systems." A notable change to the science content is that it includes biochemistry knowledge typically learned in a one-semester biochemistry class, whereas the old MCAT didn't require science knowledge outside of that presented in lower-division biology, general chemistry, organic chemistry, and physics courses.

The Verbal Reasoning section has been reinvented as the Critical Analysis and Reasoning Skills section. Like the current Verbal Reasoning section, this part of the test is entirely passage based, so you don't need any outside knowledge to answer the questions. Passages discuss topics in the humanities and social sciences as well as in areas such as ethics, philosophy, and population health. Gone are the natural sciences and technology passages that were fair game on the Verbal Reasoning section.

With all this new content, the length of the test certainly hasn't gotten shorter. Where past test-takers could expect to spend over five hours in the testing room, the 2015 MCAT takes nearly seven hours to complete, including a lunch break.

Table 6-2 gives an overview of the expected order and length of each section of the updated MCAT as of this writing; be sure to check the AAMC site (`www. aamc.org`) regularly for any updates.

Table 6-2	MCAT 2015 Sections and Expected Length	
Section		*Time*
Biological and Biochemical Foundations of Living Systems (67 questions)		95 minutes
Chemical and Physical Foundations of Biological Systems (67 questions)		95 minutes
Psychological, Social, and Biological Foundations of Behavior (67 questions)		95 minutes
Critical Analysis and Reasoning Skills (60 questions)		90 minutes

These changes reflect the evolution of medicine in recent years. For example, schools now seek applicants who understand the importance of the social and cultural context of medicine, not just the science behind it, which means that future physicians must have an understanding of the behavioral sciences. At the same time, changes in the content of the science sections mirror trends in medicine such as the increasing importance of biochemistry and molecular biology to the field. Although you may be nervous about facing the revised version of the MCAT, the changes are also aimed at bringing the MCAT more in line with undergraduate premedical education, which may actually make preparation for the test easier because your course work may better align with test content.

Gearing up for the new test

Premedical students planning to take the new MCAT need to take additional courses that weren't required for the older version of the test. Before spring 2015, the content a test-taker needed to know was that typically covered during two semesters each of general biology, general chemistry, organic chemistry, and physics. However, you need take the following in addition to those courses to be ready for the 2015 MCAT:

- ✔ One semester of biochemistry
- ✔ One semester of introductory psychology
- ✔ One semester of introductory sociology

The biochemistry course provides you with the foundation in that discipline you need for the updated science sections, and the sociology and psychology classes give you a knowledge base for the new behavioral sciences section. Taking either version of the MCAT, old or new, prior to completing all of your prerequisite isn't a wise plan, so make sure that you allocate space in your schedule for all these classes described before you take the exam.

One thing that isn't changing about the MCAT is that it will still test both knowledge and critical-thinking skills. Therefore, you can apply the general tips I provide in the earlier section "Preparing for the MCAT" to the 2015 MCAT as well. However, an additional step you should take is to read all the information provided online by the AAMC about the new MCAT. In addition to informational materials, do every practice question and full-length exam released by the AAMC to help students get ready for the 2015 MCAT. These steps are the best means you have of knowing what the updated test is like so you won't be caught by surprise on test day.

Chapter 7

Choosing Medical Schools

*A*s a premedical student, you may be thinking that you don't care where you go to med school as long as you're admitted *somewhere*. However, crafting a strategic list of schools actually helps ensure that you optimize your chances of admission overall without requiring that you apply to a ridiculously large number of schools. An effective list also lets you try for some top schools while providing backup options in case those don't come through. No matter where you stand in the applicant pool, you benefit from having a carefully researched list that is tailored to you.

In this chapter, you find out not only why putting together your list carefully is important but also how to determine the number of schools to include on it. You also discover what to look for when you research schools as well as find strategies for compiling your list.

Researching Schools

Because your list is so important, you should start researching schools and making preliminary selections early rather than waiting until you're in the midst of studying for the MCAT, writing your personal statement, and doing numerous other application-related tasks. If you start early, you may not know your MCAT score; however, you can always adjust your list after that information is available. A good time to start looking into schools is during the fall of the academic year in which you plan to apply.

The following sections explain where to get the information you need and list a number of factors to consider as you research.

The importance of a strategic list

Consider the case of Abby, a hard-working chemistry major with a 3.68 GPA and a 32 on the MCAT. She's done extensive physician shadowing and has spent over a year participating in research in a biochemistry lab. She's also volunteered in several departments in a university hospital and is an all-around solid applicant. Always organized, Abby submitted her primary application within days of the opening of the cycle, turned around her secondaries within a week of receipt, and then waited patiently for interviews. By spring, she'd been offered only one interview, after which the school put her on the alternate list, forcing her to wait yet again. Because that alternate spot never turned into an acceptance, she ended up scrambling to make plans for her unexpected and unwanted gap year while also putting together her application for the next cycle.

From the description of her background, Abby sounds like a competitive applicant. Her GPA and MCAT scores are both good, although not stellar, and coupled with her list of extracurricular activities, they seem like they'd be enough to get her into at least one medical school. So what happened? The answer lies in what I didn't mention as part of Abby's story: She applied to only five schools — her state school, two top-tier private schools, and two public schools in other states. Because her state school is highly competitive, it didn't serve as a safety school, and the rest of the schools either were out of her range or were ones where her out-of-state residence put her at a severe admissions disadvantage. All the things she did right as a premedical student and applicant didn't secure her a spot in a med school because of the two things she did wrong: apply to too few schools and apply almost exclusively to schools that were out of her reach. Had she applied to 15 or more schools, focused on private schools (with the exception of her own state school), and included at least 5 safety schools, she would've had a far better chance of being admitted. In fact, she'd probably have been spending the next fall in the anatomy lab with her med school class rather than on the interview trail.

I've met many applicants similar to Abby who were seeking my help after a failed first application cycle. Lucky for you, you don't have to learn this type of lesson through trial and error. Instead, make your initial list as close to ideal as possible, both in terms of the number and mix of schools, so that the first time you apply is hopefully the last.

Using school websites, admissions offices, and other resources

To gain a comprehensive view of a school, gather information from multiple sources, including both written materials and individuals such as admissions officers, advisors, physicians, and medical students who can share insights with you about various schools. Some of the major resources to use are as follows:

✔ **School websites:** A medical school's website usually includes information about the program's curriculum and philosophy and resources available for medical students. If you check the admissions page of a school's site, you can find the requirements for admission, application procedures, and often statistics about the demographics and average GPA and MCAT scores of the student body.

- ✔ **The Medical School Admission Requirements (MSAR) guide:** The MSAR Online database contains a wealth of information about allopathic schools, including cost, class size, selection factors, and statistics about accepted applicants. You can purchase access to the MSAR through the Association of American Medical Colleges (AAMC) site at `www.aamc.org`.

- ✔ *The Osteopathic Medical College Information Book:* This publication is a valuable reference for applicants interested in DO schools. You can download it for free or purchase a printed copy at `www.aacom.org/resources/bookstore/cib/Pages/default.aspx`.

- ✔ **Visits to the schools:** After you've read the basic information about schools, delve further, especially for schools you're highly interested in. Some schools host open houses for prospective applicants. Check with the admissions office at a school to find out whether it offers these events or whether you can arrange an informational meeting with someone in admissions. Although not all schools accommodate requests for visits, some are willing to arrange for a tour and/or a meeting with an admissions officer.

When you visit a medical school, present yourself in a professional manner and approach the interaction with the same care as you would an interview. Some applicants mistakenly behave too casually in contacts with admissions staff prior to interviews.

- ✔ **Your premedical advisor:** Check with your premedical advisor to find out whether she has compiled information about medical schools for advisees to use. Advisors often have institution-specific information, such as where students from your college have been accepted in recent years, that can help you narrow down your list.

- ✔ **Physicians and medical students you know:** Check with your contacts in the field about the schools they attended or currently attend. Their firsthand perspectives offer insight into less-tangible aspects of a program, such as the environment, accessibility of faculty, and quality of life for students.

Considering a few factors

When you know where to look for information, you next have to determine what information you're seeking. Because medical school is a long, expensive undertaking, you have to investigate the education you'll receive, financial considerations, and the location of each program as you compile your list. In the following sections, I discuss the most important factors that you should check into before placing a school on your list.

Type (public/state versus private)

One of the first pieces of information you should gather as you research schools is whether a school is public or private. A common, and critical, mistake that applicants make in compiling their lists is improperly balancing the mix of public (also called *state*) and private schools they select. To understand the error I'm about to describe, you first have to understand a crucial difference between public and private medical schools:

- ✔ *Public schools* receive state funding.

- ✔ *Private schools* don't.

Translation: Public schools give preference for admissions to applicants who are residents of that state. Public schools may be mandated to fill 90 percent or even 95 percent of their class with state residents, and some public schools accept no out-of-state residents at all certain years. Private schools don't give a preference to applicants based on state of residence. Therefore, to optimize your chance of admission, focus on public schools in your state as well as private schools in any state. If you're extremely interested in a public school outside your home state, add it to the list, but don't use more than few slots for such schools.

This advice may seem obvious, but students are often lulled into adding far-away state schools because they misinterpret admissions statistics. While browsing through school websites, an applicant may come across a public school for which the average MCAT is 32 and the average GPA is 3.6. The applicant looks at the school and thinks, "I have a 31 and a 3.5, so I'm not that far off. I've probably got a reasonable chance at this school." In reality, though, the averages for the subset of accepted applicants who are state residents and the averages for out-of-state residents are likely to be different, with the nonresidents having significantly higher average numbers than accepted applicants as a whole do. Because public schools give preference to residents, those nonresidents who are admitted are generally very strong applicants. Some public schools are more out-of-state-friendly than others, but overall, your best bet by far is private schools if you're looking out of state.

When researching state schools, check the fine print regarding admission requirements. For example, the University of New Mexico considers only applicants who have been residents of New Mexico for at least a year or who have strong ties to the state. If you've never been west of the Mississippi, your application fee is likely wasted if you apply there.

Rank

Every U.S. medical school is a good school. Any one of them will get you to your goal of becoming a practicing physician as long as you finish the program, pass the licensure exams, and do a residency. Keep these thoughts firmly in mind as you make your list. Of course, differences exist among schools. Some are more prestigious, others less so. However, the difference between the best medical school and the worst medical school is much narrower than the difference between the most and least selective undergraduate institutions. Therefore, don't overlook schools that you haven't heard of before; a lot more is out there than just Harvard and Hopkins.

Granted, going to a big-name medical school can help pave the way for the next step, which in the case of a medical career is residency. However, you certainly don't have to attend a top-tier school to enter even the more competitive medical specialties. Making the most of your time in medical school, no matter where you attend, is what's most important in making yourself competitive for residency programs.

Although no universally agreed-upon set of rankings exists for medical schools, many students find the one compiled by *U.S. News & World Report* (www. usnews.com/rankings) helpful as a guide to determining how selective a school is. With any ranking list, don't focus on the exact place a school occupies on a list; instead, view the list as a rough gauge of where the school stands. And remember, the best school to someone else may not be the best one for you.

Cost

According to a report from the AAMC, the average debt for recent medical school graduates tops $160,000, so cost is a major factor to consider. By minimizing the cost of medical school, you can keep your debt down and decrease the possibility of having loan payments so burdensome that they affect critical decisions in your life, such as which specialty you pursue or when you start a family. (Head to Chapter 18 for information about calculating and paying the costs of medical school.)

The least expensive route to obtain a medical education for many applicants is attending their state's public school. In addition to giving in-state applicants preference for admission, public schools also charge lower tuition to state residents. According to data from the AAMC, in-state tuition averages around $25,000 at public schools, while the mean for tuition at private schools is over $40,000. However, tuition isn't the only expense you have during medical school; housing, transportation, food, and other living expenses need to be factored in. Therefore, as you're comparing costs for schools, realize that a school in the Midwest with slightly higher tuition may end up being less expensive to attend overall than one located in the middle of New York City even if the latter has a lower tuition. The estimates that schools provide of the per year cost to attend medical school, including tuition and basic living expenses, are a good guide to use when comparing schools.

When assessing the potential cost of medical schools, also look at the average indebtedness and percentage of students who receive financial aid at a school (you can find this information in the MSAR for MD schools and the Osteopathic Medical College Information Book for DO schools). Private schools may be more generous about awarding scholarships than public ones, so in some cases a private school that has higher tuition than a public school may actually turn out to be the less expensive option after financial aid.

Curriculum

Although all medical schools impart the same essential body of information to their students, the way in which they teach that information varies from school to school. One of the biggest differences among curriculums is the extent to which they use a lecture format versus problem-based learning.

- ✔ The *lecture format* is one that you're likely to be familiar with from your undergraduate education. With this structure, the instructor delivers lessons to students in a classroom or lecture hall that may contain hundreds of students. This format is instructor-led and usually preferred by students who learn best in a highly-structured environment.

- ✔ For *problem-based learning* (PBL), students meet in small groups (usually eight to ten students) with a facilitator. Learning is focused around patient cases. In one session, the group begins by discussing the case to establish what's known, what potential diagnoses are, and what further information is required to solve the case. Tasks are divided among the group so that each student is responsible for researching particular learning issues to present to the group during the next meeting. This type of learning is student-led, although the facilitator ensures that the group stays on track and that learning goals are met. Students who learn more effectively in a small group and prefer a more active approach to learning tend to favor this format.

Many schools don't exclusively use lecture or PBL but instead utilize a combination of both. However, the ratio of lecture to PBL varies widely by school. The two approaches are quite different, and if you prefer to have material delivered to you in a very straightforward way or strongly prefer studying on your own rather than working intensively with your peers, a PBL-heavy school may not be the best fit for you. Conversely, if you find yourself losing focus during lectures, a school that requires students to spend five hours a day sitting in the lecture hall is likely a poor match for you.

Other aspects of the curriculum that you should keep in mind as you check into schools include these:

- ✔ **Organization of the curriculum:** The traditional approach to medical education is to present information organized around a discipline such as anatomy, physiology, or genetics. However, many schools have switched to an organ systems-based approach that studies all facets of an organ system together. For example, during a block dedicated to the cardiovascular system, students study all aspects of that system, including its anatomy, physiology, pharmacology, and pathology.

- ✔ **Integration of clinical medicine into the curriculum:** The first two years of medical school are often referred to as the *preclinical years* and the last two as the *clinical years* because first- and second-year medical students spend most of their time learning in classrooms and from textbooks or computers, whereas third- and fourth-year students are immersed in clinical rotations in hospitals and outpatient settings. However, the recent trend has been toward earlier introduction to patient care, with some schools giving students hands-on experiences as early as the first week, or even first day, of medical school. These early experiences help reinforce the lessons learned in the classroom and keep students motivated; after all, the opportunity to work with patients is the reason most students want to practice medicine in the first place.

✔ **Opportunities to pursue a concentration or area of interest:** Some schools have particular tracks or concentrations for students interested in primary care, public health, administration, or research. If you have a particular interest or career goal, check to see whether the schools you're investigating have opportunities for you to nurture that passion.

In addition to curriculum, grading systems also vary among schools. Some schools use a pass/fail system and may give "honors" or "high honors" to students who excel. Other schools use a system of letter grades. The way in which a school evaluates students may differ between the preclinical and clinical years. Make sure you look into each school's method of evaluating students as you're also checking out its curriculum. Also keep in mind that some schools use systems of evaluation that don't include letter grades but still categorize a student's performance in a course beyond a simple pass or fail. For example, some schools award each student with a fail, low pass, pass, high pass, honors, or high honors for each course.

Mission/focus

Although all medical schools aim to educate knowledgeable, competent, and compassionate physicians, particular schools emphasize different facets of medicine or seek to fulfill a need in the healthcare system. Programs may place a priority on research, primary care, social justice, and/or service to disadvantaged populations.

From reading about and visiting a school, you can determine whether the school's mission aligns with your interests. Schools look for applicants whose backgrounds and experiences demonstrate that they'd be good fits for the program, so your chances of admission are typically better at a school where you're a great fit. Also, selecting schools that nurture your interests helps ensure you're happy where you end up. After all, when the initial exhilaration of your acceptance wears off, you may have second thoughts about a program that emphasizes rural medicine if your idea of a day in the country is a bike ride around Central Park.

Size

The smallest medical school classes contain 50 to 60 students; the largest top 300, with a class size of about 150 being typical. The size of the class affects the dynamics of the group as well as the learning environment. The feel of a program with 300 students in the class is different from one with only 50 students. However, with small-group learning as a component of most medical school curriculums (and the dominant component for some), even a large student body doesn't necessarily equate to large classes. Also, some larger schools actually distribute students on different campuses, resulting in a smaller learning group.

One of the benefits of a smaller class is that the group tends to be more tightly knit, although if you're the type who prefers more privacy, the small-town atmosphere a more intimate class size creates may not be to your liking. A larger group of students also offers greater diversity and opportunities for friendships. As you make your way through the schools' websites and the MSAR, take note of the class sizes; although a less-than-ideal number may not be a deal breaker if the school is otherwise a good match for you, it's still a factor to consider as you make your decision about where to apply.

Location

You spend four years living in the area where your medical school is located, so make sure it's somewhere you're happy settling for a while. Location is less important than what the program offers, but you're more likely to be productive and enjoy medical school if you like where you're living. In particular, note the following as you consider location:

✔ **Region:** If you're a lifelong Floridian, your first winter in a school in New England may be a rough one. Although I certainly don't advise choosing medical schools based on climate alone, many California applicants have asked me to focus on "warm" states when helping them craft their list of schools. In addition to climate, the demographics, subculture, regional cuisine, and many other factors differ among regions of the United States.

On the other hand, schools value regional diversity, so if you're open to venturing to a different part of the country for medical school, that may work to your advantage when the committee is evaluating your candidacy.

✔ **Setting:** I've advised applicants who were adamant about living in or near a large city and others who craved easy access to open space. The urban, suburban, or rural location of the school affects not only your time outside of class in terms of cultural and recreational activities but also the clinical education you receive. For example, if you envision returning to your hometown in rural Wyoming to practice, a med school located in or near a rural area can provide you with a head start on discovering what practicing in such a setting is like and what factors affect the health of populations in that kind of area.

✔ **Proximity to family and friends:** You build a new support system in medical school made up of your peers and mentors in the program; however, if being near family — or at least closer than cross-country — is important to you, focus on schools closer to home. Or perhaps you lived at home during your undergraduate years, and now you're eager to venture farther afield and relish the adventure of moving to a different part of the country. Either way, how far you're willing to relocate is another factor to think carefully about as you determine which schools to choose.

Determining How Many Schools to Include on Your List

"How many schools should I apply to?" "Is more always better?" "How many schools are too few?" These commonly asked questions are important ones because picking the number of schools to apply to can be just as critical, and almost as difficult, as selecting specific schools.

Beware the dangers of applying to too few schools and too many schools:

✔ **If your list is too short, you don't have enough space to include a few dream schools, a sufficient number of safety schools, and a healthy number of schools that are comfortably in your range.** Therefore, with a short list, you risk not being admitted anywhere or being left wondering whether you could've gotten into a better school if you had tried for a wider range of programs. (The sidebar "The importance of a strategic list" in this chapter explains the disadvantages of a short list.)

✔ **Applying to too many schools gets expensive and time-consuming.** When you factor in fees for both primary and secondary applications, someone applying to, say, 30 schools faces several thousand dollars in application fees. In addition, completing secondary applications for a large number of schools may be overwhelming because many schools require multiple short answer or essay questions as part of their secondaries (see Chapter 9 for details on secondary applications). The expense and effort to apply to a very large number of schools may not pay off because of the law of diminishing returns. After you use up the schools that you have a good chance of admission to, you have to dig into the less-likely prospects to find more schools to include. At that point, you're better off investing your effort into the schools that you have the best chance of admission to rather than adding schools that are long shots.

So what is the right number? As a starting point, aim for 15 schools. You should then increase or decrease the number based on your circumstances, as I explain in the following sections.

When to include fewer than 15 schools

Applying to fewer than 15 schools is reasonable if

✔ **The public medical school(s) in your home state isn't/aren't highly competitive.** If your state school offers you an excellent option as a safety school, you may be comfortable with a shorter list.

✔ **You're a highly competitive applicant who isn't aiming solely for top-tier schools.** If you're a very strong applicant applying to mostly mid-tier or less-competitive schools, you can apply to fewer schools than a typical applicant.

✔ **You're very particular about where you're willing to attend.** Take an honest look at each school on your list and ask yourself, "If this school was the only one I got into, would I rather go to this school or apply to other schools again next year?" If the answer is "reapply," remove the school from your list. Although I recommend having an open mind about schools, if you really don't want to go somewhere, don't apply there.

Before discounting a school that you have a good chance of admission to, think long and hard about whether you'd really prefer to reapply rather than go to a school that's not one of your top picks if push comes to shove. Some applicants start out being very selective about which schools they're willing to attend, but as it gets later in the cycle, they rethink their strategies and become open to a broader range of schools if they haven't received any acceptances.

Even applicants who meet some or all of the criteria listed should try to include at least ten schools on their list.

When to include more than 15 schools

You should consider applying to more than 15 schools if

✔ **The public school(s) in your home state is/are very competitive.** For example, the public schools in California are extremely difficult to get into and by no means constitute a backup plan. Applicants who are residents of such states should aim for a list of 20 or so schools unless they're highly competitive applicants.

✔ **You have many reach schools that you want to try for.** If you have numerous *reach* schools that are likely out of your league but that you still want to try for, make your list longer overall instead of replacing schools that are more in line with your application package with dream schools. This way, you won't have regrets; you can still apply to your reach schools without risking being shut out entirely because your list was too top heavy.

✔ **You want to minimize the risk of not being admitted and can handle the extensive work that a large number of secondaries entails.** Some applicants, particularly those who are only marginally competitive, prefer to apply to 25 or even more schools so that they don't miss out on the one school that may admit them. As I note earlier, though, the returns diminish as the list gets longer and you start adding schools that you only have a remote chance of admission to.

Because medical school admission is so competitive, erring on the side of a slightly longer list is usually better. For most students, the priority is to get in the first time they apply, and the additional cost or work that applying to more schools requires is preferable to potentially having to go through the application process again.

You can add schools after your primary application has been submitted. As Chapter 6 indicates, schools you add after your primary application has been verified usually receive your application very quickly.

Creating a Balanced List: A Mix of Dreams and Practicality

To craft your list of schools, you need two things: a goal and a strategy. The goal is to put together a group of schools that gives you the best chance of receiving an acceptance by the end of the cycle without aiming too low. A good list also should be a manageable length so that you don't end up inundated with secondary applications that you can't turn around quickly. Here's a step-by-step strategy to help you achieve that goal:

1. **Write down all the schools you may be interested in applying to.**

   For tips about researching schools, see the earlier section "Considering a few factors."

2. **Divide the list into three categories.**

   You then split your list into groups based on how likely you are to be admitted to each school:

   - **Group 1 schools:** Schools that are reach/dream schools for you. These schools have average MCAT scores and GPAs that are higher than yours; you're unlikely to be admitted to these programs, but you want to try for them anyway.

   - **Group 2 schools:** Schools that you have a reasonable likelihood of being admitted to based on your numbers and the overall strength of your application package.

   - **Group 3 schools:** Safety schools. These schools are ones you're a strong applicant for.

3. **Determine the number of schools you want to apply to.**

   See the earlier section "Determining How Many Schools to Include on Your List" for details.

4. **Eliminate or add schools as needed to achieve your target number of schools.**

Note: Formulating a list of schools isn't always a neat 1-2-3-4 process, so you may perform some of these steps in a slightly different order. For example, if factors such as finances limit the number of schools an applicant can apply to, she'd start with a max number, and then she'd make and divide her list from there.

The categories don't necessarily need to contain equal numbers of schools. To maximize your chance of admission to at least one medical school, focus mostly on Group 2 and Group 3 schools. For example, a list of 18 schools may include 4 Group 1 schools, 8 Group 2 schools, and 6 Group 3 schools.

Keep the following in mind as you go through the preceding steps:

✔ **Gaining admission to a public school as an out-of-state applicant is very difficult.** As I indicate in the earlier section "Type (public/state versus private)," public schools give preference to in-state applicants; see that section for more details. Public schools outside your home state are the first ones you should eliminate if your list is too long.

✔ **Overapplying is better than underapplying.** If you're aiming for 18 schools but are struggling to get the list below 22, apply to more schools initially. If you find you can't manage all the secondaries, withdraw your application from some of the schools. Although this approach costs you more in primary application fees, it ensures you have your primary submitted early for all the schools you're considering and lets you see how many secondaries you can manage before you decide on the final number of schools.

✔ **All allopathic medical schools in the U.S. are highly competitive.** Even the least-competitive allopathic schools are very difficult to gain admission to. Therefore, applicants whose GPA and MCAT scores are only borderline-competitive for any allopathic school should consider adding some osteopathic medical schools to the list because admission to these schools is generally less competitive. (For more info on the osteopathic option, check out Chapter 12.)

✔ **Different applicants may put the same school in a different category.** Your friend with a 33 MCAT and a GPA of 3.8 may consider a particular school to be a Group 2 school, while that same school is a Group 1 school for you.

✔ **Your premedical advisor or a mentor who is familiar with medical school admissions is a great resource.** An advisor can suggest schools you've overlooked as well as give you an objective opinion about your list to determine whether you've overreached or have underestimated yourself. You can read about the benefits of premedical advising in Chapter 5.

Chapter 8

Putting Together Primary Applications

· ·

In This Chapter

▶ Familiarizing yourself with the primary application basics

▶ Creating a compelling personal statement

▶ Submitting details on work and activities

▶ Giving the scoop on your course work

▶ Examining the many kinds of GPAs calculated

· ·

The primary application is your letter of introduction to medical schools. It contains your course work, personal statement, list of experiences, and myriad other details about you and tells schools you have what it takes to go from flashcard-toting premed to stethoscope-wielding physician. A strong application is essential in making it to the interview stage.

Doing a superb job with the primary application also means submitting early. Early applicants have the advantage of a class that is wide open, whereas those who push against the deadline may find themselves competing for only a few remaining spots, or worse, for the waitlist only.

This chapter familiarizes you with the three types of application services and provides you with strategies for completing primary applications on time and well. I provide special guidance on the most challenging aspect of the primary application: crafting an engaging personal statement. Note that each school has thousands (or in some cases, over 14,000) applications for 150 or so spots. You need to make yours stand out.

Beginning with the Basics of Primary Applications

Centralized *primary applications* allow you to apply to multiple medical schools by submitting one universal application. This setup saves you from having to fill out tens of applications to separate schools (although you need to do shorter secondary applications for each school later in the cycle; see Chapter 9 for details).

The instructions run up to 75 pages long, so filling out a primary is no simple matter. Schools want to know everything from how many siblings you have to how many hours of volunteer work you've done, along with the name, title, credits, and grades for every course you've ever taken at any college or university.

Think months, not days, when tackling the primary application. One applicant I know enthusiastically stated that she was ready to begin her application and that she'd submit right on June 1, the day the cycle opened. Her plan would've been ideal had it not already been May 25 at the time!

In the following sections, I provide an overview of the three application services so that you know which one (or more) you need to use. After that, I break down the parts of the primary application, talk about timing the application process, and give you tips for your application strategy.

Sorting out application services

AMCAS, AACOMAS, and TMDSAS are terms you've probably heard as a premed student. They're the acronyms for the three primary application services, and to secure a spot in medical school, you have to use at least one of them. The prospect of filling out more than one type of primary may be daunting, but the information each requires contains a lot of overlap. With some modifying, you can use the same personal statement and list of activities, so you don't have to start fresh with each application.

Most allopathic (MD) schools use the American Medical College Application Service (AMCAS), while osteopathic (DO) schools utilize the American Association of Colleges of Osteopathic Medicine Application Service (AACOMAS). Texas has its own application service, the Texas Medical and Dental Schools Application Service (TMSDAS), for Texas public MD and DO schools.

All three applications are electronic; you can find them online at the following sources:

✔ AMCAS: `www.aamc.org/students/applying/amcas`

✔ AACOMAS: `aacomas.aacom.org`

✔ TMDSAS: `www.utsystem.edu/tmdsas`

Check out these sites now, even if you aren't applying until a year or two down the road. You can become familiar with what you'll need to do when the time comes, plus find valuable resources about medicine and the admissions process.

Breaking down the primary application

Medical schools want to know anything about you that is remotely relevant to determining your suitability for the medical profession. In addition to writing a personal statement, you need to provide a laundry list of details on the application, such as the dates you volunteered at a homeless shelter your freshman year and the name of the art history course you took at a community college two summers ago. Mistakes or omissions, particularly in the academic record, can delay the processing of your application, so making sure your materials are accurate and complete is essential. The following list focuses mostly on the parts of the AMCAS application (for future osteopathic physicians, the AACOMAS application is covered in Chapter 12).

✔ **Personal statement/personal comments essay:** You have ten minutes to convince the admissions committee to give you an interview. What would you say? Those words belong in the innocuous-sounding personal statement section. You have anywhere from 4,500 to 5,300 characters, depending on the primary application, to state your case. Use this space tell your story — why want to be a physician, what experiences have shaped you, and what qualities make you suited for the profession. The Texas schools also allow for two optional essays of up to 2,500 characters each in which to discuss unique or challenging experiences. (I provide details on putting together your personal statement later in this chapter.)

✔ **Work and activities:** In this section, you list your clinical activities, research, work, and volunteer experience as well as honors, awards, and extracurricular activities. Describe each experience and reflect on what you learned or gained from it. (The later section "Completing the Work and Activities Section" gives you the scoop on writing these descriptions.)

✔ **Standardized tests:** This section includes the dates and scores for the MCAT as well as other tests, such as the GRE (required for certain dual-degree programs). If you've already taken the MCAT once or more, the information about your test(s) will automatically be included on your AMCAS application, so all you need to do is check those entries for accuracy. (For TMDSAS and AACOMAS, you must release your scores to the application service through the MCAT Testing History System.) If you haven't taken the MCAT yet or will be retaking it, enter your planned test date. Chapter 6 has more about the MCAT.

✔ **Academic record:** The primary application requires an exhaustive academic history. You need to list each college you've attended and your major and minor, plus each course you enrolled in with credits and grades earned. (Check out the later section "Entering Course Work and Understanding GPAs" for more info on filling out this section.)

✔ **Identifying information and biographical information:** Each primary application requires your name, address, family information, date of birth, state of residency, and other background information. Some information in this section may help the schools to determine whether you're socioeconomically disadvantaged. Don't hesitate to provide any information here that may enhance your admission. (See Chapter 17 for information geared toward disadvantaged applicants.)

✔ **List of schools:** Your primary application is sent only to the schools that you designate in this section.

The temptation may be to check off the few schools you know as well as a bunch of others you're only vaguely familiar with. That approach is a quick way to get your list done, but the next year will go by very slowly if you end having to go through the whole process again because you didn't apply strategically. A balanced, realistic list is critical. Yet even with the best-researched list, new information or a change of heart may inspire you to add more schools after submitting the primary, and for an additional fee, you can. (Flip to Chapter 7 for guidance on compiling a targeted list of medical schools.)

✔ **Certification and payment:** The certification functions as a legal signature and is considered to be a binding agreement between you and the application service. It consists of your reading and agreeing to the terms of the application service. You also have to pay the necessary fees before submitting. Table 8-1 notes the fees you have to pay to AMCAS and AACOMAS for schools you select at the time of your initial application (these fees are for the 2012–2013 cycle). As of 2013, TMDSAS charges a flat fee of $135 for all applicants (in-state and out-of-state) no matter how many schools they apply to.

Table 8-1	2012–2013 Fees for AMCAS and AACOMAS	
Application Service	*First School*	*Each Additional School*
AMCAS	$160	$34
AACOMAS	$175	$32

Timing your applications

Two applicants I worked with had MCAT scores in the low 30s, GPAs of 3.6, and similar lists of extracurricular activities. By spring, one had three acceptances in hand while the other was sitting on four waitlists. The difference: timing. The first applicant submitted the primary and secondary applications early and took the earliest interview dates she was offered. Meanwhile, the other procrastinated until fall for the primary application and sat on each secondary application until the last minute. The moral of the story? If you're an all-nighter type who thrives off a caffeine-fueled adrenaline rush and a dramatic last-minute finish, now is the time to change your strategy.

So what is "early"? And when and how should you start to prepare in order to hit your target dates? The following tips, along with the overall application timeline in Chapter 5, can help keep you on track and sane throughout this long process:

✔ **Be ready for a long haul.** The application cycle takes almost a full year. If you plan to go straight from college to medical school, you submit your application at the end of your junior year, interview and hear decisions from fall to spring of your senior year, graduate in the spring and start med school that fall. If you instead apply at the end of your last year in college, you have a *gap year* (refer to Chapter 5) prior to starting medical school.

✔ **Start researching the admission process and medical schools the year before you apply.** The year you apply, you have your hands full managing the application process, gathering letters of recommendation, and taking the MCAT. Use the year prior to start perusing the application instructions, digging up details on the schools, plotting your strategy, and identifying and correcting weaknesses while you still have time.

✔ **Take the MCAT by the end of May of your application year in order to have the scores available when AMCAS and AACOMAS open.** As of 2013, scores take approximately 30 days to be released. If balancing your classes plus MCAT studying is too much during the school year, you can take the MCAT the same summer you submit the application. If you take this route, you need to decide whether to wait for the results or to submit the application while your score is still pending.

Note: As I discuss in Chapter 6, you can submit the primary without MCAT scores; however, this strategy has some risks. MCAT scores are critical to getting accepted, and if you receive lower scores than expected, you may end up opting to apply the next cycle. Also, knowing which schools you're competitive for without scores is very difficult. Some applicants handle this situation by initially selecting only one or two schools and then adding the rest of the schools when the scores come out. Others take the opposite approach, applying broadly and withdrawing their applications from some schools after receiving their scores and narrowing the list. Weigh your decision carefully and determine whether the benefits outweigh the drawbacks of each; see Chapter 6 for more guidance.

✔ **Aim to submit your application as close to the first day of the cycle as possible.** AMCAS and AACOMAS begin accepting applications in early June; TMDSAS opens in May. Know, though, that the application process isn't precise enough that a few days or even a few weeks during the first part of the cycle will make a significant difference. If waiting until mid or late June allows you to finish up finals so that you can devote your full attention to producing a superb application, you should hold off until then.

✔ **Start filling out your application ahead of the cycle.** AMCAS and AACOMAS applications become available online in early May, approximately one month before they may be submitted. This timing means that you can begin entering your information onto the application then so that you're ready to hit "submit" when the cycle opens.

✔ **Allow at least a month to complete the application, and longer if your time is split among multiple activities such as school, MCAT preparation, and work or volunteering.** You should start the personal statement at least two months before you plan to submit, especially if you're out of practice writing anything more creative than an abstract for a scientific paper.

Planning your strategy

"What do I do first?" After reading reams of instructions and realizing how many steps lie between you and an acceptance, you may not know where to start. Begin by reviewing the application and gathering the information you need to fill out each section. Break down the application into manageable parts and start the most-difficult sections early. Because the personal statement is the most time-consuming aspect of the application, start brainstorming for ideas several months before you plan to submit (see the next section for much more about the personal statement). As you're generating ideas for the personal statement, you should also be taking the following steps:

✔ **Develop your list of schools.** This step can begin a year or more before you plan to apply. When researching schools, go beyond reading the school websites. Is the doctor you met volunteering in the ICU an alumnus of your favorite school? Ask him about it. What did he like (or not) about the program? What does the program look for in prospective students? Would you be a good fit there? Contact the friend of a friend who is a third year in med school to get the insight on his program even if it's not on your list of dream schools. (Chapter 7 explains how to compile a strategic list of schools.)

✔ **Two months before you plan to apply, order a copy of your transcripts for yourself from every college or university you've attended.** Check these documents carefully for mistakes. Although rare, errors do occur on transcripts. One applicant had the unwelcome surprise of finding a course on his transcript that he'd never even enrolled in. The worst part: the F grade that came with it. Fortunately, this story had a happy ending, but getting the mistake corrected took weeks. By reviewing your transcripts a couple of months before the application is due, you have time to address any problems you find.

Have official transcripts sent to the application services when they begin accepting them, usually in May. If you're still in school, you may need to wait until the spring semester ends and your latest grades are posted if you want those grades included in the AMCAS GPA.

✔ **Collect the information that you'll need to fill out the application.** This step may require you to look up everything from the name of the volunteer coordinator for the ER to the number of hours you put in during a summer research internship. Get all the data in place and organized so that you aren't scrambling for information you need to finish the application.

✔ **Register for the application service online so that you can begin entering information into the application as soon as it becomes available.** As I note in the preceding section, you can begin working on the AMCAS and AACOMAS applications about a month before you can submit them.

Crafting a Strong Personal Statement

Your GPA is respectable, and your MCAT scores are solid — maybe even much better than that. You've shadowed four different physicians, comforted the sick, served meals to the hungry, and run gels in the lab late into the night. But what are you actually like? Why do you want to spend four years of demanding study followed by three to seven more years of grueling training? What or who influenced you to make this decision? Letting the admissions committee glimpse who you are and what brought you to where you are now — with the help of your personal statement — distinguishes you as an individual and makes you more than a set of numbers and a list of experiences. A shoddy personal statement can detract from even an applicant with stellar MCAT scores and a top GPA, while a compelling statement may propel an average applicant into the interview stage.

In the following sections, I note the length limits of the personal statement, explain how to use the statement effectively, and walk you through the steps of putting together the statement. (Here, I focus on the personal statement for MD schools, but in Chapter 12, I discuss putting together a personal statement for DO schools.)

Being aware of length limits

The length limit and instructions for the personal statement for AMCAS, AACOMAS, and TMDSAS are slightly different. The length limits, including spaces, are

✔ **AMCAS:** 5,300 characters

✔ **AACOMAS:** 4,500 characters

✔ **TMDSAS:** 5,000 characters

These length limits equal about one to one and half pages of single-spaced text. The application doesn't allow you to enter text beyond designated number of characters, so cut your statement down to the correct length before you enter it or you may end up having to do some last-minute editing.

If you're applying through more than one service, start with the one with the longest statement and then cut back and modify for the other application(s).

Using the personal statement effectively

You've probably seen those computer-generated images formulated to represent the ideal woman's face. Her features are perfectly symmetrical, her eyes the optimal distance apart, and her nose precisely sculpted. Yet something always seems off; the visage looks flat, bland, and lifeless. A technically perfect personal statement that lacks personality and a clear voice is a lot like this computerized image: You can't find anything specifically wrong with it, but it doesn't engage you, either.

Your personal statement must tell your story and reflect your individuality. By the end of the personal statement, the admissions committee should know the following:

- ✔ Why you want to become a physician
- ✔ Why you'll make a great physician

The personal statement should include elements of your background or experiences that aren't present elsewhere in the application or discuss experiences in more depth or from a different perspective than in the work and activities section (which I discuss later in this chapter). In addition to developing the content and structure that convey your message to the committee, you need to ensure that the personal statement is well-written, organized, descriptive, and clear.

Be sure to avoid the following when crafting your personal statement:

- ✔ **Getting way off topic:** You can include aspects of your background that aren't directly related to your interest in becoming a physician, but don't stray too far from the topic of medicine. An entire essay describing the summer you attended clown school will make you stand out, but probably not in a good way.

- ✔ **Being overly negative:** The statement is an opportunity to address weaknesses in your application, but don't let negatives dominate the essay. The semester you got mono and your grades suffered may merit a brief mention, but spend most of the space emphasizing your strengths.

✔ **Sharing inappropriate information:** Note that whatever you say cannot be unsaid. This essay isn't the place to reveal personal information, your deepest secrets, or quirky insecurities. Save those for your best friend.

✔ **Repeating your activities list:** Don't list every activity, experience, and award you've ever had. Your personal statement isn't a resume; it's a chance to add depth and a personal touch to your application.

✔ **Being too off-the-wall:** Don't be overly creative; some creativity is fine, but this essay isn't the time to take risks.

✔ **Focusing too heavily on childhood experiences:** If you write about childhood experiences that shaped your interest in medicine, make sure you also write about adult experiences. You want the admissions committee to view you as an adult who's made a fully informed decision to pursue a career in medicine, not just as a kid who loved playing with a toy stethoscope.

Tackling the personal statement step by step

Like the Verbal Reasoning section of the MCAT, the personal statement takes premedical students out of their comfort zones of facts and formulas. You aren't just being asked to write; you have to write about yourself. Procrastination or a haphazard approach makes for a long, painful writing process and, worse, a mediocre final product. You need a systematic approach, especially in the early stages of writing. The following sections are a step-by-step guide to going from promising ideas to a fully developed, dynamic personal statement.

Brainstorming for ideas

Even if you've wanted to be a physician from a very young age, you weren't literally born knowing medicine was your life's calling. At some point, you made the decision to pursue medicine. Why? What experiences led to this choice? What influences shaped you as a person? What makes you unique? The writing process shouldn't begin with your sitting down facing a blank screen to answer these questions in your first draft. Instead, the first step is to bring ideas and experiences to the forefront of your mind and jot them down over a period of days or even weeks.

Here are some additional questions designed to help you get the ideas flowing:

✔ What attracts you to the medical profession?

✔ How have your experiences contributed to your understanding of the qualities a physician needs?

- ✔ What qualities do you possess that will make you a good physician? How did you develop these qualities?

- ✔ Who have been your role models or mentors?

- ✔ How have you explored the field of medicine?

- ✔ What challenges have you faced in life?

- ✔ Who or what has had an impact on you?

- ✔ What do you excel at?

- ✔ What is unique about you or your background?

- ✔ If you were face to face with the admissions committee, what would you tell it?

Along with thinking generally about these topics, you need to produce specific anecdotes and examples to illustrate your points. For example, in response to the first question in the preceding list, your first thought may be that volunteering in the ICU your freshman year of college reinforced your budding interest in medicine. Don't stop there; instead, develop your idea in greater depth. What was the environment in the ICU like? What did you notice about the way the medical staff interacted with each other and with the patients? What specific experiences did you have with patients or physicians? How did your perspective on medicine change as a result of the experience? What was the most memorable day you had on the unit? Why?

At this stage, don't edit your ideas; simply jot them down. Some of your thoughts will make it into the final draft; many won't. Start with plenty of material so that you can choose the items that most effectively tell your story. Brainstorming also helps you get back into the mode of writing and out of the memorizing-and-regurgitating approach you perfected to get through your premed classes.

Choosing a theme

With your list of ideas and examples for inspiration, you're ready to choose a theme for your statement. The best personal statements are those unified around a common theme. Read through the list of ideas you brainstormed. Which ones are most important? What's the thread that ties them together?

A theme seemingly unrelated to medicine can be an excellent choice because it can set apart your essay from the sea of others that revolve around "I want to help people" or "I love science." For example, as one applicant I worked with looked through his list of ideas, he noticed that many of his experiences reflected his strong sense of independence and desire for adventure. He believed this attribute was rooted in growing up in a military family that moved around every few years, including overseas. This applicant could build an essay around these ideas by describing how the characteristics he developed at an early age informed his later experiences and motivated his interest in medicine. Even a single experience, such as the first time you watched a surgery in action or a patient who profoundly impacted you, can serve as a theme.

Themes are great, but don't be too heavy-handed with the subject, or you may end up making the reader roll his eyes. Talking about playing the violin in the opening paragraph and then using each subsequent paragraph to compare medical specialties to different types of instruments is something even the strongest writer probably couldn't pull off. Skillfully handled, a theme is a framework for the essay that may recede into the background at times only to reemerge later.

Developing a structure

With your ideas and theme in place, the next step is to organize them so that you're presenting a clear, logical story. An essay that makes a weak start, jumps around, or trails off won't do its job even if the content is stellar. Before you start writing, determine the topic of each paragraph and the order you'll present them in. You don't need to make an exhaustive outline if that isn't your style, but without a basic road map in place, you may end up writing along only to realize you've hit a dead end.

Follow these principles to generate an effective structure for the statement:

- ✔ **Start with your strongest material.** The first paragraph is the one that makes the reader either eager to move forward to see what happens next or so bored he skims just to get through. If you saved three children from drowning, won an Olympic medal in pole vaulting, or job shadowed the surgeon general, don't begin your statement by talking about the time you dissected a frog in 7th grade biology class, even though that occurred first. Not presenting the topics in chronological order does make the transitions more challenging, but the payoff is worth it. So although you shouldn't bounce around in time every time you switch paragraphs, going for a great opening and then transitioning the reader to the back story is okay.

- ✔ **Have a goal for each paragraph.** Each paragraph should have a function; if it doesn't, it shouldn't be there. The length limits leave no room for fluff (check them out for yourself earlier in this chapter), so every paragraph must count, and none should be redundant or overly similar to another. If you don't know what you're trying to say in a paragraph, neither will the admissions committee. Select the best ideas from your list and determine what function they can serve in the essay and how you can build a paragraph around them.

  For example, one paragraph may focus on the theme of understanding the realities of medicine and not just its rewards. The paragraph may include a discussion of your volunteering in hospice, a setting in which physicians face end-of-life issues on a daily basis, as well as a description of job shadowing a surgeon and seeing the sheer stamina it takes to stand in the OR for long hours performing an incredibly intense and demanding job. The goal of this paragraph is to discuss qualities you possess — such as perseverance, a strong work ethic, and adaptability — that will allow you to succeed in these challenging situations. *Remember:* Part of the paragraph's goal includes giving examples discussing how you've demonstrated or developed these qualities to make the point convincingly. (I discuss this technique of showing and not telling in the next section.)

✔ **Aim for five to seven paragraphs.** This number is enough to allow you to cover plenty of topics so that your story will have breadth but not so many that you end up with a choppy essay. This range isn't a hard-and-fast rule but rather a guide. Some writers are so capable of transitioning seamlessly from one topic to another that even using eight or nine paragraphs works beautifully. Others have a style that fits better with fewer, more-robust sections. Work with your writing style and the material you have to come up with an optimal number.

✔ **Keep the conclusion concise.** Don't attempt to introduce a bunch of new ideas at the end or do an exhaustive recap of what you've already covered. You can use the conclusion to finish a story you started in the first paragraph, allude to the beginning in some other way to bring the essay full circle, or provide final words about your commitment to medicine and suitability for the profession.

Writing the first draft

You can only do so much plotting and planning before you just have to start writing. With a basic structure, your overarching theme, and your list of ideas, you have the tools to write your first complete draft. *Complete* doesn't mean "perfect" or even "great". It just means "done." So don't agonize over every sentence or word. The first draft is just the starting point and is meant to get the process going.

Give yourself a block of a few hours, sit down, and generate a rough draft of every paragraph you plan to include. Start with a draft that is too long and then condense later. Aiming for a first draft that is between 120 percent and 150 percent of the final length gives you room to simply write but isn't unmanageably long. During the revising steps I describe in the next section, you eliminate any unnecessary material in stages until you have a tightly written essay in which every word matters. The rough statement won't look much like its final form for another few drafts, but it gives you a foundation to work from.

Here are some guidelines now that you're into the actual writing:

✔ **Show, don't tell.** This advice may not be very novel, but it's absolutely critical. A statement such as "I spend a lot of time shadowing in the hospital and really enjoy it" is not only boring but also vague. Instead, draw a picture with your words that allows the reader to come to the conclusion about what you did or learned. For example, say, "I watched intently as the surgeon made a single, precise incision." The reader can easily infer that you were deeply engaged in your OR experience and that you've taken the time to explore medicine firsthand.

✔ **Be descriptive.** This tip is closely related to the preceding point. Through imagery, you can create a scene and place yourself within it. A phrase such as "brightly lit operating room" makes the setting more vivid than simply saying "the operating room." Instead of saying that "I volunteer at the front desk of a busy clinic," try "Arriving for my shift at the front desk each morning, I pass through the clinic's bustling waiting room." The first statement sounds generic and isn't particularly informative. The second helps the reader easily visualize you in a medical setting; the "bustling waiting room" signals that the clinic is busy without directly stating so.

✔ **Have strong transitions between topics.** Link a paragraph to the previous one through the transition sentences. By moving smoothly from topic to topic, your statement will read as a unified whole, not as disparate subjects. For example, if one paragraph discusses your work at a medical mission in Costa Rica and the next one focuses on your volunteer work in a clinic serving primarily Spanish-speaking patients, you can link the two paragraphs through a sentence such as "I arrived back in the United States a month later, eager to use my greater fluency in Spanish to serve communities closer to home." This sentence ties together two adjacent paragraphs by mentioning the main topic of each. In the next sentence, you can go on to discuss your volunteer work at the community clinic without making the reader feel jarred by the switch to a new subject.

✔ **Be clear and direct.** Aim for clarity in your writing. Filling the essay with deliberately complex sentences and pretentious vocabulary doesn't make you sound smarter. It just makes the essay frustrating to read.

✔ **Vary your sentence structure.** A statement with too many similarly structured sentences is akin to a person speaking in a monotone voice. Therefore, don't start several sentences in a row with any single type of structure, such as "I [verb]." Intersperse brief sentences among longer ones; too many short sentences together sound choppy, while too many long ones clustered are difficult to follow.

✔ **Use your own writer's voice.** Your writing is as unique as your actual voice. Your distinct voice will come through in your statement as long as you don't let it get watered down by too many suggestions from other people. Getting input from one or two trusted advisors or friends is fine, and having someone else proofread your statement is essential (as I explain later in this chapter), but writing isn't something that is done by committee. With four or five different people involved, you're likely to get conflicting opinions and to end up with a disjointed piece of writing that lacks personality. This statement should include what is meaningful to you, in your words.

✔ **Be accurate.** Applicants often worry that their backgrounds aren't exciting enough to create a great personal statement. The misconception is often that they should've had a single life-changing moment to discuss in the essay. For most people, though, the decision to become a doctor was a gradual one and didn't take place one dark and stormy night. If you try to force your story to be something it's not, that will show in your writing. Keep in mind too that the personal statement is frequently a source for interview questions, and even the most carefully spun tale comes apart under pressure.

✔ **Don't criticize physicians.** Reading an applicant's personal statement that discussed the incompetence of the cardiologist treating her father and her vow to "never be like him," I could only wonder what the applicant was thinking. That the approach of attacking a profession she hoped to join would win her points for her daring? That she'd be seen as medicine's savior? At best, evaluators may see an applicant's criticizing physicians from the outside as naïve; at worst, it will make physician-readers defensive or annoyed. Stick to discussing positive physician role models and the enormous good that medicine does. You can still acknowledge the challenges physicians face, but this essay isn't the place to air your grievances. If you aspire to affect change, you can do it much more easily in a few years with "Doctor" in front of your name.

✔ **Take breaks between drafts.** A fresh look at your statement will make it easier for you to spot weaknesses and to correct them. If you get stuck or feel that you're becoming stale, set the essay aside for a few days.

Revising and cutting, over and over again

You read your first draft. You then compare this rough-around-the edges piece of writing to the gleaming personal statement you read online. You consider hitting "delete" and/or crying. See where this is going? Applicants sometimes expect their rough draft to resemble the final product, but much of the real work of writing comes down to revising: reworking paragraphs, restructuring sentences, refining, polishing, and editing. If you have a draft that contains the essential ideas you want to include, the best approach is to stick with it and mold it into a sparkling piece of prose. Only if you're seriously off-track should you scrap it and start over.

As you begin to revise the essay, eliminate sentences that lack purpose and expand areas that show promise. Take at least a few days between drafts, or even a week if possible, so that you can read your work with fresh eyes. Continually ask yourself whether there's a better, clearer way to make each point. Assess the tone of the writing. Do you sound enthusiastic, confident, and determined? Tentative and indifferent? Step back and look at the overall structure. Are the topics presented in an order that allows the story to unfold logically and naturally? Or is the narrative choppy and confusing? Work through each part of the draft, cutting, moving, changing, and altering until a new, improved version emerges. When you're done with the first round, go back and do it again.

Repeat the revising process over and over, honing the writing each time. Continue to pare down the length to fit the application's requirements. Generating a great personal statement typically takes eight to ten drafts, but that number can vary greatly.

After the statement is fairly established, get feedback from a premedical advisor, professor, or physician familiar with the application process. Too much feedback can actually inhibit your ability to write a statement that reflects your story, but you need to see how your work impacts someone else. Did it hold his attention? Was he left wanting to learn more about you? How would he describe you after reading your statement? Does he envision you as someone capable of succeeding in medical school and as a physician? Address major weaknesses before you invest the time to perfect the wording and other details of the essay.

Don't forge ahead if you recognize that the message of the statement is fundamentally weak. Could someone who has never met you read your draft and understand why you've decided to become a physician? Or be convinced that you have the necessary qualities to be a good physician? Look past the sentences that need polishing and the slightly-too-long length at this stage to see whether the fundamental theme and content of the essay are sound. If your essay doesn't answer these questions or doesn't encompass the message you want to tell the committee, consider starting over. Pushing ahead with the wrong approach will end up costing you more time than beginning again or will result in a lackluster statement. If the foundation of your statement isn't strong, no amount of editing can create a piece of writing that is truly compelling. If you need to make a fresh start, revisit the list of ideas you generated during your brainstorming for inspiration to find a new mix of topics or a different theme.

Proofreading

Nothing wrecks a great story more than run-on sentences, misspelled or misused words, and incorrect punctuation. These errors detract from the impact of the essay and leave the impression that attention to detail isn't your strong suit. Therefore, in addition to proofreading relentlessly on your own, find someone with impeccable grammar to read your statement. (It should be a different person from the one who read your essay earlier on. A person who is very familiar with the text is more likely to miss a small error than a fresh reader.) Good sources of help include an English teacher or your college's writing center.

When the proofreading is done and you're happy with the statement, don't start second guessing yourself. If you start making last-minute changes, you risk introducing errors. If you do have a great inspiration and must make changes, proofread again and give the statement to back to your proofreader as well.

Transferring the personal statement into the application

You have two options for entering your personal statement into the application:

- ✔ Write it in a separate document and then copy and paste it onto the application.
- ✔ Type directly onto the application.

I strongly recommend the former approach. If you type the statement directly onto the application, you'll have to proofread again in case you make typographical errors (and the application doesn't have a spell check function). Instead, perfect the essay in a word processing program, save it as a text-only document, and copy and paste it in that format onto the application. The text-only part is important; the primary applications don't support special fonts or formats (including simple bolding and italics), and pasting in anything other than a text-only version may cause problems with the format of your statement on the application.

Sifting through Personal Statement Examples

As I mention throughout the chapter, showing rather than telling is a great way to get your point across. I use that technique in this section by providing you with examples of what great personal statements look like. I also give you an example of a weak personal statement to illustrate mistakes to avoid as you create your own statement. As you read on, keep in mind that your statement will be unique to you both in terms of content and style.

Example 1: Taking an artistic approach

The compelling personal statement in this section tells the story of an applicant whose decision to enter medicine was the culmination of many experiences. It also demonstrates how to effectively integrate an outside interest, in this case art, into a personal statement.

I once imagined becoming an artist. My immediate family members work with their hands in ways both creative and practical: My father is a skilled carpenter, my mother sews intricate quilts, and my sister's fingers fly across the strings of her violin to create music of remarkable beauty. With the fine motor skills bestowed by my parents' genes and an eye for the nuances of color, I embarked on a series of drawing and painting classes starting at the age of eight. Though I was technically proficient, I eventually realized _that creating masterpieces was not my calling. I began to explore my talents and strengths and found my inspiration in unexpected places: in the halls of the hospital, at the side of an ill patient, or in the elaborate diagrams of an anatomy book. I also learned that medicine is its own kind of art and that my original vision of my future was not far off after all._

As a teenager watching a television show about a "real-life ER," I was amazed at how the doctors faced one life-or-death situation after another. During the entire action-packed hour, lives were saved or, on occasion, lost. The nondescript hospital I drove by each day on the way to school was a place I now viewed as the scene of high drama. Intrigued, I signed up as a volunteer. I quickly discovered that life is not much like TV, especially reality TV. Our small community hospital was not a major trauma center and seemed more calm than chaotic. However, I soon learned that life-changing events occurred every day within the hospital's walls as patients arrived to deliver a baby, undergo a surgery, or visit a loved one. These events were mostly unaccompanied by sirens or dramatic scenes, but the difference between "before" and "after" was equally profound.

My days as a volunteer were filled with small moments — some routine, others unforgettable. Through delivering ice chips and blankets or making rounds with a cart full of books, I was able to make patients' stays a bit more comfortable. I most looked forward to the times I spent reading or talking to patients. I vividly remember the World War II veteran with renal disease who loved to play cards and the young mother who suffered from complications of multiple sclerosis and worried about her three children at home. Sometimes patients spoke with me about their physicians. The arrival of the physician brought relief; someone caring, competent, and knowledgeable was there to help. I admired these men and women in their white coats; yet, becoming one of them seemed a distant dream more akin to an abstract painting than a realistic sketch of my future.

Shadowing doctors in the emergency room, operating room, and clinic confirmed my desire to join their ranks. These experiences illuminated the mix of technical expertise and humanism that defines the profession. I peered over the surgeon's shoulder as he bypassed the regions of the coronary artery that could no longer effectively deliver blood to the heart. Like a painter with a brush or sculptor with chisel in hand, the physician manipulated the surgical instruments with precision and grace. I marveled when, following the procedure, the physician walked out of the operating room still in his scrubs to speak with the patient's family. I witnessed the honest, accessible, and empathetic communication with which the doctor comforted the patient's worried wife and grown children. This remarkable ability to connect with people is one that I've noticed is common to all great physicians. I have always been most gratified by work that allows me to form a bond with others, and the opportunity to forge such connections with patients drives my desire to practice medicine.

Knowing that any composition is formed a single brush stroke at a time, I took the next step toward my goal of entering medicine by declaring a biology major. My science courses have honed the critical-thinking skills I use in my volunteer work in a primary care clinic and allow me to better understand the approach of the physicians I observe. Each week I perform tasks from measuring patients' blood pressures and temperatures to weighing infants and making reminder calls to patients with upcoming appointments. Between patients, the physicians sometimes explain their craft to me, discussing how electrolyte results are interpreted or which questions to ask when assessing a patient for diabetes. I see too that the hands-on nature of a physician's work is not limited to the operating room but includes manipulating a stethoscope to listen for the telltale wheezes of asthma, irrigating a wound to prevent infection, or touching a patient's shoulder to offer comfort. A physician's mind and hands are equally essential tools, and the tactile skills I have developed through my art training will be invaluable to me in caring for patients.

Performing a complex surgery, making a difficult diagnosis, and spending time at the bedside of a patient are all art with the highest purpose: to comfort and heal. My experiences as a student, volunteer, and observer have revealed medicine as infinitely complex, endlessly challenging, and deeply rewarding. I am confident that I possess the determination, compassion, and creativity to contribute to a field that is, without doubt, both an art and a science.

Analyzing why Example 1 works

This applicant immediately grabs the reader's attention by starting with a concise, definitive statement. The first sentence is about art, not medicine, yet as the statement progresses, the author weaves the two topics seamlessly together. The description of his family and his childhood art classes immediately establishes the applicant as an individual, not an ID number or list of grades and achievements. He revisits the theme of art throughout the statement but always keeps the focus on medicine. He uses specific experiences, such as hospital and clinic volunteering and physician shadowing, to illustrate his motivation to become a physician. This applicant is showing and not telling the reader why he wants to be a physician. His use of specific detail allows the reader to envision him talking to a patient or watching, enthralled, as a surgeon operates. The applicant is very confident in his decision to enter medicine and is enthusiastic and eager to learn from his experiences. Finally, the writing is clear and unpretentious. This applicant is someone the admissions committee will want to meet.

Example 2: Showcasing an adventurous applicant

The example of a strong personal statement in this section illustrates how to use a particularly meaningful experience to anchor a statement while also incorporating other important elements of the applicant's background into the essay.

The climb sounded like the perfect start to summer. My roommate, Justin, had asked me to join him and two friends on a trip to the Eastern Sierras. The route would be challenging but manageable even for a novice like me. Eager to get an early start, we made the six-hour drive to Bishop and camped near the trailhead the night before the climb. We were up by 6:00 a.m. and after a quick breakfast headed into beautiful Sierra backcountry. After an easy hike, the climb up Mt. Goethe started simply enough, with a few sections requiring careful maneuvering. As we got higher, we ran into snow remaining from an early summer storm. My thought that this was no big deal was shattered by a sudden sliding noise followed by a scream. In a matter of seconds, Justin had gone from 200 feet above me to just 20 feet away. I reached him quickly and saw that his right arm was misshapen and likely fractured. I grabbed the first aid kit and used one of my hiking poles to fashion a splint as the rest of our group went for help. Observing my friend's pale complexion and clammy skin, potential signs of shock, I repositioned him and kept him hydrated. Five hours later, the sound of the helicopter broke the silence of the wilderness, and within 20 minutes Justin was being hoisted up by rescuers. As I made my way back to the trailhead, I reflected on what had just happened: For a brief time, I had been responsible for the health of another human being. This, more than any other experience, crystallized my understanding of what it would mean to be a physician.

I returned to school that fall with the newfound perspective that providing even basic medical care required more than just science knowledge. It also demanded composure, compassion, and good judgment. Yet I still appreciated that it is science that gives doctors the tools to alleviate symptoms, treat injuries, and cure disease. Eager to contribute to the scientific foundation that underlies medicine, I began working in a lab whose area of investigation is the virulence factors of Helicobacter pylori, bacteria involved in peptic ulcer formation. Because the group's principle investigator was a physician, I had the privilege of occasionally observing while he treated patients in a GI clinic. I watched in awe as he deciphered the history, symptoms, and test results to uncover the cause of a patient's condition and formulate a treatment plan. Though I deeply enjoyed shadowing, I also craved greater patient interaction than observing would allow. To satisfy my desire for hands-on experience I began volunteering in both inpatient and outpatient settings.

Although each of my volunteer experiences was rewarding, none matched the level of satisfaction I gained from working at Mid-City Clinic. Because the clinic is extremely busy, I performed whatever tasks were needed, from setting up examination rooms to checking in patients and stocking supplies. As I became more experienced, I was entrusted to take vital signs and basic patient histories. Through volunteering as a clinic assistant, I confirmed my comfort in a clinical environment and learned more about the nature of the physician-patient relationship. I witnessed interactions such as the one between a pediatrician and a three-year-old girl with symptoms of an ear infection. Although the child seemed frightened at first, she soon responded to the physician's calm, reassuring manner. After determining that the girl had an infection and explaining the needed treatment, the doctor spoke with her mother about the child's overall health, nutrition, and development. This broad scope of practice and the opportunity to develop a relationship with a patient over years or even decades reaffirmed my growing interest in primary care, although I am still eager to explore other areas of medicine.

Through my own interactions with patients, I learned that even small gestures can make an impact. One young woman from whom I was gathering intake information began talking about the recent loss of her job as well as her worsening symptoms of an autoimmune disorder. I listened as she described her feelings of frustration and helplessness, which were compounded by her inability to get regular medical care. I responded by saying that it sounded like she was going through a difficult time and assured her that the staff and volunteers would help in any we could. As she left the clinic following her consultation with the physician, she sought me out and thanked me for taking a few minutes to listen. I know that as a physician there will be many demands on my time, but that to treat each patient with compassion and kindness will be essential.

A year after our adventure on Mt. Goethe, Justin has only a small scar and a good story left to remind him of his slide down the mountain. When he told me that he will be back to climbing this season, I couldn't help but think that his doctors had done their job well. My friend was back to life as usual, and for a patient and his physician, that is the ultimate goal. That day on Mt. Goethe, I had only a wilderness first aid course and the best of intentions to guide me. With a physician's training and skills, I will be equipped to provide those in need with comprehensive care and the ability to climb their own mountains.

Assessing the intriguing elements of Example 2

This applicant made the most of his climbing adventure as a hook to open the statement. By the end of the first paragraph, the committee knows that this applicant isn't afraid to stretch his limits and can keep a level head when a crisis arises. He then moves on to discuss more-conventional premedical pursuits, such as conducting basic research, shadowing a physician, and volunteering in a clinical setting. He chooses to dedicate two paragraphs to his clinic work, which reflects the importance of this experience in his developing interest in medicine. He approaches his clinical experience from several perspectives: as a new volunteer in an overburdened clinic, as a premedical student observing a physician, and as a more seasoned volunteer connecting with a patient.

Unlike the art theme in used in Example 1, climbing isn't a topic that is carried through the entire statement but rather a device used only in the opening and closing paragraphs to frame the essay. At the end of the statement, the applicant returns to the story begun in the first paragraph, describing how his friend is doing a year after his fall. Picking up the thread of the story in the concluding paragraph effectively unifies the statement. The applicant then ends with a strong message about his desire to become a physician and his belief that with a doctor's skills and training he'll be truly ready to help others who are in need.

Example 3: Seeing what not to write

The statement in this section provides you with an example of what not to do when you write your personal statement. This applicant manages to pack just about every "don't" for the personal statement into six paragraphs.

My parents have always expected that I would become a doctor, and because of this, I started learning about the field when I was very young. My father, an esteemed surgeon, is the third generation in his family to be a physician, and my mother is an internist. They brought me with them to work when I was quite young, and from that I developed an interest in medicine and an understanding of the importance of carrying on the family tradition in this respected field. I also want to be a physician because I have a great love of science, I want to help patients, and I enjoy working with people. For these reasons, I made the decision to apply to medical school.

Intelligence and mastering medical knowledge are the top priorities for a doctor; therefore, I have cultivated my academic credentials in preparation for medical school. Although I received two Cs in science classes my freshman year in college, I attribute this to the fact that I was adjusting to being at college and unknowingly chose chemistry courses given by a professor with a reputation for being notoriously difficult. Out of 60 people in each of my chemistry classes, only 10 got As the first semester and 8 the second. My sophomore year I received a 3.6, and I achieved an even higher GPA this year as a junior. My MCAT score of 31 is also evidence that I am prepared to handle the challenges of medical school. My scores in the sciences were particularly strong, and I do not believe that my verbal reasoning score of an 8 reflects my true potential in that area. I tend to focus on subjects that are most interesting and relevant to me, and thus scored better on the science sections, as these topics are most important in medicine.

I believe that it is important for a future physician to know what it means to be a good physician. I have seen both good and bad doctors, which has helped me to understand how I can be a better doctor in the future. A close friend of the family was in a serious car accident last year, so I visited him in the hospital several times. During one visit, his mother told me that the doctor had not clearly explained what was going on with her son or how long he would be in the hospital. I was in the room on one occasion when the doctor came in, and I watched as my friend's parents tried to ask the doctor questions. The doctor seemed rushed and answered them abruptly. He spent most of the time talking to the intern and residents who were with him and did not conduct himself as a professional. I am determined not to be a physician like the one I saw that day. I have the good judgment and caring manner to ensure that I always treat my patients with respect.

I know that volunteer work and clinical experience are important and have done many hours of both. Doing community service in a homeless shelter has reminded me how much I enjoy working with people. Volunteering in the hospital seemed to be an exciting opportunity as the hospital environment is one I enjoy. I was assigned a position in the playroom entertaining pediatric patients. Although this position was not the one I had hoped for as I do not have a particular interest in pediatrics, I did enjoy working with the kids I met. I also found volunteering with Dr. Bass, a dermatologist, to be very intriguing. I have been interested in surgery for as long as I can remember, but watching Dr. Bass, I began to consider dermatology as a potential field. I believe that balance is important in life, and as a dermatologist, I could achieve a work-life balance and still make a difference in patients' lives by treating skin cancers and other dermatological disorders. Radiology is another area that interests me, and I am working to find a radiologist to shadow. Through shadowing, I have learned more about the various specialties, as well as how different ways doctors practice medicine and the sacrifices doctors make for their careers. To me, it is important to know as much as I can about the field I choose to pursue so that I can make an educated decision.

Another area I am interested in is medical research. I believe that I am suited to a career in academic medicine because a career that involves seeing patients, teaching, and research would provide me with variety. After applying to several labs, I secured a position in a neuroscience lab several months ago. Since that time, I have gained training in basic laboratory techniques such as gel electrophoresis and PCR. These will provide me with the foundation I need for future research endeavors as an undergraduate and in medical school.

By becoming a physician I can contribute to one of the most important fields that exist while also being part of a tradition in my family. Through research, teaching, and clinical practice, I can use my experience to help advance the field of medicine. Although I do not yet know what specialty I will ultimately select, I know that I will make a difference in whatever I area I choose to pursue.

Dissecting what went wrong in Example 3

This statement starts off wrong, and things only get worse from there. The applicant's opening words are a turnoff; parental expectations aren't a valid reason to go into medicine. The other reasons he states pertaining to his interest in medicine, such as loving science and wanting to work with people, sound generic. The second paragraph with its litany of numbers and attempt to blame his mediocre performance on his professor or his lack of interest in a subject serves only to highlight the weaknesses in his application. He would've been better off focusing on experiences and achievements that led to his decision to pursue a career in medicine.

After this bumpy start comes an even bigger mistake: criticizing a physician. Instead of concentrating on positive role models in medicine, this applicant decides the best idea is to make negative remarks about a physician and then state how much better he'll do when he's a doctor. As a writer, he has reversed the "show, don't tell" creed and states directly that he has "good judgement" and a "caring manner" without any evidence or examples to back up his contentions.

Although he does mention his volunteer experiences, his discussion of them is cursory and he soon turns to talking about his interest in specialties that will give him "balance," which is likely to be as interpreted as "I'm not even in med school and I'm already looking for the specialty with cushy hours." Next, the applicant throws in a research paragraph that is poorly developed and seems unrelated to the rest of the statement. Finally, he closes the statement by alluding to the opening and family tradition, thereby ending on the same weak note that he opened. Is this an applicant you want to meet? The admissions committee probably won't want to, either!

Completing the Work and Activities Section

All three primary applications have a section in which to enter your paid employment, clinical experiences, research, volunteer experiences, honors, and other activities.

- ✔ AMCAS allows a maximum of 15 entries and up to 700 characters, including spaces, for each description. Applicants may select up to the three experiences to be designated as "most meaningful." For these items, you get an additional 1,325-character space in which to reflect more deeply on the experience. You have to choose an "Experience Type" from a drop-down list to describe each experience. For certain activities, such as a paid research position, you may find that more than one designation applies. However, you may only choose one, so you must decide which category is the best fit.

✔ AACOMAS gives you 750 characters, including spaces, for each description, with the exception of the honors, awards, and scholarships section. You also choose a broad category for the experience type. For honors and awards, you list only the name of the award and the sponsoring organization; you don't get space to describe them.

✔ TMDSAS has a shorter limit for descriptions, with a maximum of 300 characters, including spaces, per entry. You have to focus more on the essentials, such as responsibilities and accomplishments for each activity, and limit the amount of discussion and reflection. Another difference between the Texas application and the other primaries is that you can list activities more than once if they fit under several categories. For example, a paid job in a research lab may fall under "Employment" and again under "Research Activities."

The work and activities section functions as your resume (though it isn't formatted like one) and frees you from feeling as though you must squeeze every accomplishment you've ever had into the personal statement that I discuss earlier in this chapter. In the following sections, I explain how to fill out this section properly.

You don't have to fill every bit of the space allotted for the descriptions. Busy admissions officers don't want to waste time reading text that was added simply to use up space. If you truly need to use the entire space, that's fine, but your focus should be on the quality of your description, not the length. Blank space isn't the enemy.

Choosing activities and deciding which are most meaningful

You don't have to fill up all 15 spaces in the work and activities section allotted by AMCAS. In fact, some of the strongest applications I've seen contained fewer than 15 entries. Schools look for depth, not dabbling. Plus, admissions officers read thousands of pages of documents, and wasting their time with filler won't win you any points. If you have 15 substantial activities, that is fine, but don't include trivial items just to have a full list.

The activities you choose should be primarily those that you took part in after graduating from high school. However, if you began an activity in high school and continued on into college, include it. Also, a particularly relevant or meaningful accomplishment from high school may make the list, but for the most part, focus on your more recent activities. If you have more than 15 activities, select those that are the most closely related to medicine, that demonstrate leadership or other qualities desirable in a future physician, or that you were most deeply involved in. You may also select a couple that represent your personal interests.

You need the following information on hand in order to complete this section:

- ✔ The name of the organization
- ✔ The dates and number of hours you took part in the activity
- ✔ The location
- ✔ The contact information for an individual who can verify that you participated in an activity, received an award, worked at a job, and so on

To decide which entries merit the designation "most meaningful" on the AMCAS application, read through your list of activities and ask yourself the following questions:

- ✔ Did this activity have an impact on my decision to apply for medical school?
- ✔ Did the activity play an important role in my personal development?
- ✔ Is this an event I want to discuss in detail?

Using these questions, narrow down the list to up to three activities you want to designate as most meaningful. *Tip:* If you're having difficulty deciding, focus on choosing three that show different facets of your portfolio, such as one about a clinical experience, another about a research experience, and a third describing a leadership role or outside interest. You can also try drafting essays for the top contenders and then make the decision based on the strength of the ideas you're expressing. It's not just what you did that's important; what you have to say about the experiences is crucial as well.

Writing the descriptions

Some applicants dedicate months to creating the perfect personal statement and then hastily throw together the descriptions of their activities in a matter of days, thinking that this section isn't very important. However, the application is a complete package, meaning that every section is critical. The work and activities entries give you the chance to discuss the many facets of your background that don't fit into the personal statement, including experiences reflecting your professional, academic, and personal development. In the following sections, I guide you through writing both the standard-length and most-meaningful entries and provide examples of each type. (Check out Chapter 12 for details about writing descriptions for DO schools.)

Standard activity entries

For up to 12 of your activities, you have only the 700-character space to explain what you did and why it was important to you. Because the space is so limited, you should prioritize explaining the context of your experience and your duties. For the more relevant and important standard activities, include a sentence or two of reflection even within the 700 character entries. Straightforward entries, such as one for an academic award, may take less than the maximum space.

You don't need to attempt to turn the descriptions into mini-personal statements, nor should they be a list of bullet points as in a resume. Write a single, fluid paragraph and use complete sentences.

Here's an example of a standard entry about emergency department shadowing:

> *Each Saturday, I am immersed in the controlled chaos of the emergency department at an urban county hospital. As a volunteer, I bring blankets and ice chips to patients, direct visitors, and assist the ED staff. Through this work, I have learned about the diversity of patients treated in the ED and the roles of the physician, nurses, and other members of the medical team. During several of my shifts, one of the emergency medicine physicians invited me to observe her work. I witnessed her diagnose fractures, suture a laceration, and assess a patient with symptoms of a stroke. Through my experiences, I discovered that I thrive on the fast pace and high intensity of the ED environment.*

Here's a second example of a standard activity entry describing a swim team assistant coach position:

> *At the age of eight, I took part in my first swim meet. By ten, I was swimming year round, practicing five days a week, and competing at meets on weekends. Swimming was not just a sport; the team became my second family. I have returned to my hometown for the past two summers to work as an assistant coach for a local team. Along with other staff members, I develop practice regimens, lead swimmers in the mastery of skills, and supervise during practices and meets. My coaching philosophy emphasizes teamwork, sportsmanship, and setting personal goals. Through coaching, I have sharpened my communication skills and learned to adapt my teaching style according to the needs of the individual.*

Most meaningful activity entries

For the three most meaningful activities, you can use the entire 700-character space to describe your duties, your accomplishments, or the context of the activity because you have another, separate space in which to reflect on why the activity was meaningful to you. As you prepare to write these expanded descriptions, consider the following: What did you learn or gain from the experience? How did it affect you? What made it memorable or influential? Here's an example:

(standard description)

Rose Avenue Clinic is an outpatient health center providing medical care to low income patients. Initially, I volunteered my time at Rose Avenue, but within a year, I advanced to a paid position as a clinic assistant. I continue to work in this capacity two days each week, taking vital signs, recording patient histories, and performing administrative tasks such as scheduling appointments. Because many of the clinic's patients speak limited English, I am sometimes called upon to act as a Spanish interpreter for the medical staff. I have recently begun assisting in the organization of outreach efforts such as health fairs to increase awareness of the clinic's services.

(expanded description)

I once viewed medicine as a series of straightforward steps: Take a history, diagnose a patient, and prescribe a treatment. As long as I studied hard and applied what I had learned, I could help a patient; it was that simple. Two years ago, when I walked into the Rose Avenue Clinic, my perception changed. Within my first days as a volunteer, I discovered that factors not covered in my biology book or chemistry notes can affect a patient's ability to recover from an illness. No medication would work if the patient didn't understand how to use it or did not have transportation to the pharmacy to buy it. As I watched the clinic physician assess and treat patients, my view of the practice of medicine was revolutionized. Primary care doctors asked about everything from a child's performance in school to how a new mother was adapting after the birth of her child. Even with medically complex cases such as an elderly man with a history of hypertension and heart disease, the broader context of the patient's life was never lost. Working with physicians as they practiced their craft reinforced that dedication, compassion, and perseverance are essential qualities of a doctor.

Entering Course Work and Understanding GPAs

Entering course work sounds like a relatively simple administrative task, but it can be a lot more tedious than you may realize. You have to think back to every college you've attended: community colleges, universities, summer classes, and study abroad. Then add post-baccalaureate or graduate work. You need to list every course you enrolled in at these institutions, as well as credits earned through other sources such as Advanced Placement examinations, in the course work section of the application. I explain how to do so in this section and note how each application service takes your course work and calculates its own GPA for you.

Note: Accuracy is essential on this part of the primary because your entries will be matched against the information on your official transcripts as part of the verification process after you submit the application. The sheer volume of information and attention to detail required make this section another challenging one, although you may find this part of the application a relief from all the writing the personal statement and activities sections demand!

Wading through course work information

Although the format of the course work section differs slightly among the three application services, they all ask for the same essential information: the institution the course was taken at, course number and name, academic year and term, your class status (for example, freshman), credit units/hours, transcript grade, and course classification. On the AMCAS application, the *course classification* section requires you to choose the subject of the course from a list of categories such as chemistry, English, or mathematics. Special designations are available for situations such as Advanced Placement credit, repeated courses, course withdrawals, or course work that's planned or in progress. The other centralized application services require you to classify courses as well, although the details of the systems used by each service differ.

Entering your course work as efficiently and accurately as possible requires gathering the information in advance, understanding the requirements of the section, and allowing yourself enough time to get the job done right. The suggestions in the following list familiarize you with this area of the application and help you complete it as quickly and accurately as possible:

- ✔ **Use an official copy of your transcript to work from as you enter the courses.** Unofficial copies or other lists of course work, such as degree progress reports, can differ from the official transcript. Order transcripts from every college you've attended at least two weeks before you'll need them.

- ✔ **Read the instructions carefully before you begin filling out this section.** Errors or omissions can result in a delay in your application being processed. Though the reviewer may correct minor discrepancies, larger ones can land your application back in your hands for revision.

- ✔ **Allow several hours to enter the courses.** After you've saved the information, return to take a fresh look at it another day in order to proofread what you've entered.

Getting a handle on GPA calculations

Medical schools don't just look at a single GPA; they also consider subsets of your grades, such as your GPA in science or nonscience course work, performance in a given class year, the trend in your performance from year to year, and undergraduate versus graduate grades (if applicable). Therefore, the application services calculate your GPA in different ways. AMCAS generates the following GPAs based on your course work:

✔ Individual GPAs for each year in college (freshman, sophomore, junior, senior)

✔ Post-baccalaureate undergraduate GPA

✔ Cumulative undergraduate GPA

✔ Graduate GPA

The *cumulative undergraduate GPA* includes work done in your freshman through senior years, as well as post-baccalaureate work that is undergraduate level. Withdrawals (Ws) aren't factored into the GPA.

For each category, AMCAS generates a total GPA as well as a *BCPM (biology, chemistry, physics, and math) GPA* and an *AO (all other) GPA* for courses not classified as BCPM. The BCPM is sometimes known as the *science GPA* and the AO as the *nonscience GPA*. Medical schools most heavily consider the overall undergraduate total and BCPM GPAs, although because the GPAs are also broken down by year, the schools can easily spot a trend in the grades. A weak start with an upward trend is viewed more favorably than a decline in GPA over time. AACOMAS also generates multiple GPAs, including science, nonscience, and all-course-work GPAs.

As I mention earlier in this chapter, you must classify your course work on your applications, but the application services may classify them differently when calculating your GPAs. For example, on the AMCAS application, neuroscience falls under biology and a statistics course under mathematics, which may not match up with the department that offered your class. Consult the charts for the services you're using (they're provided as part of the application instructions) to understand which courses will be used to calculate your science GPAs.

One major difference between ACOMAS and AMCAS is that AMCAS counts both grades for a repeated course, whereas AACOMAS only counts the most recent grade for a repeated course. This nuance can make a big difference for an applicant who repeated multiple courses, especially if the initial grades were Ds or Fs.

Like the other two application services, TMDSAS calculates both an overall GPA and separate science and nonscience GPAs. These calculations also include separate sets of GPAs for undergraduate and graduate work.

As an example of the various permutations of GPAs, consider the AMCAS GPAs generated for Kyle for his freshman year of college:

✔ BCPM: 3.43

✔ AO: 3.68

✔ Total: 3.56

Kyle's cumulative freshman GPA as calculated by AMCAS is a 3.56; his GPA for biology, chemistry, math, and physics classes is slightly lower and his GPA for all other courses higher. (That's a common pattern.) If Kyle checks his transcripts, he may notice that the GPA his undergraduate institution calculates is slightly different because many colleges have a grade forgiveness policy for repeated courses or because of other nuances in the way the GPA is calculated.

Chapter 9

Looking at Letters of Recommendation and Secondary Applications

In This Chapter

▶ Comparing types of letters and selecting evaluators

▶ Requesting and submitting letters of recommendation

▶ Preparing secondary applications

*A*fter seeing what the primary application entails (refer to Chapter 8), you may think that med schools couldn't possibly want to know anything more about you. However, for your file to be considered complete, you also need to supply the schools with letters of recommendation and usually a secondary (supplemental) application. Only when a school receives all elements does it consider your file ready for review.

Letters of recommendation are an especially challenging aspect of the application process because they require you to rely on someone else to submit information on your behalf. Meanwhile, the sheer number and variety of secondaries make this step of the application process a pitfall for applicants who aren't vigilant. View letters of recommendation and secondary applications as additional opportunities to show admission committees that you're an excellent candidate for their schools, and you'll be motivated to start on these steps early and to hit them out of the park.

To help you make the most of these aspects of the application, this chapter walks you through each part of obtaining great letters of recommendation, from choosing evaluators to submitting your letters, and covers the information you need to know to about secondaries, including what they contain and when to submit them.

Using a Premedical Committee Letter versus Seeking Individual Letters

You have two options for obtaining letters of recommendation (also known as *letters of evaluation*) — getting a letter from your academic institution's premedical committee or using individual letters:

✔ If your school provides a committee letter, you should take that option; medical schools prefer, and sometimes even require, that you use a committee letter when it's available.

✔ However, if your school doesn't have a premedical committee, don't worry; mine didn't either. Individual letters work very well as long as you follow the requirements medical schools set regarding the number and type of letters to be submitted.

In the following sections, I discuss the differences between committee and individual letters before stepping you through the logistics of obtaining letters later in this chapter.

In a group: Premedical committee letters

Many undergraduate schools have a *premedical advisory committee* or *Health Professions Advisory Committee* (HPAC) typically composed of a school's pre-health advisor and one or more faculty members who oversee the premedical advising process. The school's premed committee usually has an established process in which it evaluates a med school applicant and then produces a letter of evaluation known as a *premedical committee letter* or *HPAC letter*.

Although the details vary by school, a committee letter often contains information about an applicant's academic achievements; clinical, research, leadership, and community service experiences; and other activities. Quotations from letters submitted on the applicant's behalf by professors, physicians, or other evaluators are included in some committee letters, and/or entire letters from individual evaluators are added to the committee letter. In addition, the letter usually provides an overall assessment of the strength of the applicant's candidacy for medical school, and some schools even rank applicants in comparison to each other.

The committee may ask you to submit some or all of the following to help the members prepare the letter:

- A curriculum vitae (cv) or resume
- A draft of your personal statement
- Letters of recommendation from faculty and others who have supervised you in academic, clinical, research, or other professional-type settings
- Responses to a committee-provided questionnaire where you describe your applicant's activities and discuss your reason for pursuing a career in medicine, your strengths and weakness, and other relevant information

After the committee collects and reviews the information, you usually undergo an interview with one or more committee members. The process culminates with the committee writing a letter of evaluation on your behalf and submitting it to application services or medical schools.

Note: At some institutions, the prehealth advising office doesn't provide a true committee letter; however, the advisor may still coordinate individual letters of recommendation. In this case, faculty, physicians, and other evaluators send letters to the premedical advisor, who usually writes a cover letter and sends it plus the individual letters as a single packet to the application service or medical schools. Applicants using this kind of letter packet need to follow the guidelines medial schools set for individual letters when selecting evaluators.

If your college offers a committee letter and you submit individual letters instead, medical schools may request a written explanation about why you haven't submitted a committee letter. Excuses such as missing the deadline for obtaining a letter or believing that individual letter writers can do a better job than your committee aren't valid reasons for circumventing a committee and may hurt your application.

Check with your premedical advisor about the process of obtaining a committee letter at the beginning of the academic year in which you plan to apply. Schools start the committee letter process as early as fall, and you don't want to be stuck scrambling at the last minute to obtain needed documents or worse, to lose out on the opportunity to obtain a letter at all. (Check out Chapter 5 for an introduction to getting help from a premedical advisor.)

Conscientiously follow whatever procedures the premedical committee sets for obtaining a letter because committee letters sometimes mention when a student has demonstrated poor planning or an unprofessional attitude during the committee letter process.

Singled out: Individual letters

I attended a college that didn't offer committee letters and have advised many applicants in the same situation. Applicants who attend schools that don't offer a committee letter are sometimes concerned that they're at a disadvantage in the application process. Good news: Not having a committee letter is a potential problem only if your school offers a letter and you don't obtain one. If the option for a committee letter isn't open to you, using individual letters doesn't reflect negatively on your application.

The major issue to be aware of with individual letters is that you must check with each school you plan to apply to about its letter requirements. Schools may have requirements regarding both the number and type of letters.

Med schools usually require a minimum of two to four letters and may or may not have a maximum. Some schools require that one or two of the letters be from science faculty but don't put any restrictions on letters beyond that. Others are more stringent; they may stipulate that one or more evaluators must be individuals with whom you've taken a class (versus faculty with whom you've only done research) or that at least one letter be from a faculty member from the same department as your major. A small number of schools ask for a nonscience faculty letter, which can be a challenge to obtain for science majors who have taken very few nonscience courses. (See the later section "The key to great letters: Getting to know your potential evaluators" for tips about developing relationships with referees to ensure that you have plenty of options when you're ready to ask for letters.)

In addition to the required letters, you can choose to send extra letters to the schools as long as you don't go above any maximum number allowed. Even if a school doesn't have a max guideline, consider limiting the number you send to no more than five or six. Inundating admissions committees with a large number of letters may make it harder for the most substantive letters to stand out or may even be viewed as excessive. Extra letters may come from the following sources:

- ✔ Additional science or nonscience faculty
- ✔ Researchers who have supervised your work in basic or clinical research (Chapter 4 has details on types of research experience)
- ✔ Physicians with whom you've shadowed or volunteered
- ✔ Supervisors from paid employment or volunteer positions
- ✔ Advisors for clubs or other organizations with which you're involved

Not all letter sources are created equal. Don't obtain letters from family members or friends; your letters should be from individuals who know you in a professional capacity. Also, don't get letters from teaching assistants; academic letters should be written by faculty. If the TA for the course knows you well, he or she can provide input for the professor to include in the letter, but the evaluator must be a faculty member, not a graduate student or even a post-doctoral fellow, for the letter to hold weight.

If you won't have your list of medical schools finalized until late spring or summer of the year you plan to apply because your MCAT scores won't be available until then, obtain a range of letters to cover almost any combination a school may require. Letting a particular letter go unused is much better than searching frantically for someone to write a letter at the last minute after discovering that a school you're a great fit for needs a type of letter you're lacking.

Choosing Evaluators and Requesting Letters

Whichever type of recommendations you're submitting to medical schools (see the earlier section "Using a Premedical Committee Letter versus Seeking Individual Letters"), the letters you solicit from professors, physicians, and so on need to show that these folks have a strong grasp on you and your strengths. Translation: Your recommenders need to be people you've cultivated a strong relationship with over time. By the time you actually need the letters, it's far too late to develop a strong relationship with your endorser. A letter from a professor who barely remembers you or didn't know you well in the first place is going to be a mediocre one at best.

To obtain strong letters, get to know your professors, physicians you shadow, and other potential evaluators as you make your way through your classes and outside activities instead of, say, rushing to visit office hours for the first time a couple of weeks before hitting up your professor for a letter. With a diverse group of recommenders to select from, you can choose those who fulfill the requirements for the schools on your list. After you choose whom to ask, you need to approach your potential evaluators in a way (and on a timeline) that's most likely to yield you a strong letter, providing the writer with the materials she needs to do the job well. You also need to be prepared to take action if a potential evaluator isn't enthusiastic about writing a letter.

The key to great letters: Getting to know your potential evaluators

A superb letter can only be written by someone who knows you well and can provide specific details and examples about your achievements, performance, and personal qualities. (Find more about what makes a great letter in the section "Discovering the Characteristics of Strong Letters of Recommendation" later in this chapter.) Here's a sample recommendation; judge how well it meets the criteria:

> *Erica received an A in the physiology class I teach. This course is very rigorous, and this grade is evidence that she has the intellect needed to succeed in medical school. She also attended office hours on two occasions. Based on these interactions with her and on her performance as a student in my course, I believe she will make a good medical student.*

Unconvincing? Weak? Ineffective? This letter is all these things and more. Even with an added paragraph introducing Erica and incorporating some tidbits from her resume and a conclusion saying a few more nice things about her, this letter seems to be from someone who barely knows her. The reader is left questioning Erica's judgment in selecting evaluators; is this really the best she could do? If so, the committee has reason to be concerned.

To avoid this situation, make an active effort from the start of your premedical years to build relationships with the professors teaching your courses, physicians you shadow, and others who supervise you in some capacity. The best way for this camaraderie to happen is organically; the more active you are in class participation, volunteering, shadowing, and research, the greater the opportunities for potential evaluators to see your work directly and learn about your motivation, skills, and personal qualities.

Getting to know professors

If you attend a university that relies mostly on large lecture classes, getting to know your professors can be extremely challenging. As a graduate of a large public university, I understand that you have to do more than just succeed in a course to distinguish yourself in a class of hundreds of students. Here are some strategies for forging a relationship with faculty:

- ✓ **Participate in class discussions.** If sitting in the back of the class and passively listening is your style, you may have a hard time making yourself known to the professor. You don't need to transform yourself into the type that sits in the front row and chimes in every few minutes with a question or comment, but offering to answer a question, participating in discussion sections, and generally taking an active part in the class is the first step in getting to know your instructor.

✔ **Attend office hours.** Office hours provide an opportunity to meet with the professor one-on-one or as part of a small group. Use this time to ask questions or discuss material in greater depth with the course instructor.

✔ **Do research with a professor at your school.** I don't advocate doing research for the sole purpose of obtaining a letter, but if you have an interest in research, working in a lab or doing clinical research on campus allows for much greater interaction with faculty than a classroom setting does. (Chapter 4 has more information on doing research.)

✔ **Become a teaching assistant.** Some colleges utilize undergraduate teaching assistants who work closely with the course instructor to perform tasks such as running discussion, review, or laboratory sections; proctoring exams; and grading tests and assignments.

✔ **Enroll in a subsequent course taught by the same professor.** If you enjoyed a course taught by a particular professor, consider signing up for a second class with that same instructor. A professor who has interacted with you over a longer period of time will have a better chance to know you and can more effectively reflect on your development.

✔ **Select smaller, discussion-based courses if you can.** Upper-level, more specialized courses in particular may offer the opportunity for you to be part of a smaller class.

Making a good impression on other potential evaluators

In addition to faculty letters, letters from physicians with whom you've shadowed, from advisors of clubs or other organizations you're active in, or from supervisors at a your place of employment are also valuable. By picking a few long-term activities to focus on, you really get to know the individuals you work with, and (even more importantly) they get to know you. When shadowing a physician, for example, don't just passively observe; ask questions between patients and offer to assist in any way possible. Even someone who participates in an activity for years won't get a great letter of recommendation if she appears bored, lacks initiative, or is clearly just putting in her time so that she can list an experience on her application. Head to Chapter 4 for details on finding appropriate extracurriculars, including shadowing and club opportunities.

It's time: Deciding when to ask for letters

If you're obtaining a premedical committee letter, follow the guidelines and timetable set by your school's committee. As I note in the earlier section "In a group: Premedical committee letters," the applicant evaluation process begins early in the academic year at some schools, so check with your advisor about your institution's schedule and stick to it precisely.

For individual letters, I can't emphasize enough how important asking early is. I have counseled many applicants through crises resulting from promised letters that arrived late or never arrived, thus preventing the applicant's file from being reviewed by the med school until later in the cycle than was ideal. With *rolling admissions* (where a school begins reviewing applications before the deadline), every week's delay while you await the arrival of your letters may mean interview slots are being filled. (Read more on rolling admissions in Chapter 5.)

Asking for letters by early spring gives your evaluators plenty of time to write and submit them so that they're available for the secondary stage of the application process. (If you submit your primary applications early in the cycle, you'll start getting secondaries by mid-summer as described in the timeline in Chapter 5.) Having faculty letters safely in hand early is especially important because instructors may not be on campus in the summer, making them much more difficult to track down. If you ask early and someone doesn't come through, you still have time to seek a backup. ("Submitting Your Letters of Recommendation" later in this chapter provides options for banking your letters if you obtain them prior the opening of the application cycle.)

Step by step: Approaching a potential evaluator

Students are sometimes unsure of how to approach an evaluator and of exactly what to say when requesting a letter. How you ask is important; by approaching a letter writer in a professional manner and providing her with the information she needs to write a great letter, you give yourself the best chance of having a strong letter submitted correctly and on time. To obtain your letters, take the following steps:

1. **Arrange to meet in person with the individual from whom you're requesting a letter.**

   If you've already graduated and no longer live near your alma mater or for some other reason are located at a distance from your letter writer, contact the person to set up a time to speak with her by phone.

2. **Bring to the meeting a copy of your resume or cv and your personal statement as well as information about when and where to submit the letter.**

If you don't have at least a good draft of your personal statement at the time you ask for the letter, offer to send it later.

3. **During the meeting, explain that you're applying to medical school and want to know whether the person can write you a strong letter of recommendation.**

   The key word here is *strong*. Don't simply say "Would you be willing to write me a letter of recommendation?" By specifying that you're looking for a strong letter, you provide an easy opening for the evaluator to decline if she doesn't feel she can write an effective letter for you.

   When you meet with your evaluator, explain to her why you decided to ask her for a letter of recommendation. For example, if you had interesting and enjoyable discussions with a professor about a certain topic or did a project or paper that you found particularly meaningful (and for which you received a high grade), mention these reasons to provide a context for your request for a letter and jog her memory about possible topics for discussion.

4. **If the writer agrees to write you a strong letter, give her the items in Step 2 and ask whether she also wants you to e-mail her the information.**

5. **Give the writer a specific date by which you want the letter to be submitted.**

   The date should be between four and six weeks from when you ask for the letter. Given too little time, a busy professor or physician may not have an opportunity to write an optimal letter; with too much time, she may put off the task until she forgets about it.

6. **Before concluding the meeting, offer to provide any additional information that the evaluator wants and to meet with her again to discuss your candidacy for medical school.**

   For example, an evaluator who is outside of academia, such as a community physician you've shadowed, may need guidelines about what medical schools are looking for in a letter and perhaps an outline of topics to cover. (You can find this information in "Discovering the Characteristics of Strong Letters of Recommendation" later in the chapter.)

7. **After the meeting, follow up with an e-mail thanking the writer for agreeing to write you a letter and providing her with any additional materials she may need to submit your letter.**

   Specific materials vary depending on the submission method you use; they may include matching forms, links to instructions for uploading or mailing letters, or ID numbers. See the later section "Submitting Your Letters of Recommendation" for information on the logistics of sending letters.

   In addition, make sure you advise your recommender that the letter must be written on official letterhead and signed, as required by many medical schools.

The details of these steps vary depending on how well you know the letter writer and the direction the conversation takes, but by following this overall framework, you have a strategy to work from and adapt as needed.

Send your evaluator a thank-you note after she's submitted your letter. Professors, physicians, and other evaluators are taking time out of their schedules to write a letter on your behalf, so acknowledging their efforts is important.

In all honesty: Handling a less-than-enthusiastic response

Hopefully, all your potential evaluators meet your recommendation request with an enthusiastic "I'd be happy to write you an outstanding letter of recommendation!" However, be prepared to deal with a response that indicates the letter writer isn't sure she can write you a great letter. Although rejection in any form is disappointing, it's better to know up front that a letter you get from this person may be weak. Anyone who is direct about not being able to write you a great letter has done you a favor: By being honest, she's allowed you to avoid having a lackluster letter in your file.

Let me repeat this point one more time: If a potential letter writer shows any hesitation or you doubt her ability or willingness to write a great letter, don't get a letter from that person. Tell the evaluator that you appreciate her honesty, that you want your candidacy for medical school to be as strong as possible, and that you understand that she can't provide you with the type of letter you're seeking. This situation is unlikely to occur with letter writers you're well acquainted with, but if you're in the position of having to ask for a letter from someone you don't know extremely well, you're more likely to find that the person can't give you what you need. Some professors are more accommodating than others, so keep trying until you find someone who understands the dilemma students face when trying to find enough letters and who will go out of her way to write a good letter.

Discovering the Characteristics of Strong Letters of Recommendation

The goal of all the planning, preparing, and strategizing I describe earlier in this chapter is to ensure that you obtain letters that aren't just okay but rather are able to help convince the committee members that you'd be a valuable addition to their school and that you possess the qualities needed to succeed in medicine. But what differentiates an average letter from a stellar one? What specifically do medical schools look for as they evaluate letters? Knowing the answers to these questions is important, especially if any of your recommenders hasn't written many letters of recommendation for med school applicants previously; those folks may ask you for guidelines for writing the letter. Some letter writers even request that the applicant write a draft of the letter so they have a foundation to work from. By becoming knowledgeable about what constitutes a great letter, you're in a position to make sure your letters are an asset to your application package.

Effective letters don't simply tell the reader about an applicant; they show what the applicant is like by providing specific supporting examples. (This "show, don't tell" advice also comes up in Chapter 8, where I discuss how to write a compelling personal statement.) A great letter of recommendation tells medical schools that you're someone the evaluator knows well and describes both your personal qualities and your performance in your interaction with her. In summary, the best letters of recommendation do the following:

- ✔ Clearly state the capacity in which the recommenders know you (for example, the instructor for a class you took or the principle investigator of a lab in which you performed research)

- ✔ Discuss your academic potential, interpersonal skills, leadership qualities, personal traits, and character as demonstrated in the context of your interaction with the evaluators

- ✔ Use examples, anecdotes, and details to illustrate your characteristics and accomplishments

- ✔ Provide information comparing you to your peers, such as "Emma's superb problem-solving skills, professionalism, integrity, and strong work ethic place her among the top 10 percent of undergraduate researchers I have mentored over the past 15 years."

- ✔ Conclude forcefully with an unreserved recommendation of you as a candidate for medical school

Note that a particular letter may focus only on certain items listed in the second point. For example, a letter from your biochemistry professor may emphasize academic accomplishments and leadership traits, while one from a supervisor at a hospital you volunteered at may focus on the communication skills and personal qualities you demonstrated through interactions with patients and members of the medical team. Taken as a whole, though, the letters should give a well-rounded and thorough picture of what you offer. The best way to understand what a great letter of recommendation looks like it to read one, so check out Figure 9-1 for a sample letter of recommendation.

TOP STATE
UNIVERSITY

May 12, 2014

Dear Admissions Committee:

I am extremely pleased to recommend Amy Applicant as a candidate for your medical school. I have known Amy for more than two years, first as a student in my introductory genetics course and later as a teaching assistant for general biology. In the 20 years I have been a faculty member at this institution, Amy is one of the most talented and motivated students I have encountered.

As a sophomore enrolled in Introductory Genetics, Amy immediately distinguished herself not only through her academic performance but also through her enthusiasm and contributions to the class. Amy's overall grade was the second highest of the 60 students in the course and was a reflection of her genuine interest in the material. Amy was especially eager to learn about the application of genetics to medicine and visited my office hours frequently to discuss this topic, demonstrating an impressive understanding of molecular medicine. She was a valuable contributor to class discussions, offering her insights and asking pertinent questions while also being respectful and encouraging to her peers. Recognizing that Amy possessed the mastery of the subject and interpersonal skills necessary to guide other students through the course, I offered her a position as a teaching assistant for my general biology course the following semester.

During her three-semester tenure as a teaching assistant, Amy has demonstrated her outstanding communication skills, her dedication to helping others, and a sense of initiative. While helping to lead laboratory and review sections, Amy was apt at recognizing which students needed help and using a clear, accessible approach when explaining the material. Although TAs are required to offer only one review session prior to each exam, Amy developed a second session based on her knowledge of areas that she noticed students found particularly challenging. Amy also made herself available to students outside of class, even tutoring several students regularly on a volunteer basis. She did not seek recognition for her extra efforts; I was made aware of them only when two students told me at the end of the course that Amy's help had been significant to their success in the class. The desire to help others evident through Amy's actions is in keeping with her history of volunteerism, which includes three years of work at a local women's shelter and two years of service in the post-anesthesia care unit (PACU) of University Hospital.

Through observing Amy in her role as lead TA this semester, I have witnessed that she is a natural leader. Providing leadership among one's peers is challenging for most students; however, when training other TAs, answering questions, or resolving conflicts, Amy's friendly but direct approach meets with success. Although her engaging personality makes her well-suited for positions of leadership, she is equally comfortable taking direction from others who are more experienced or knowledgeable than she. Amy possesses a rare combination of confidence and humility that will be valuable as she undertakes medical school.

Amy's achievements are especially impressive in light of her heavy schedule. Neuroscience, her chosen major, is one of the most challenging areas of study offered by the university. However, Amy has maintained a GPA of 3.7 while also working toward an English minor. Along with a full academic schedule and volunteer commitments, Amy works part time in the campus career center. Her ability to manage these commitments is attributable to her strong organizational skills, high level of energy, and upbeat attitude.

Amy is a bright, dedicated, and curious student as well as a mature and compassionate individual with a strong sense of integrity. She is also deeply dedicated to pursuing a career in medicine, and I believe that she will be an asset to any program she enters. It is without reservation that I give my highest recommendation to Amy for consideration for a place in your medical school.

Figure 9-1:
An example
of a strong
letter of
recommen-
dation.

Sincerely,

Benjamin Brilliant

Benjamin Brilliant, PhD
Professor, Department of Biology

Research Hall • College City, NJ 57875 • 222-333-4444 • www.topstateuni.edu

Illustration by Wiley, Composition Services Graphics

Submitting Your Letters of Recommendation

As I explain in the earlier section "Step by step: Approaching a potential evaluator," you must provide your letter writers with information about when, where, and how to submit the letters. Several options may be available to you for submitting letters depending on the institution you attend and the schools to which you're applying. Your choices include

- Having letter writers submit the letters directly to the primary application service

- Using your undergraduate institution's premedical advising office or career center to coordinate the letters

- Using a *commercial letter service* (which accepts and transmits letters to designated application services or schools)

In the following sections, I describe each of the preceding options and provide tips to help you decide which to select. I also discuss the decision to waive your right to have access to your letters.

Sending letters to application services

The two primary application services for MD schools — the American Medical College Application Service (AMCAS) and the Texas Medical and Dental School Application Service (TMDSAS) — accept letters of recommendation and transmit them to medical schools, thus saving premedical committees and individual letter writers from having to send letters to each individual school.

- For AMCAS, committee and individual letters can be uploaded directly by advisors or letter writers, be mailed in, or be sent to AMCAS through a letter service. (See the next section to find out about letter services.) AMCAS accepts up to ten letters and allows applicants to designate which school(s) receive(s) a particular letter.

  Note: As of the 2012–2013 application cycle, Duke University School of Medicine and Louisiana State University Health Sciences Center School of Medicine in Shreveport are the only two U.S. schools that use AMCAS for the primary application but don't accept letters of recommendation sent through AMCAS. Check with these schools individually for instructions regarding submission of letters.

✔ For TMDSAS schools, either a committee packet or two individual letters are required, although TMDSAS accepts a third, optional letter as well. Advisors can upload a committee packet to TMDSAS or send it by mail or through a letter service. Letters from individual letter writers are accepted by TMDSAS through either mail or Interfolio (a commercial letter service).

If you're obtaining individual letters, carefully read all instructions provided by the application services so that you can give your letter writers any necessary matching forms, evaluation forms, or ID numbers per the service's specifications. Doing so ensures that the letters received are matched to your application file and that the schools receive all necessary information.

Both AMCAS and TMDSAS begin accepting letters in May. This means that any letter writers sending the letters directly to either of these application services have to wait until May to do so. If you're really on the ball and have your letters before then, you can have your premedical advisor or career center coordinate the letters or use a commercial letter service to safely store your letters (and give you peace of mind) and then have the letters sent to AMCAS and/or TMDSAS when the application cycles open. Check with your school about the available options.

Unlike AMCAS and TMDSAS, the American Association of Colleges of Osteopathic Medicine Application Service (AACOMAS) doesn't handle letters of evaluation. Therefore, for AACOMAS schools (DO schools), letters must be submitted directly to the schools by your advisor, by a letter service, or by the letter writers as part of the secondary application process. You can read about all three application services in Chapter 8.

Coordinating your letters through your premedical advisor or a letter service

Using either your premedical advisor or a commercial letter service as a means of coordinating your letters of recommendation offers several advantages:

✔ **Corralling letters received early:** These options allow you to ask for recommendations before AMCAS and TMDSAS cycles open without worrying about completed letters getting lost in the shuffle.

✔ **Making life easier for letter writers:** If you're applying to DO schools (see Chapter 12), using your premedical advising office, career center, or a commercial letter service saves your letter writers the huge hassle of sending letters to many schools individually. Therefore, I strongly recommend one of these approaches for applicants to osteopathic schools in particular.

> ✔ **Keeping old letters on hand for reapplication:** In the event you need to reapply to medical school (see Chapter 16), you'll have to submit letters again. If you decide you want to use one or more of the letters from your previous application, you can request to send them again through a letter service or your advisor.

Check with your premedical advisor about the services she offers regarding letters of recommendation. Even if your school's advising office doesn't provide applicants with a committee letter, your advisor may coordinate letters written by individual evaluators. If your school doesn't have a premedical advisor or letter services aren't offered by the advising office, find out whether your institution's career center handles letters of recommendation. If your school doesn't offer any such services, you can use a commercial letter service.

Interfolio is a commercial letter service that accepts letters of recommendation, stores them, and transmits them to application services and/or individual medical schools. AMCAS and TMDSAS accept letters from Interfolio, as do most (if not all) osteopathic schools. Therefore, you can establish an account with Interfolio and then instruct your letter writers to upload or mail your letters to your account. When the application cycle opens, you can have the letters transmitted to application services or schools that you select. Details about fees and signing up for Interfolio are available at www.interfolio.com.

Waiving your right to see your letters

Depending on the method you use to submit your letter, you may be asked whether you want to waive your right to have access to your file. Schools generally prefer that you don't have access to your letters so that evaluators feel comfortable giving an honest evaluation of you without concern that you may see the letter. I recommend waiving your right to see your letters so that the med schools are confident the integrity of the letters hasn't been undermined. If you're so worried that someone may write a negative letter about you that you hesitate to waive your right to see your letters, that's a good sign that you shouldn't ask the evaluator(s) in question for a letter.

Some letter writers send applicants a copy of their letters or even ask an applicant for her input for the letter as it's being drafted. Therefore, waiving your right to see a letter doesn't necessarily mean you never get to see all the great things your evaluators wrote about you. It just means that you've waived your legal right to see the letter, so you can't legally demand to see it. In this scenario, letter writers retain the right to voluntarily show you the letter; however, as a point of professional etiquette, never ask a letter writer to see the letter if you have waived your right.

Grasping the Basics of Secondary Applications

Although you may be ready to celebrate when your primary application is submitted, you're not quite done filling out forms and writing compelling essays. In addition to requiring a primary application through AMCAS, TMDSAS, or AACOMAS, most medical schools have a school-specific *secondary* (supplemental) application as well. The secondary application constitutes the second of the three major steps of the admissions process described in Chapter 5. Secondary applications range from very brief, requiring only that you pay a fee and submit your letters of recommendation, to extremely long, including multiple essay questions.

Handling secondaries is very much about time management, especially for applicants who apply to a large number of schools. This step of the process is where you can either retain your early application advantage or lose it. As you get ready to tackle secondaries, focus on both writing great responses and strategizing so that you can submit effective, well-written secondaries as early as possible. In the following sections, I cover both the essentials for completing secondaries and tips for prioritizing and organizing your time during this important phase of the admissions cycle.

Even though filling out secondaries can seem like an overwhelming task, you have the comfort of knowing that the end is in sight. After all the forms, essays, and letters are in, you're in the running for an interview offer and, after that, a possible acceptance.

Knowing what to expect from secondaries

At a minimum, during the secondary phase you need to submit a fee (paid directly to the school, not to the application service) and your letters of recommendation. If the schools you're applying to accept letters through TMDSAS, your letters are transmitted electronically. For AMCAS schools, you should follow each school's instructions on submitting recommendations. For AACOMAS schools, you need to send your letters of recommendation directly to the schools during the secondary application phase using one of the methods I describe in the earlier section "Coordinating your letters through your premedical advisor or a letter service."

Schools use secondaries as a means to gather information that isn't included on the primary application or to request some of the same information organized into a different format. Therefore, in addition to a requiring a fee and letters of recommendation, secondaries may ask you to provide the following:

✔ A list of the courses that you've taken or plan to take that fulfill the pre-requisites for the school (versus the comprehensive list of courses you entered on the primary).

✔ Responses to prompts about your interest in medicine, the school, or about your background. Examples include "Why have you chosen to apply to this school?" and "Describe a challenge you've faced and how you overcame it." See the later section "Perusing common secondary prompts" for more examples.

✔ An opportunity to explain weaknesses in your record such as a low GPA or multiple withdrawals from courses

✔ A section to discuss how you're spending your time if you have one or more *gap years* between college and medical school. (Flip to Chapter 5 for more on the gap year concept.)

Surveying the screening process

Although most programs send secondaries to all applicants who have sub-mitted a primary to their schools, some schools only send secondary appli-cations to applicants who have passed through a screening process. How rigorous a school's screening is varies; some schools send secondaries to more than half of the applicant pool, while a few only send secondaries to applicants they've selected for an interview. The screening may be based solely on GPA and MCAT scores or may involve a more overarching review of the applicant's credentials.

When you receive a secondary quickly after verification of your primary, it's very likely from a school that sends supplemental applications to all appli-cants rather than only to screened applicants.

Check school websites, the Medical School Admission Requirements (MSAR) online database (available for subscription at `services.aamc.org/30/ msar/home`), and/or the *Osteopathic Medical College Information Book* (down-loadable for free or available for purchase as a printed copy at `www.aacom.org`) to see which schools screen before sending secondaries and which don't. That way, when you receive an application from a school that screens, you have the satisfaction of knowing you've made it through the first cut.

Perusing common secondary prompts

Some schools get creative with the questions they ask on secondaries, but many stick with versions of tried-and-true topics. Examples of questions and prompts similar to those commonly found on secondaries are

✔ What are your career goals in medicine?

✔ How will you contribute to the medical school community?

- ✔ What has been your greatest achievement?

- ✔ What experiences in a clinical environment have been most important to you?

- ✔ What do you want the admissions committee to know that isn't stated elsewhere on your application?

- ✔ Provide a brief autobiographical statement.

- ✔ How will you contribute to the diversity of the student body and of the medical profession?

- ✔ Describe your hobbies and interests.

- ✔ Discuss a scholarly activity or research project in which you've participated.

- ✔ What do you believe makes you a good fit for this school?

- ✔ How do you envision your life 15 years from now?

- ✔ Describe your activities during any periods following high school during which you weren't attending school full time (excluding summer and other regular breaks from school).

- ✔ Describe experiences during which you've demonstrated leadership.

- ✔ What type of practice setting do you imagine working in?

- ✔ What extracurricular activity has been most rewarding to you?

- ✔ How have you contributed to your community?

- ✔ Describe a time when you failed at something.

- ✔ How do you resolve conflicts?

- ✔ What are some of the challenges facing physicians in the United States?

The length limit you have for a particular secondary largely dictates how you approach writing your responses. Some secondaries allow only a few lines for a response; others give you a page or more. For the longer answers, you have room to incorporate plenty of details and examples as described in the discussion about writing the personal statement in Chapter 8. However, even for shorter responses, make sure that you don't fall into resume mode and just list your experiences (unless a list of experiences is specifically what the prompt asks for). If the question asks you to discuss an activity or give an example of a certain type of experience, such as your greatest achievement or biggest failure, include some reflection to give the response depth instead of just describing the experience.

Because the primary application is so thorough, you'll find that on secondaries you end up discussing some of the same topics and experiences as you did in the primary application. You can differentiate your responses on your secondaries from the material on your primary application by going into greater depth about a particular aspect of an experience or by using new examples to support your discussion. If you've undertaken new activities since submitting the primary application, you may be able to use these as the basis of your responses for some secondary application questions, which will give you a chance to let the school know about your latest endeavors as well as provide fresh material to write about.

Knowing that timing is everything

After you submit your primary application, you have a break anywhere from a few days to more than six weeks as you await verification of your application. After your verified application is received by the schools, expect a wave of secondaries (because very few schools send secondaries to applicants prior to verification).

Expect to receive a steady stream of secondaries over the next few weeks before the pace slows. After that, you may not receive the last few secondaries until weeks or months later, when the schools that screen prior to sending a supplemental application have completed their reviews of your file.

Note: For schools using TMDSAS, the system and timing of secondaries is different. You should submit your secondaries to the schools immediately after you submit the TMDSAS application (although not all TMDSAS schools have secondaries). For details see the TMDSAS site (`www.utsystem.edu/tmdsas/`) and specific school websites.

Every step of the application process, including secondaries, should be completed as early as possible. Deadlines for secondary applications vary, and can be as soon as two weeks from the date of receipt to as long as several months later. You may hear different recommendations regarding the target time to submit secondaries: Some advisors recommend a 48-hour turnaround time, while others say within two weeks is fine. I recommend aiming to submit each secondary within one week of receipt unless you're so inundated with applications that such a fast turnaround would mean compromising the quality of your applications.

Overall, the sooner you submit the better, but the earlier in the cycle it is, the more flexibility you have. An applicant who receives a secondary on July 10 and takes two weeks to submit is in a much better position than an applicant who receives a secondary from that same school on September 20 and submits it two days later. Keep in mind that with rolling admissions, an early application equals early review and potentially an early interview and admission.

Some schools use secondaries as a way to narrow down their applicant pools to only those students who are most seriously interested in enrolling. Applicants who are less serious about a school may decide to skip a long secondary or do a cursory job with the answers. Being one of the applicants who spends time answering even the most tedious essay questions carefully can pay off.

Managing secondaries

You come home from a day in the lab you're interning at for the summer, sit down at your laptop, and open your e-mail. Waiting for you in your inbox are eight secondaries. This morning, you had none.

This scene isn't an unrealistic one; after the primary application is verified, you may be hit with a slew of secondaries. When that happens, you need to be ready with a plan to manage your applications, especially if you've applied to a lot of schools. The following are some tips to help you keep on top of your applications as the secondaries roll in:

- ✔ **Use a spreadsheet or other record to track your applications.** Include the name of each school you've applied to, whether you've received a secondary from that school, the date you received the secondary, the date the secondary is due, your target submission date, the date you submit the secondary, and whether the school has notified you that your file is complete and ready for review. This way, you can easily keep track of looming deadlines or be aware if you still haven't heard from a school.

- ✔ **Knock out the easy secondaries first.** Send out secondaries that have few or no questions immediately. If all a secondary requires is that you send in an application fee and fill out a short form (or no form at all), you can quickly finish it and check that school off your to-do list. Confronting the more difficult secondaries is easier knowing that you've got at least a couple of applications finished.

- ✔ **Prioritize the remaining secondaries according to deadline and your level of interest in the school.** Complete secondaries for the schools that you're highly interested in first. Those are the schools that you want to have the greatest advantage at in terms of admissions, so submit secondaries for those programs early to get the review of your application underway as quickly as possible. At the same time, be aware of deadlines for all the schools because some may be soon after receipt. If a lower-priority school has a deadline coming up quickly, you may need to complete the application for that program before those for top-choice schools with later deadlines. Note that some schools have deadlines for secondaries that may be months away, so you often need to set closer deadlines for yourself rather than relying on knowing that an application is due soon to get you motivated.

- ✔ **Modify responses that you wrote for one application to use for another if the prompts for the two are similar.** Different schools often ask similar questions, so you don't need to start fresh with the writing for each supplemental. *Warning:* If you use this strategy, don't take shortcuts and try to use an old response wholesale for a prompt it doesn't quite fit. It's obvious when an answer doesn't match the question asked. An answer that isn't tailored to a question is a sign that the applicant either didn't read the prompt carefully or isn't interested enough in the school to write a response to the question and instead recycled a response to use.

A good strategy to ease the time crunch created by secondaries is to begin working on responses to essay and short answer questions even before you receive secondaries. Frequently, schools use the same or very similar questions for their secondaries year after year. Your premedical advising office may have copies of secondaries from previous years on file, or you can check with friends who have applied to medical school in the past couple of years for copies of the questions. Focus on schools that don't screen prior to sending secondaries so that you don't waste your time writing answers to a secondary you may never receive. If you use this approach, check each secondary you receive very carefully when it arrives in case it's different from the version you used to formulate your responses.

Chapter 10

Acing the Medical School Interview

. . . .

In This Chapter

▶ Considering the importance of the interview in admissions

▶ Surveying interview formats

▶ Preparing effective responses to interview questions

▶ Planning your trip and picking your interview attire

▶ Interviewing and following up

. . . .

*A*fter months of filling out forms, writing application essays, and endur-
ing uncertainty as you wait to hear something from medical schools,
you receive your first interview offer. Your hard work has finally paid off:
Only the most serious contenders are offered the opportunity to interview,
so this invitation represents a significant step toward your ultimate goal of
becoming a physician.

The interview stage is also exciting because it's when the medical school
application process finally starts to feel real for many applicants. Walking
through the halls of a medical school, meeting faculty, and chatting with
medical students are aspects of interview day that give you a glimpse of the
place you may be studying at for the next four years.

However, after the initial thrill of having been offered an interview subsides,
applicants sometimes find themselves full of questions (and even anxiety)
about the interview process and unsure of what to expect or how to prepare.
Yet a strong performance on interview day is essential because even an applicant who is great on paper will likely be denied entry to medical school if he
fails to present himself in person as someone with the makings of a future
physician. Therefore, to help you turn your one-day visit to a school into an
invitation to attend, this chapter covers every aspect of the interview from
what a typical interview day is like to interview formats used and typical
questions asked.

Assessing the chances of acceptance at the interview stage

Landing an interview isn't an easy feat, but after you have an invitation in hand, you've cleared a major hurdle on the road to an acceptance. Of the hundreds or even thousands of applicants vying for a spot at a medical school, only a small proportion are offered an interview. At most schools, only between 10 and 20 percent of those who apply are invited to interview. The odds are much better for in-state applicants to public schools that receive fewer than 1,000 applications from in-state residents; for a few schools, around 90 percent of in-state applicants are interviewed (although these odds are definitely the exception).

Most medical schools accept less than ten percent of the applicants to their programs. However, schools typically accept 20 to 60 percent of applicants whom they interview. Depending on the school and the strength of your application, your chances at an individual school may be significantly higher or lower than that number, but one thing is for sure: After you get an interview, you're much closer to making it into a med school.

Looking at the Interview's Role in the Admissions Process

Your application package was strong enough to pique a medical school's interest, and now the committee members want you to visit in person so they can meet the human being behind the test scores, grades, and letters of recommendation. After all, medicine isn't a job performed in isolation; as a physician, you interact with people from all walks of life during some of the most difficult times in their lives. You also make potentially life-saving decisions and work under what are sometimes high-pressure and stressful conditions. Therefore, your communication skills, personality, and motivation for pursuing such a challenging field are all important factors in the decision of whether to admit you.

Although some information about your personal characteristics and communication skills can be gleaned from other areas of your application, the interview provides a school with a more direct means of assessing who you are as a person, whether you've got what it takes to be a successful medical student, and whether you're a good fit for the program. In addition, interviewers may try to gauge your level of interest in the school and the likelihood that you'll accept an offer of admission to the program. The amount of weight each school places on an interview varies, but regardless of how little or how much emphasis the interview is given, a stellar performance can be an asset to your application and a poor one detrimental.

The interview is usually only one of many factors that determine whether an applicant is ultimately offered admission, not the sole deciding factor after an applicant reaches the interview stage. In other words, not all applicants are on equal footing when they walk into an interview. Applicants with less-competitive overall application packages sometimes hope that when they've made it to the interview stage, their GPA, Medical College Admission Test (MCAT) score, or other elements of the application won't matter anymore; after all, they think, why would a school bother to interview them if they didn't think they were qualified to attend?

Although it's true that schools don't want to waste their interviewers' time with applicants who don't have a good chance at admission, that doesn't mean that everyone who interviews is considered equally competitive and that whoever does the best on the interview will be offered a spot. Instead, the decision-making process often follows this outline:

1. An applicant's file is reviewed and a decision is made to offer an interview, place the file on hold for potential review again later in the cycle, or to decline the applicant for admission.

2. The interview takes place, and the applicant is evaluated by the interviewer(s).

3. The admissions committee considers the applicant's entire file, including the results of the interview.

4. A decision is made about whether to admit, reject, or waitlist the applicant.

Schools vary in the specific details about how they handle the application process, but the important point is that doing well during the interview doesn't guarantee acceptance. Still, that doesn't mean that the interview isn't important. If the school has offered you an interview, it wants to find out more about you, and a great interview can push a marginal applicant into the "accept" group. Similarly, an applicant with sterling credentials who comes across as arrogant, bored, or immature may be declined admission. Therefore, always approach the interview as though it will make the difference in whether you're in or out, because it very well may.

Becoming Acquainted with Interview Formats

When envisioning a medical school interview, most applicants imagine sitting across a table from a faculty member and talking one-on-one about their application. Although this picture may be accurate for many medical school interviews, it doesn't represent the full the range of interview formats used by schools. At some schools applicants face multiple interviewers at once, interview alongside other applicants, or participate in a multiple mini-interview (MMI), which involves rotating to a different station every ten or so minutes.

Even if a traditional interview format is used, the amount of information the interviewer knows about an applicant varies from school to school. At one school, an interviewer may know nothing more than your name; at another, he has access to every piece of information you've submitted during the application process.

If the school uses an MMI, it will very likely inform you in advance to expect this format. However, you may not be told the details of a traditional interview format, such as whether it's one-on-one, panel, or open or closed file, until the day of the interview. By familiarizing yourself with the many setups you may encounter during interview season, you'll be prepared to shine no matter what method a school favors for assessing applicants.

One-on-one and panel interviews

Although the variety of interview formats has increased in recent years with the introduction of the MMI, most schools still use a *standard-format interview,* which utilizes either a one-on-one or a panel setup.

- ✔ In a *one-on-one interview,* an individual interviewer meets with a single applicant at a time. The interviewer is usually a member of the school's faculty or staff, a medical student, or a physician from the community. In the most common format, a student has interviews with two different interviewers, with each session lasting anywhere from 20 minutes to over an hour, although 30 to 45 minutes is typical.

- ✔ In a *panel interview,* the applicant faces a panel of two or three interviewers instead of meeting with one interviewer at a time. With a panel interview, a single applicant may interview alone or with one or more other applicants at the same time.

Although panel interviewers tend to be more intimidating than individual ones, the essential approach to preparing for the two is the same. Therefore, the steps I describe in "Getting Ready for a Traditional Interview" later in this chapter apply to both formats.

Open file, closed file, and semi-closed file interviews

When you walk in the door, what does an interviewer know about you? Your interview will fall into one of the following categories based on the answer to that question:

- ✔ **Open file:** In an *open file* interview, your interviewer has access to your application file, so he may ask you questions about particular activities you've listed, inquire about weaknesses in your application, or ask you to elaborate on topics discussed in your personal statement.

✔ **Closed file:** A *closed file* or *blind interview* means the interviewer knows very limited information about you — perhaps only your name. An interviewer may begin a closed file interview with a broad prompt or question, such as "Tell me about yourself" or "Why do you want to be a physician?" because he doesn't have any specific information to work from at the outset. The intent of a closed file interview is to eliminate the *halo effect,* in which an interviewer may be biased by your credentials. For example, an interviewer may be primed to be impressed by your answers if he sees that you nailed a 38 on the MCAT and have been published in a prestigious journal, while those with less-impressive records are stuck facing a more skeptical audience.

✔ **Semi-closed file:** A hybrid of the two types of approaches is the *semi-closed interview,* in which schools give interviewers some information from your file, such as the personal statement and/or activities section (see Chapter 8 for more about these parts of the primary application) but withhold your MCAT score and GPA. This approach allows the interviewer to be familiar with some aspects of an applicant's background but prevents bias based on the quantitative factors.

If you have multiple one-on-one interviews at a school, one of your interviews may be open file and the other closed, or all interviewers may have access to the same amount of information. For panel interviews, all members of the panel may have read your file, or only one of the interviewers on the panel may have been given your full application while the others have limited or no background information about you. Even if you know the interview is open-file, don't assume the interviewer has memorized your application.

How familiar the interviewer is with your background affects the type of questions you're asked and how you respond to them. Some schools tell interviewees in advance whether an interviewer has access to their files. Other times, an interviewer may reveal to the applicant at the beginning of the interview whether he has read the application. When in doubt, err on the side of assuming that the interviewer hasn't read your file so that you don't leave gaps in your story or gloss over relevant information that the interviewer may not be aware of.

The multiple mini-interview

The *multiple mini-interview* is very different from a traditional one-on-one or panel interview. With an MMI, you don't meet with one or more interviewers for an extended length of time and discuss standard questions such as "Why medicine?" and "What are your strengths and weaknesses?" Instead, you rotate through a series of stations, encountering a different case, question, task, or role-playing scenario at each.

After being developed by McMaster University in Canada as a tool for medical school admissions in 2002, the MMI has gained popularity among U.S. medical schools in recent years as an alternative to traditional interviews. This type of interview is probably unlike anything you've encountered before. However, you may be reassured to know that many applicants actually prefer it to the standard interview format. In fact, more than one applicant I've spoken to has described it as "fun," which isn't a word usually associated with any part of the med school application process!

The following sections list typical stations, go over the basic setup of MMIs, and explain why some schools are switching to MMIs.

Surveying station types

If you interview at a school that uses an MMI, expect to be part of a group of applicants rotating through six to ten stations, each lasting eight to ten minutes. During a station, you usually interact with an interviewer (usually referred to as a *rater*), though in some stations, the rater observes your interaction with another person. Every station you rotate through during an MMI presents you with a new challenge; however, although the exact details of each will differ, certain types of stations are commonly used. These include the following:

- **Role-playing:** For a role-playing station, you get a scenario involving an individual who's played by an actor or community member. You may need to give the person bad news, confront him about a problem, or resolve a conflict. Many applicants consider these stations to be among the most difficult, but the same problem-solving and communication skills used for the other stations apply here as well.

- **Ethical scenarios:** For these stations, you receive a case or scenario and must discuss the ethical issues involved and/or how you'd handle the situation. The situations often involve medicine and *bioethics* (a branch of ethics that focuses on issues relevant to medicine and to research in biological sciences), although some revolve around everyday issues such as academic dishonesty.

- **Critical thinking:** Some stations call on your critical thinking skills by asking you to analyze a proposal or discuss how you'd approach a problem.

- **Teamwork:** Stations may require you to work with another individual who is part of the interview team or with another applicant to complete an assigned task, such as drawing a picture.

In addition to these more exotic stations, an MMI may include a station that involves standard interview questions. That means that just because you're doing an MMI doesn't mean you can necessarily escape answering "Why did you apply to this program?" and other old favorites.

Exploring the structure of MMIs

The description of a station and instructions are usually posted outside the room. You typically get two minutes to read this information and think about how you'll approach the station before a buzzer sounds, signaling applicants to enter their designated rooms. When you enter the room, you discuss your thoughts about the prompt with the rater. After you're inside, you have six to eight minutes to complete the station before the buzzer sounds again, indicating it's time to move on to the next station. During the discussion, the rater may ask probing questions to follow up on your response. Some stations also use visual aids, such as video clips or photographs, in lieu of or in addition to a written description. For example, a video may show two people arguing; your task is to discuss the interactions between the two individuals and how you'd respond if you witnessed this conflict.

Candidates usually aren't permitted to take notes during an MMI, so you need to get used to generating and remembering the framework for your response without writing it down, a process that is perfected through practice. Don't worry, though; you don't have to memorize the prompt or station instructions because you usually find one copy of the prompt on the door and another inside the room for you to refer to during the station.

Understanding why some schools are making the switch

You may be wondering why some schools use an MMI instead of sticking with the way things have been done for decades. Here are a few reasons:

- ✔ **Evaluating personal characteristics:** A major part of the answer has to do with what medical schools are seeking in applicants. Schools don't want students who are merely book smart; they want individuals who also possesses social intelligence, integrity, and compassion and who demonstrate professionalism, all of which are essential to the practice of medicine. MMI stations are designed to help schools assess the various skills and qualities they're seeking in applicants.

- ✔ **Standardizing interviews:** MMIs are an attempt to make the interview process fairer. With traditional interviews, some applicants may be interviewed by "easier" interviewers than others. With an MMI, the same rater remains at a particular station throughout the session, evaluating each applicant that comes through the station, which makes the process more standardized.

- ✔ **Lessening the impact of one bad round:** In a traditional interview setting, an applicant's evaluation lies in the hands of one or two individuals. If the applicant and interviewer don't click, or if one interview simply doesn't go well, the applicant's chances of admission may be significantly adversely affected. If an applicant performs poorly in one station out of ten in an MMI, his overall score is less likely to be tanked.

Examining the Elements of a Strong Interview

A successful interview reinforces to the admissions committee that you have clear, substantive reasons for wanting to become a physician, possess a genuine interest in the school, communicate effectively, and have the characteristics needed to make a good physician. A weak interview leaves the committee unsure about why you even want to be a physician and doubtful that you have the nonacademic skills needed to make a great one. The interview can be either a means of helping you attain a spot in the class or a reason that you end up on the waitlist or in the rejected pile.

Regardless of the format, the interviewer will gather information about you during the interview not only from the content of responses you give but also from the way you deliver them. By understanding the various elements that constitute a positive performance, you can address each so that you shine on interview day. The three major areas that you should focus on when preparing for any med school interview are the following:

- ✔ **Content of responses:** Good answers have substance, are well organized, provide supporting details or examples when appropriate, and contribute to a consistent overall picture of you as an applicant. To answer some questions, you need to elaborate on items mentioned in your application, while others require you to tackle outside topics or to think on your feet. (Check out the later section "Crafting Your Responses" for details about how to formulate effective answers to interview questions.)

- ✔ **Communication skills:** It's not just about what you say in an interview; it's also about how you say it. Even if the content of your responses is excellent, you'll leave the interviewer unimpressed if you deliver your answers in a way that is unclear, digressive, or dry. Both verbal and nonverbal communication skills are important, so everything from the way you sit (no slouching!) to the amount of eye contact you make and the level of enthusiasm you display can add to or detract from your performance.

- ✔ **Professionalism:** Schools look for applicants who are able to present themselves in a mature, professional manner, especially because early clinical exposure — putting medical students into contact with patients as soon as the first semester of school — is the trend. Wearing professional attire (see the later section "Choosing Your Interview Attire" for tips about selecting an outfit), addressing the interviewer with respect, and maintaining composure under the stress of an interview all reflect how you'll fare in your role as a student physician.

Getting Ready for a Traditional Interview

Preparation for a one-on-one or panel interview (described earlier in this chapter) begins with information gathering. Before you compile responses to specific questions, you need to do research about the school, current issues in healthcare, and bioethics topics and make sure that you know every aspect of your application well. With this raw material to work with, you have the foundation to respond to many of the interview questions that come your way. Mock interviews never hurt, either. The following sections walk you through preparing for a standard-format interview.

Taking a few basic steps

Here are some specific steps to take to ensure that you're ready for commonly asked questions:

- ✔ **Do your homework about the school.** In Chapter 7, I discuss how to approach researching medical schools in order to formulate a list of schools for your application. Now's the time to revisit your notes about a school's curriculum, mission, educational philosophy, and location as well as to dig deeper into what the school offers by doing more reading and talking to anyone you know who's affiliated with the program. Schools want to select applicants who genuinely desire to attend their programs, so be ready to give a thorough, convincing response about the nature of your interest in the school.

- ✔ **Review your application.** You should also go back and read about *yourself.* Sound silly? When you consider the amount of information on your application, some of which describes classes and activities that took place years ago, refreshing your memory about your credentials isn't such a far-fetched idea. An interviewer may choose to focus on any aspect of your application and ask about the sculpture course you took on a whim as a freshman rather than your more recent accomplishments. Revisiting your application can save you from being stumped if you're faced with such a situation.

- ✔ **Research topics in healthcare.** With the ongoing debate about the U.S. healthcare system, interview questions about an applicant's knowledge of issues facing healthcare and potential solutions for them aren't unusual. You don't have to become an expert on the Patient Protection and Affordable Care Act, but you should know the basics about hot topics in healthcare.

In addition to keeping up with regular news sources, check out articles and publications from professional organizations such as the American Medical Association (AMA) and the American Osteopathic Association (AOA) for the latest on issues affecting physicians.

✔ **Prepare for bioethics questions.** To get ready to tackle questions involving issues such as patient autonomy, end-of-life issues, and informed consent, spend some time becoming familiar with the terminology and major topics in the area of bioethics. Books and websites that include cases involving ethics issues are good sources to use during your preparation. The University of Washington School of Medicine's page on bioethics topics is an excellent resource that includes cases with discussion. Go to `depts.washington.edu/bioethx/topics/index.html` to check it out. Although bioethics questions are more commonly found as part of an MMI, they're part of some traditional interviews as well.

Study all sides of bioethics issues, particularly those issues that evoke strong opinions, such as healthcare reform, physician-assisted suicide, and other potentially controversial topics. Acknowledging concerns or arguments that someone who disagrees with your view may have allows you to present your perspective while making it clear that you respect others' opinions even when they're different from your own. Interviewers don't expect you to necessarily share their views, but they do want to know that you think critically about difficult issues and keep an open mind. If you're asked such a question, you can give your opinion, but make sure that you support it, and definitely don't denigrate supporters of the other side.

Tackling common interview questions

Schools and individual interviewers have their own styles. Some lean toward a more relaxed, conversational approach, asking applicants about their classes, interests, and hobbies. Others are tougher, quizzing applicants about every aspect of their applications and closely probing their motivations to enter medicine. Despite these differences, certain questions endure and are ones you'll likely be asked again and again in some form on the interview trail. Here's a sampling of some of these commonly used questions and topics:

✔ Why do you want to be a physician?

✔ Tell me about yourself.

✔ How have you explored the medical profession?

✔ Why did you apply to this school?

✔ What are your greatest strengths and weaknesses?

✔ Tell me about the [specific activity] listed on your application.

✔ What would you do if you weren't accepted to medical school this cycle?

✔ What qualities do you have that you think would make you a good physician?

- ✔ Is there anything that you want the committee to know that isn't on your application?

- ✔ What are your hobbies?

- ✔ If you couldn't be a physician, what career would you consider?

- ✔ What was the last book that you read?

- ✔ Where do you see yourself in 15 years?

- ✔ What are some of the major challenges facing physicians in the United States today?

- ✔ What are some of the drawbacks to being a physician?

- ✔ Are you a leader or a follower?

- ✔ What accomplishment are you most proud of?

- ✔ What has been the most challenging experience you've faced?

- ✔ Why did you get a *C* (or lower grade) in this class?

- ✔ Why is your score on the MCAT (or a particular MCAT section) low?

- ✔ Why should we accept you to our program?

- ✔ What questions do you have for me?

Some schools also include *behavioral interviewing* questions. These questions ask you to discuss situations you have faced in the past and how you handled them. Behavioral questions often begin with "Tell me about at time when . . . " or "Describe a situation when . . ." Here are a few specific examples:

- ✔ Tell me about a time when you had to make a difficult ethical choice.

- ✔ Describe a time when you made an unpopular decision and how you dealt with the result.

- ✔ Tell me about a time when you had to deal with someone you didn't like or who didn't like you.

Crafting your responses

The key to formulating great answers is having in mind some major points you want to include for particular topics as well as a general framework for answering questions. Don't compile an exhaustive list of responses and attempt to memorize them, which not only is impractical but also results in your sounding rehearsed rather than natural. The following sections provide you with tools to use for answering a wide range of interview questions as well as tips about how to make a good first impression and finish strong.

Responding to interview questions with a few basic guidelines

Keeping your answers focused and organized will display your communication skills and ensure that you convey your ideas effectively. You also need to strike a balance between giving a thorough response and going on for too long. Accomplishing all this plus being ready to go with the flow of the conversation rather than doing an information download on the interviewer takes some practice but sets you up to make a positive impression during your interview. The following tips help you to develop your overall approach to answering interview questions:

- ✔ **Be concise.** Ideally, an interview isn't an interrogation; it's a conversation between the applicant and interviewer, and nothing kills the flow of the discussion faster than a long-winded monologue by a candidate. In general, keep your responses to no more than two minutes, although a very open-ended question, such as "Tell me about yourself" may merit a (slightly) longer response.

- ✔ **Focus on discussing one or two points in depth rather than trying to cram too much into an answer.** This tip is closely related to the previous one. By picking a few important things to focus on, you don't lose the listener and are able to more thoroughly develop your most important ideas. Quality over quantity definitely applies here.

- ✔ **Organize your answer.** A rambling response that jumps from topic to topic, digresses, and is difficult to follow won't win you points with your interviewer. Verbal communication should be organized much the way written communication is: Start with a thesis sentence, move on to addressing the topics comprising the body of your answer in a logical order, and finish with a brief, forceful conclusion.

  At the same time, don't get so hung up on structure that you pause for more than a couple of seconds before responding to a question. Practice responding out loud to different types of questions and do a mock interview so that you get the hang of responding right away with a clear, organized answer. Occasionally taking some extra time to consider a question that you find especially challenging is fine, but pausing too frequently is awkward. (Find out more about mock interviews in the later section "Doing a mock interview.")

- ✔ **Be flexible.** Although you may have ideas in mind about items you want to discuss during your interview, such as your undergraduate research or a medical mission you did in Haiti, the interviewer may be more interested in hearing about your fly-fishing hobby or the dog-walking business you operate. In that situation, run with those topics instead of trying to force the conversation to fit a predetermined agenda. Keep in mind that the admissions committee already has an application listing your credentials, and the interviewer may prefer to use the time to discuss areas unrelated to academics or even medicine. No matter what the topic of conversation, an interviewer can still gauge your communication skills and personality.

Adding depth through details and examples

Without supporting details and examples, your responses come across as unconvincing, superficial, or just plain boring. Details, anecdotes, and examples enrich your answers and engage the interviewer, encouraging them to ask follow-up questions that allow you to discuss an experience in greater depth. To see how details can transform a response, consider the answers of two different applicants to the following question: "How have you explored the medical profession?"

Applicant A:

> *"I've learned about medicine through hospital volunteering, research, and physician shadowing."*

Applicant B:

> *"I began my exploration of medicine in high school as a volunteer in the oncology and emergency departments in a local hospital. In college, I gained further exposure to the profession by assisting a psychiatrist in a clinical research project and by shadowing both primary care physicians and specialists. My shadowing experience with Dr. Jackson in his cardiology practice last summer was especially valuable in helping me understand what a physician's job entails. During that time, I witnessed patient care in both inpatient and outpatient settings, observed several procedures, and had the chance to attend grand rounds."*

Although Applicant A answers the question, the response sounds generic and reveals virtually nothing about him. By contrast, Applicant B's response gives the interviewer a clear picture of the type of experiences he has had and puts them in context by emphasizing a particularly meaningful one. Although Applicant B's response contains some detail, it's not excessively long. Adding detail doesn't mean that a response needs to be long-winded. Where Applicant A says "research," Applicant B states "assisting a psychiatrist in a clinical research project," which only adds seven words to the total but makes a much greater impact.

Thinking of details and examples on the spot can be challenging, so before the interview, peruse your application and think back to memorable experiences you've had; patients you've seen; and challenges and events you've learned from. Bringing these stories to the forefront of your mind and jotting them down will prime you to recall them when you need to. Don't expect to use all, or even most, of the examples you come up with, but the more thinking you do in advance, the greater the range of material you'll have to draw from when the time comes.

Starting strong and closing with confidence

The initial impression you make on the interviewer can be either a positive one that you build upon throughout your time together or something you spend the rest of the interview overcoming. Shaking the interviewer's hand weakly, mumbling "hello," and looking terrified doesn't exactly inspire confidence that you're ready to take on med school. Many applicants walk into the interview imagining that the person on the other side of the table is looking for a way to trip them up with trick questions or pick apart their applications in hopes of finding a reason for rejection; that vision understandably makes it difficult to enter the interview room with confidence and enthusiasm. In reality, interviewers are generally fair-minded people who genuinely want to get to know you. By viewing the interviewer as a potential ally rather than as an obstacle to admission, you can enter the interview with composure.

When you meet the interviewer, shake his hand, make eye contact, and introduce yourself, using his title and last name: "Hello, Dr. Ravi, I'm Steve Applicant." And smile. The simple act of smiling conveys that you're happy to have the opportunity to interview and excited at the prospect of potentially attending the school. It may also help you relax and feel more comfortable.

During the interview, the conversation may flow easily, leaving you feeling almost as though you're chatting with a friend. Other times, however, you may find yourself worrying that you and the interviewer aren't hitting it off. If the latter occurs, keep in mind that the way an interviewer reacts may be a reflection of his personality and style rather than of your performance. Just because an interviewer seems stoic doesn't mean he isn't engaged in the conversation. Some people simply aren't easily readable or prefer to maintain a neutral demeanor when interviewing an applicant.

If you find yourself facing someone who you aren't sure is responding positively to you, don't become unnerved or rush through your responses. Maintain a friendly attitude and give the same thorough (but not overly verbose) answers you would when talking with a more congenial interviewer. If you keep your composure, an interview you thought was a flop may just be one that yields an acceptance.

After the interview, make sure that the last impression you leave the interviewer with is a positive one. Hopefully, things went well and you're feeling more relaxed than you were when the interview began. In any case, though, thank the interviewer for taking the time to meet with you, shake hands again, and walk out knowing you did everything you could to ace the interview.

Doing a mock interview

After browsing through lists of interview questions, thinking about how you'd respond to them, and answering questions out loud to yourself so often that your roommates become concerned, it's time to practice with another human being. Doing a practice or mock interview is a great way to replicate the interview experience and gives you a chance to work the rough spots out of your delivery and identify problems with the content or presentation of your responses. You'll also be more comfortable going into your first interview if you've simulated the experience before.

Ideally, a mock interview is conducted by someone who is familiar with medical school admissions and who can provide objective feedback about your performance. Some prehealth advising offices offer mock interviews, and if yours does, I strongly recommend that you take advantage of the opportunity. If you're obtaining a premedical committee letter (described in Chapter 9), you're likely to have to go through an interview with one or more members of your committee. That experience also provides practice for the medical school interview; often, the types of questions asked in committee interviews are similar to those used for medical school interviews.

If you don't have access to a prehealth advising office that provides mock interviews, check with your school's career center to see whether it can help. At some institutions, the career center assists not only students preparing for job interviews but also those applying to graduate or professional schools. Other options for practice include asking a physician, mentor, or professor to work with you. Going through interview questions with a willing friend or family member also gives you the opportunity to practice your responses, although that person's knowledge of what medical schools are looking for is going to be much more limited. Yet even without specific insight into the admissions process, whoever you practice with can give you feedback to help you hone your overall presentation by pointing out habits you may not be aware of, such as saying "um" before every sentence or fidgeting in your seat.

If possible, wear your interview attire to the mock interview. Because a suit isn't exactly everyday attire for a premedical student, you may feel a bit awkward at first in your interview outfit. By donning the clothes you'll wear on interview day, you more closely simulate the real experience and become more comfortable wearing professional attire. (For tips on putting together a polished look, head to "Choosing Your Interview Attire" later in this chapter.)

Going a Little Further to Prepare for an MMI

Even if the school you're interviewing at uses an MMI (described earlier in this chapter), a good way to begin your preparation is by going over the guidelines for traditional interviews that I outline in the earlier section "Taking a few basic steps." By completing those tasks, you gain the foundation needed to excel at stations requiring you to analyze ethics scenarios as well as to respond to questions at a short standard-format interview station, which is a part of some MMIs. Studying up on healthcare issues is valuable as well; doing so gets you thinking about how to approach the task of analyzing a policy or proposal, an important skill for stations that require critical thinking. The following sections lay out some MMI-specific considerations and give you some sample MMI stations.

Taking a few additional steps

Despite the similarities between MMIs and standard-format interviews, your preparation for an MMI also needs to reflect the distinct differences in the formats. Additional actions you should take before an MMI include

- **Practicing under timed conditions:** The timing for an MMI is much more stringent than for a traditional interview. A traditional interview has no per-question time limit, whereas during an MMI, each station is strictly timed. After two minutes of reading the prompt and thinking, you must be ready to enter the room and tackle the task at hand during the next six to eight minutes. To succeed on an MMI, you need to be able to analyze a prompt and develop a mental outline for your response within the typical two-minute time limit.

  To get used to operating under such parameters, practice under timed conditions, using sample scenarios that are sometimes provided by schools for interviewees or that can be found online. Team up with a partner to practice, and switch off being in the interviewee and rater roles. During your practice sessions, make sure you stop the station when the timer sounds, whether you feel you're done with your answer or not.

- **Developing a strategy for role-playing stations:** Although you can't predict the exact role-playing scenarios you'll face, you can still fine-tune your communication skills and develop general approaches to use during role-playing scenarios by thinking through some potential situations you may face. For example, if you're given the task of speaking to someone about a problem they're confronting, you first need to consider how you'd begin the conversation. After that, what questions would you ask to gather information about the situation? How would you convey empathy for the person's situation or react if he became angry or upset? How would you suggest solutions or next steps to take in resolving the problem? Running through a few scenarios helps you understand the challenges you may confront during these stations and how to best overcome them.

During an MMI, you may encounter an interviewer who becomes confrontational or challenges your opinion. Stay calm and use reason rather than emotion to respond the situation; remember, one of the skills that MMIs in particular assess is conflict resolution. (However, this advice is good for any type of interview.)

Schools keep their MMI stations under wraps, often requiring interviewees to sign an agreement not to disclose details about the MMI, which makes finding practice stations challenging. However, your focus should primarily be on general approaches to station types rather than on specific scenarios. Success on an MMI relies more on your ability to communicate, think critically, and problem solve than on your knowledge of the particular topic raised or task to be performed. Because a good performance during an MMI requires skills and characteristics developed over the long term, this type of interview is generally more difficult to prepare for than a standard-format interview. However, by familiarizing yourself with this format and thinking about how you'd handle different station types you may encounter, you'll feel more comfortable when the buzzer sounds and the first round begins.

Checking out examples of MMI stations

The earlier section "Surveying station types" lists some common station types to expect. The following examples build on that information to provide you with a more specific idea of what the prompts and instructions used in an MMI may look like:

Role-playing:

> *You are a supervisor at your place of employment. You have been informed that two employees in your group, Madeline and Andrew, do not get along, yet they need to work together as part of a team for many projects. You have arranged a meeting with Madeline to discuss the situation. She is waiting inside the room.*

Teamwork:

> *You and another applicant will be working together to perform a task. You will be provided with a sketch; the other applicant will not have a copy of the sketch. Using verbal communication only, describe to the other applicant how to draw the sketch. During this station, you and the other applicant will be seated so that you are unable to see one another.*

Ethical scenario/critical thinking:

> *You are a physician. An elderly patient under your care has been suffering from weakness, and tests determine that the cause of his symptoms is a progressive neurological disease for which there is no effective treatment and that is ultimately fatal. At the patient's request, you discuss the outcome of the diagnostic tests with his family first, before you talk to the patient about them. During your discussion with the family, family members state that they do not want the patient to be told the diagnosis. They say the family has recently emigrated from another country and that in their country of origin, it is common for a serious diagnosis to be withheld from a patient, especially if he is elderly, in order to avoid upsetting him.*

> *What ethical issues are raised by this situation?*

> *What steps would you take to address this situation?*

Dealing with Logistics

After you've received an invitation to interview, you not only need to prepare for the actual interview (as I explain earlier in this chapter) but also have to take care of details such as scheduling an interview date and potentially making arrangements for travel, lodging, and transportation for your visit. Because you may be juggling trips to various parts of the country with attending classes, taking tests, and other obligations, things can get complicated fast. In addition, the expenses incurred during interview season can be significant after you account for the cost of plane tickets, car rental, hotels, and meals.

From choosing an interview date to picking your mode of transportation and your accommodations, you're faced with many options as you make your interview plans. The following sections help you to sort out the choices so that interview season goes smoothly and doesn't break the bank.

Scheduling your interview

If you're offered several options for interview dates, you should rely on the same principle that applies to filling out primaries (see Chapter 8) and submitting secondaries (see Chapter 9): Do everything as early as possible. Securing a spot early in the interview season gives you the best chance of having your application come before the committee for a final review while many spots are still available in the class. If you need to delay by a week or two because of examinations at school or in order to cluster interviews at schools in the same city together, that's fine. However, delaying by a month or more is generally not advisable, especially late in the cycle.

Check a school's website and any info you may have received with its secondary to verify what its rescheduling policy is. Most schools understand that students have to work around class schedules, jobs, and other commitments, and they generally try to be accommodating regarding interview scheduling. If the assigned date or dates you're given to choose from won't work for you, notify the admissions office immediately; some schools are more flexible than others, and you may be able to reschedule. (Take the next available date that fits with your schedule, though.) However, some schools state that they rarely reschedule interviews or limit rescheduling to one time.

To cut costs, you can try to schedule interviews in the same city for within a few days of one another in order to have to avoid making two or more trips to the area. However, such coordination isn't always possible because one school may review your file and offer you an interview long before the other has made a decision about your candidacy.

You may hear about applicants who make *in the area* calls or e-mails to medical schools they're hoping for an interview at. With this strategy, an applicant contacts a school that he hasn't yet heard from regarding his interview status but that is located in the same geographic area as another school he already has an interview at. The idea is that the admissions office, knowing that the applicant will be coming to the school's city, will review his application more quickly than it otherwise would. Although this tactic sounds good in theory, I have yet to hear a single firsthand account of it actually working. The response from admissions offices is typically along the lines of, "We'll review your application when we review it." Be prepared for the possibility of having to make two trips to the same area over the course of the interview season, even if you try the "in the area" strategy.

Getting there

After your interview is scheduled, you need to start looking into travel options if the program is located out of town. If the school is far enough away that air or train travel is required, begin shopping around for a ticket early to compare prices and hopefully get a good deal. If a city is served by multiple airports, make sure you check flights for each one to find the best price (check with the school's admissions office for a list of nearby airports). If a school is close enough to home that driving is another option, consider costs such as gas and parking when comparing the modes of transportation. (*Tip:* If you do fly, make sure you're signed up for frequent flyer programs. By the end of interview season, you may have racked up enough points for a ticket to somewhere fun for a much-needed vacation after all this admissions stuff is over!)

If you're traveling by plane or train, you also have to arrange for transportation to the place you're staying and to the school if it's not within walking distance of your accommodations. Some cities are very easy to get around by public transportation, whereas a car is virtually a necessity in others.

If you'll have a free day or half day before or after your interview, use that time to check out the city to get a feel for whether it's somewhere you think you'd be happy living. Before you embark on your trip or immediately after your arrival, find out about the best ways to get around within the city so that you can explore the area outside the school. (The hotel's concierge or your med student host is a good source for tips on seeing the city). After all, even as a med student, you won't be spending all your time within the borders of the campus.

Staying in a hotel or with a student host

If you happen to be visiting a school located near family or friends, you may luck out and have a cost-free place to stay. However, your major choices for accommodations are usually checking into a hotel or bunking with a medical student through host programs offered by some medical schools. Schools with student host programs typically include this information with the other details about the interview, or you can inquire at the admissions office about this possibility. Some benefits of staying with a student host are

- ✔ **Reducing cost:** Because boarding with a student host is free, going this route helps you to minimize your expenses associated with interviews.

- ✔ **Getting the chance to hear an insider's perspective on the school:** The students you stay with can provide you with their take on the school and answer questions you may have about the program, student life, and the community.

- ✔ **Having a contact to help you as you make arrangements for your visit:** You'll be in touch with your student host prior to your visit and can ask his advice about travelling to the city, getting around after you've arrived, and other tips for your stay. If the timing works out, you may even end up heading to the school with your host the morning of your interview as he's on his way to class.

Despite these advantages, staying with a student isn't for everyone. A hotel offers a greater level of privacy and no pressure to socialize or be "on" if you prefer to just relax on your own the night before the interview. You also may have to crash on the couch of your host's apartment, which may not make for the most restful night's sleep. The extra expense for a hotel may be worth it if you want the assurance that you'll have your own room to sleep in and won't have to worry about anyone else's late night or early morning habits disrupting your rest. Ultimately, you should choose whatever option appeals to you and that will put you most at ease going into your interview.

Choosing Your Interview Attire

Appropriate attire conveys to the interviewer, admissions officers, and anyone you encounter on interview day that you take the interview process seriously, understand how to present yourself in a professional setting, and respect the people who have set aside time to conduct an interview with you. Outfits that are inappropriate or overly casual are more than just fashion mistakes; they may be interpreted as a reflection of your judgment and attitude toward the interview. Looking polished and professional sends the message that you're ready and eager to embark on the next step toward a medical career as a first-year med student in the fall. The following sections provide pointers for men's and women's interview attire.

If you want to bring paper and a pen to take notes with during presentations given as part of the interview day, carry them in a portfolio. The portfolio also provides you a place to put any papers you want to bring, such as a copy of your application or information about the school to review during any downtime on interview day.

Men's attire

A suit is standard interview wear; anything less and you risk appearing underdressed and out of place among your more polished-looking peers. If you don't own a suit, invest in one. Stick with conservative colors; navy blue, black, and charcoal gray are all good choices. For shirts, opt for either white or light blue. You can use your choice of tie to add a touch of style, but don't go with anything too loud or whimsical; if you're unsure about your selection, err on the side of being more conservative. (Sorry, that means you should leave the rubber-duck tie at home.) Complete your outfit with black dress shoes (worn with dark socks) and a belt.

Here are a few more tips for guys who are gearing up for interview day:

✔ **Quality and fit are important.** By shopping around and seeking out sales, you can find a good-quality suit that is reasonably priced. You certainly don't need to spend an excessive amount, but a suit that is cheaply made will look it. Fit is critical too. Even the nicest suit doesn't look sharp if the pants are too long or the jacket too big. Have your suit altered as needed to ensure you look your best in it.

✔ **Pay attention to grooming.** Your interview day appearance is determined not only by the clothes you wear but also by your attention to other details. If you're in need of a haircut, schedule one before you head off for your interview. Make sure you shave and check that your nails are clean and trimmed as well.

✔ **Skip the cologne.** With cologne, you run the risk of encountering an interviewer who's bothered by the smell or, worse, of triggering someone's allergies. Also, one person's idea of "just the right amount" may be someone else's idea of "way too much," so your best bet is just to leave it off altogether.

Women's attire

For women, a suit that consists of a jacket and either pants or a skirt is appropriate. Interviewees sometimes wonder whether one (skirt or pants) is better than the other, but either is perfectly acceptable. You'll see fellow applicants in both types, so choose whichever combination you prefer. Black, navy blue, and dark gray aren't just good color choices for the guys; they're also the standbys for women's professional attire. However, lighter gray, as well as other colors, can work as long as they aren't too bright. Although white is almost always a good choice for a blouse, you can also use the blouse as a means of injecting some color into your outfit; that said, I recommend favoring more-subtle colors over very bright ones.

For shoes, select a pair of pumps with closed toes. Shoes with a moderate heel (no more than 2.5 inches) look more sophisticated than flats, especially with a skirt; however, heels also present the issue of practicality. You'll be doing a lot of walking on interview day and don't want the experience to be an uncomfortable one that leaves you limping behind the rest of the group.

If you can't find a pair of heels that you're comfortable walking in, consider bringing a pair of flat shoes to wear during the tour. That's what I did, and it worked well, allowing me to wear the great shoes I had picked out to complete my interview outfit but also to maneuver easily through the parts of the day that required a significant amount of walking.

Some other thoughts for female applicants to keep in mind include the following:

- ✔ **Make sure your hemline and neckline are appropriate.** Choose a skirt that is no shorter than slightly above the knee. You definitely don't want to have to worry about tugging your skirt down when you sit down for your interview. For shirts, the same concept applies: Stay away from anything low cut; you don't want to show any cleavage at all.

- ✔ **Avoid the bare-legged look.** Although bare legs with skirts may be in style, that look isn't professional enough for a medical school interview. Pick up some sheer hose to wear with your suit. They'll finish off your look nicely and have the secondary benefit of providing a bit more warmth if your interview day is chilly.

- ✔ **Choose a small purse in a conservative style if you carry one.** Pare down the items you bring to the interview to only the necessities so that you don't have to bring a gigantic handbag with you. Instead, select a purse that is small and professional-looking rather than oversized and flashy. Go with a conservative color such as brown or black that complements the color of your attire.

- ✔ **Take it easy with jewelry, makeup, and fragrance.** Some understated earrings and a simple necklace finish an outfit nicely; however, leave the dangly earrings, bangle bracelets, and chunky necklaces at home. Some makeup can add polish to your look, but avoid overdoing it. Skipping perfume entirely is safest because you never know whether your interviewer will have allergies.

Walking Through a Typical Interview Day Schedule

Interview day is usually composed of much more than the actual meetings with your interviewers. At most schools, you also tour the campus, hear a presentation from the admissions office, and meet medical students over lunch. All these events together may turn interview day into an all-day affair that not only allows a med school to get to know you better but also gives you the opportunity to check out the program more closely. In the following sections, I discuss what to expect on interview day as well as how to handle each step so that you can make a good impression while gathering the information you need to make your ultimate decision about where to attend.

From the moment you step onto campus until the moment you leave, you should be in interview mode. The faculty, admissions staff, and med students you encounter appreciate respect, friendliness, and enthusiasm. Conversely, an applicant who's abrupt with staff members, disdainful of fellow applicants, or seems to care only about impressing the interviewers leaves a negative impression that may make its way back to committee members or other decision makers.

Attending orientation

At many schools, interview day begins around 9 a.m. and concludes five or six hours later. Usually, the first stop is an orientation during which a member of the admissions staff welcomes the interviewees. The orientation can be as brief as 15 minutes or last well over an hour and may include presentations by faculty, staff, and medical students about the school's mission and curriculum, financial aid, and student life.

If the presentations take place before you've had your interviews, concentrating on the speaker can be difficult because you're preoccupied with worrying about what your interviews will be like and wishing you could get them over with. However, absorbing as much information as you can while you're at the school is important. Hopefully, you'll eventually receive multiple acceptances and have to choose among several schools. Although some schools offer second look visits to accepted applicants (described in Chapter 11), returning to each school may be logistically difficult and expensive, so interview day may be your only chance to visit before you have to select a program. Try to find out as much as you can about the program during this visit, and take notes to jog your memory when decision time comes.

Touring the campus

One of the most valuable parts of interview day is the tour. Most medical schools include a student-led tour as part of the agenda, allowing interviewees to see the facilities and get a feel for the campus. During the tour, you usually get to check out the library, classrooms, student lounge, cafeteria, and hospital (if it's on the same site as the med school). You may also get to sit in on part of a lecture.

In addition to listening carefully to your tour guide's explanation about what you're seeing, take note of everything around you, from how busy the hospital is (busier is better when it comes to gaining clinical exposure) to how well maintained the facilities are to whether any construction is going on that may indicate expansion or improvements being made.

Your tour guide is likely to be a wealth of information and can offer a med student's perspective of the school. Use your time with him to ask pertinent questions about topics that you won't be able to glean as much insight about from the faculty and staff. A student guide can give you his take on topics such as to how close-knit the class is, how necessary having a car is, and what the overall environment of the school is like. Of course, someone who has volunteered to be a tour guide is likely happy at the school, so he may not represent the student body at large, but you can at least get one student's view of the program.

Taking time for lunch

If interview day lasts longer than a few hours, you can expect a midday meal to be part of the schedule. The setting for lunch varies, and as a premedical student on the interview trail, I encountered everything from off-campus eateries to take-out sandwiches and even hospital cafeterias as the source of lunchtime fare. The tour guides and/or other medical students often join the lunch, providing additional opportunities to chat with people in the know about the program. The amount of time allotted for a lunch break is usually 30 minutes to an hour, and the school generally picks up the tab.

Keep a small snack, such as a granola bar, handy in case your energy starts flagging before it's time for lunch or later in the afternoon. You'll usually have downtime between some of the events during which you can eat a snack that you have on hand.

Undertaking interviews (finally!)

Although many students prefer to have their interview(s) first thing, an interview can be scheduled at any point in the day, so be prepared for anything from jumping into the interview immediately after you arrive to waiting until the end of the day for your turn. At most schools, an applicant participates in one to three interviews with faculty members, staff, and medical students; however, the interviews aren't necessarily scheduled back to back. For example, you may have your first interview at, say, 10 a.m. and then go on the tour and have lunch before a second interview at 1 p.m.

Because interviewers' offices may be located in different buildings around campus or even be situated off campus, the school builds time into the schedule to allow you to get from one place to another. If you have to make your way around campus, the admissions office will provide you with directions for how to get where you're going or assign someone to accompany you to your destination. If you're assigned to an off-campus interview site, such as a nearby affiliated hospital, you may need to take a shuttle there.

Schools can't possibly schedule the day precisely down to the minute, so you may have some downtime between interviews. Often, there's a designated area for applicants to wait between appointments, such as in the admissions office or a student lounge. These short breaks in the action are a good chance to regroup before you're off to the next event.

Although all this information may sound overwhelming, interview days are generally very well organized, and schools usually provide each applicant with a detailed schedule of the day in advance of their arrival or at the start of the day. For a look at a typical schedule, check out Figure 10-1.

Interview Schedule for Alex Applicant

8:45 a.m.–9:00 a.m.	Applicant check-in
	Location: Admissions office, Administration Building, Room 102
9:00 a.m.–9:30 a.m.	Orientation by admissions office staff
9:30 a.m.–10:15 a.m.	Information session with presentation by the director of admissions
10:30 a.m.–11:15 a.m.	Faculty interview
	Interviewer: Dr. Francis Physician, Department of Surgery
	Location: Clinical Center, Room 208
11:30 a.m.–12:15 p.m.	Student-guided tour of medical school
12:15 p.m.–1:00 p.m.	Lunch with medical students
1:15 p.m.–2:00 p.m.	Medical student interview
	Interviewer: Filene Fourth Year
	Location: Education Center, Room 127
2:00 p.m.–2:30 p.m.	Financial aid presentation
	Location: Admissions office, Administration Building, Room 102
2:30 p.m.–3:00 p.m.	Q & A session

Figure 10-1:
A typical interview day schedule.

Illustration by Wiley, Composition Services Graphics

Sending Thank-You Letters

After the interview, you're not quite ready to simply sit back and wait for a decision from the school. Instead, you have one last task: writing thank-you letters to your interviewers and other members of the admissions team involved in interview day. Although not mandatory, this final touch is one more way to connect with the school and emphasize your interest in the program. Any small step you can take to make an impact is worth taking, so set aside some time within a couple of days of an interview to draft thank-you letters or e-mails and send them off.

To have the desired effect, the letters must be well written, personalized, and professional. In the following sections, I cover the protocol concerning who should receive a letter, what information to include, and by what means to send letters in order to guide you through creating thank-you notes that will be an asset to your application.

Deciding who should get a letter

If your interview was a traditional one rather than an MMI (I discuss both formats earlier in this chapter), send a letter to each person with whom you interviewed, including medical student interviewers. With an MMI, you rotate through a series of stations and interact with up to ten raters about whom you usually know virtually nothing; this setup makes sending letters to interviewers impractical. However, for both types of interviews, consider sending a letter to the director or dean of admissions, especially if one of these individuals gave a presentation to applicants during your visit. If you had interactions with other members of the admissions staff, such as someone who coordinated the day's activities or helped you out in some way to plan your visit or after you arrived, you may send him a letter as well.

Note that these guidelines are superseded by any instructions given to you by the medical school. If you're told not to contact your interviewers, the dean, the admissions team in general, or someone in particular, *don't*. Disregarding instructions makes you appear as if you didn't pay attention to what you were told or you thought you were a special exception, neither of which casts you in a positive light.

Debating how to deliver the message

E-mail or regular mail? The answer to this oft-asked question about the best mode of communication for thank-you letters depends on the school's preference, the type of contact information you have for the recipients, and several other factors. Overall, both forms of communication are acceptable, and you may find that e-mail is the best means of communication to use for some schools and regular mail for others.

If the school states a preference for a particular type of correspondence, the decision is easy because, as noted in the previous section, instructions from admissions take precedence over all else. Often, however, the choice is yours to make, so you need to weight the benefits of each.

E-mail

Although regular mail is considered slightly more formal and is a bit more personal, e-mail has the major advantage of being faster. If you don't know when the admissions committee is meeting to review your file, using e-mail is the best means of ensuring that the message makes it to its destination before a decision is rendered on your application. Although your file may not be reviewed for weeks post-interview, it's also possible that your application will be discussed within a day or two of your visit, and a letter that arrives after a decision is made is of little use.

Another advantage to e-mail is the ease with which the recipient can respond. If all an interviewer has to do is type out a message and hit "send," your chances of hearing something back, even if the response is just a quick line or two, increases greatly. Any response you receive may be very brief, but sometimes an interviewer will offer you some words of encouragement. In addition, having even a small amount of two-way communication may help strengthen the connection between you and the interviewer.

Regular mail

If you're sure that a snail-mail letter will reach the school before the committee has decided on your file, you can opt for this more traditional means of communication if you prefer. After all, something is more personal about a letter written on paper that the receiver can hold in his hand that makes this choice tempting.

Also, you can't always look up an interviewer's or admissions officer's e-mail on the medical school's website; if all you have is an interviewer's office address, send the letter by regular mail.

Compiling a letter

When you sit down to write your letters, you may be stymied about what to say beyond "thank you." However, you can more easily overcome your writer's block if you keep in mind that along with expressing your appreciation for the opportunity to interview, a thank-you letter is your chance to briefly discuss your reasons for wanting to attend the school and summarize why you're a great fit for the program. Here are some tips to help you craft an effective letter:

- **Limit the length.** Interviewers and admissions officers are busy people and appreciate brevity. A half page often does the job; definitely don't go over one page.

- **Open with a sentence or two stating who you are and when you interviewed and thanking the person for taking the time to interview.** This way, the reader immediately knows who's writing a letter to him and why.

- **Personalize the letter by mentioning a topic you discussed with the interviewer.** You don't want your thank-you note to sound like a form letter, so individualizing it is important. Refer to information you learned from the interviewer or that you were particularly glad you had the chance to share with him about yourself during your interview. If the recipient wasn't an interviewer, refer to details from the presentation he gave or to his role in interview day.

- ✔ **Mention why you want to attend the school and how your visit reinforced your interest.** Include specific details about what you did or saw that day that reaffirmed your interest in the school. Tie these details in particular into your background experiences, interests, and/or goals in medicine to aspects of the program to show that you're a good fit for the school.

Because you're sending this kind of note in a professional context, you should type it rather than handwrite it. And definitely skip the cutesy thank-you cards; your friends and family may appreciate flowers or baby animals, but these notes don't fit the protocol of a professional setting. The same approach applies for e-mail correspondence; leave out the smiley face icons and stick with a plain background.

Figure 10-2 gives you a look at a sample thank-you letter to an interviewer, and Figure 10-3 illustrates a letter to a director of admissions.

October 10, 2013

Dr. Derek Diagnostician
Best University College of Medicine
Department of Family Medicine
121 Doctors Blvd. Suite 5
Medville, AZ 32345

Dear Dr. Diagnostician:

Thank you for taking the time to interview me on Wednesday, October 9, for a position in the fall 2014 entering class at Best University College of Medicine (BUCM). I especially enjoyed our discussion about opportunities available to medical students at SRC, the university's student run clinic. Since last summer, I have been volunteering weekly at a safety-net clinic and have found the community clinic setting to be a great fit for me. I am eager to gain more experience in similar practice settings and was excited to hear that students are involved in all facets of both patient care and clinic operations at SRC.

In addition to opportunities such as the ones offered at SRC to gain hands-on experience early in my medical training, I am drawn to BUCM for the emphasis on small-group learning as well as the collaborative environment fostered by the school. I learn most effectively in small groups that allow for active participation and discussion, and was intrigued by Dr. Foster's description of how problem-based and case-based learning are integrated into the first two years of the curriculum. I was also impressed by the enthusiasm of the medical students I encountered during the tour and at lunch. They emphasized that the tone set by the faculty encourages collaboration among students. Such an environment would be an ideal one in which for me to obtain my medical education.

My visit to the school solidified my strong interest in BUCM's program, and I appreciate the efforts on behalf of the interviewers, admissions staff, and students to make applicants feel welcome throughout the day.

Thank you again.

Regards,

Irvin Interviewee

Irvin Interviewee

Figure 10-2:
A thank-you
letter to an
interviewer.

778 Maple Avenue
Anytown, AZ 11111
(222) 458-7777
irvin.interviewee@fakeemail.com

November 4, 2014

Mr. Arnold Acceptance
Director of Admissions
Big Name Medical School
28 Hospital Drive
Doctorsville, IL 95595

Dear Mr. Acceptance:

Thank you for the opportunity to interview at Big Name Medical School (BNMS) on Monday, November 3. The presentation you gave was very helpful in clarifying how the admissions process at BNMS works as well as what to expect throughout interview day. To me, the friendliness of the admissions staff and the care taken to ensure that interview day went smoothly and was productive is a reflection of the school's commitment to its students.

My interest in BNMS was initially inspired when I attended an open house at the campus in September 2012. The school's emphasis on educating students who are not only knowledgeable about the practice of medicine but also compassionate, service-minded physicians resonated with me. Further, I was attracted to school for the opportunity it offers to work with the diverse patient population served by University Medical Center as described by Dean Long during his talk.

Through a discussion with a faculty member during the open house, I discovered that BNMS offers students the option of completing a fifth year dedicated to research or another scholarly pursuit. Two of the medical students I spoke with during my interview visit were pursuing the five-year track and discussed the encouragement that they received from the school in pursuing their unique interests. As an undergraduate student, I have participated extensively in research. I know that as a student at BNMS I could continue this involvement as part of my medical education either through the fifth-year pathway or through the many summer research opportunities available to students. This flexibility and the opportunity to obtain an outstanding medical education and to learn from the school's renowned faculty are among the reasons that I chose to apply to BNMS. Again, I appreciate the chance to visit the school yesterday to discuss my application in person.

Regards,

Percy Premed

Percy Premed

656 Spruce Lane
Small Town, PA 23232
(111) 567-8822
percy.premed@fakeemail.com

Figure 10-3:
A thank-you letter to a director of admissions.

Illustration by Wiley, Composition Services Graphics

Chapter 11

Hearing Back

*A*fter an interview, you may find yourself checking your e-mail obsessively, jumping every time the phone rings, and rushing to the mailbox as you await word from the school. When the message comes, whatever its form, you're bound to be thrilled if it's an acceptance and at least a bit dejected if it's not. No matter the outcome — acceptance, rejection, or waitlist — you need to be prepared to take the appropriate next steps.

In this chapter, I provide strategies for handling whichever response you receive, from guidance for dealing with multiple acceptances to ideas for writing a letter of update to methods for moving forward after a rejection.

You Did It! Celebrating Acceptances

A call, letter, or e-mail bearing the great news that you've been accepted may arrive anywhere from a few days to several months after you interview (see Chapter 10 for details on interviewing). The first acceptance is especially thrilling because of the sheer relief you feel knowing that you've got a program to attend in the fall. If a second acceptance follows, you've entered the territory of multiple acceptances. Now the tables are turned; instead of the medical school doing the choosing, you're in the position of scrutinizing programs in order to choose one. (Take that, selection committee!) By handling acceptances strategically, you can keep your options open while you check into the schools more deeply before making the incredibly important decision of where to attend.

Managing multiple acceptances

Allopathic and osteopathic schools handle acceptances differently, so familiarizing yourself with their admissions policies can help you successfully manage your acceptances. I outline the basics of each in the following sections.

Following the instructions and deadlines for individual schools is essential to ensure that you don't risk losing your spot. Schools may have policies and deadlines that differ from those recommended by the AAMC and the AACOM, so rely on the school's instructions as your primary source of information.

AAMC programs (MD schools)

In general, the following guidelines apply for Association of American Medical Schools (AAMC) programs:

- ✔ Prior to May 15, accepted applicants get a minimum of two weeks to respond to an offer of admission.

- ✔ You may hold acceptances at multiple schools until May 15. After May 15, you may hold an acceptance at only one school.

- ✔ Deposits to hold a place in the class are typically $100 and are usually refundable until a certain date (often May 15).

Therefore, if you have offers from more than one AAMC school prior to May 15, you can put down a deposit at each of them, take some time to think about your decision, and then withdraw from all but your top choice school by May 15 (and usually get your deposit money back). You may remain on waitlists for other schools even after May 15. If you're accepted off a waitlist at a school you prefer to the one where you already have a seat, you may opt for a place at the second school instead and withdraw from your spot at the first school.

The AAMC recommendations for policies governing admissions are known as the AAMC *traffic rules*. You can find the complete list on the AAMC site at www. aamc.org/students/applying/recommendations/applicants/.

AACOM programs (DO schools)

Managing multiple acceptances at American Association of Colleges of Osteopathic Medicine (AACOM) schools is a bit more difficult than it is for AAMC schools (refer to the preceding section). At AACOM schools

- ✔ Deposits are usually $1,000 to $2,000 and either nonrefundable or only partially refundable.

- ✔ The amount of time you have to decide about an offer varies depending on how late it is in the admissions cycle that I describe in Chapter 5. An applicant offered an acceptance in September may have three months to make a decision, whereas someone accepted in February may have

14 days. (You can find detailed guidelines in the *Osteopathic Medical College Information Book* on the AACOM site www.aacom.org; the link is on the homepage).

✔ You don't have to be holding only one acceptance after a specific deadline.

Going on second look visits

To help accepted applicants get to know their programs better, many schools host *second look* weekends in the spring. These visits usually include social events with students, faculty, and alumni; tours of the campus and city; visits to clinical sites; and talks about topics such as the school's curriculum and opportunities available to medical students. The environment is generally relaxed, and as an accepted applicant, you'll probably feel more comfortable asking the real questions you have about the school than you did on interview day (when you may have worried that too much probing about potential concerns would turn off your interviewer). Look out for e-mails from the schools notifying you about second look weekends and check out the schools' websites for details as well.

Some medical schools provide free lodging with a student host or pay for a hotel for a second look visit, but plan to be responsible for your transportation to the school, an expense that may limit you to taking second looks only at the top couple of schools on your list.

Choosing a school

The factors that you consider when compiling a list of schools to apply to (discussed in Chapter 7) are many of the same ones that you'll be weighing as you make your final decision: the school's curriculum, cost, mission, size, location, and rank. However, at this stage, you have some additional information to work with that you probably didn't have when you put your list together, including the following:

✔ **A feel for the school's culture:** Is the environment at the school laid-back and easygoing or high energy and dynamic? An institution's personality is important and helps determine how well you fit in at a school.

✔ **The perspective of some of the school's med students:** Although you meet only a fraction of the med students at a school during your visit(s), speaking even briefly with someone attending the school gives you a student's view of the program, which is something that no amount of reading or researching on your own can substitute for.

✔ **Your financial aid package:** Send in your financial aid materials early, so that you (hopefully) have your package, or at least an estimate, by May. This information is essential in making a decision because institutional grants or scholarships may bring your cost of attendance down at a school that initially appeared to be a more expensive option. (Flip to Chapter 18 for details on paying for medical school.)

As you make your decision, look for the school that is the best fit for you, even if it's a program that isn't necessarily the highest ranked among those to which you've been accepted. Four years is a long time to spend anywhere, so aim to attend a school where you can be comfortable and happy.

Oh No! Suffering Rejections

Even the strongest applicants to medical school may receive rejections, so if you end up in this position, you're far from alone. However, you can turn this setback into a constructive piece of feedback if you assess your application to determine the likely reason for the rejection and then take steps to address your weaknesses. You may be able to improve your odds of admission for the current cycle if you act quickly; even if that isn't possible, though, you'll have a head start on making yourself more competitive for the next round in case reapplying becomes necessary.

Noting common reasons for rejection

When a rejection arrives, your first question is probably "Why?", especially if you feel that you put forth your best effort for every step of the application process. However, by stepping back and analyzing your application, you may be able to determine what happened and adjust your course while you still have time to affect the outcome of the cycle.

Among the common reasons for rejection are the following:

- ✓ **A low grade-point average (GPA) and/or Medical College Admission Test (MCAT) score:** Even if your overall GPA and MCAT are high, a subset where your numbers are noncompetitive — such as your science GPA or one section on the MCAT — may be enough to tank your application. (Check out Chapter 2 to find out the numbers you need to be competitive for MD and DO schools.)

- ✓ **Lack of clinical experience:** Even if you have a 3.9 GPA and a 35 on the MCAT, schools may question your commitment to pursuing this profession if your exposure to medicine is minimal. (Find out more about the importance of clinical experience, as well as where to get it, in Chapter 4.)

- ✓ **Weak letters of recommendation:** Letters of recommendation written by people who don't seem to know you well or who don't strongly endorse your application can hurt your cause. Even an average letter doesn't stand up when compared to the effusive letters many other applicants have. (Chapter 9 explains how to secure strong letters of recommendation.)

✔ **Poor interviewing skills:** You may have all the right qualifications to be granted an interview, but if you can't convince a representative of the school in person that you have the communication skills, motivation, and personal qualities needed to succeed in medicine, you're unlikely to get an acceptance.

✔ **Aiming for schools that are out of your reach:** If you're a middle-of-the-road applicant whose list is loaded with top-tier schools, you may end the cycle empty-handed. In Chapter 7, I discuss how to compile a list that lets you dream a bit while still ensuring you have plenty of realistic options.

If you've received a rejection from a school, contact the admissions office to see whether you can get feedback about your application. Although many schools only give feedback about applications after the cycle is over (if at all), some provide an immediate analysis of your application so that you know where you fell short.

Taking the next steps

Now that you've determined why you weren't admitted, the first priority is to focus on addressing issues that you can take care of for the current cycle. Some obstacles, such as grades and MCAT scores, take months or years to remediate, but you can make headway with other items more quickly:

✔ **Clinical experience:** Although clinical experience is something that you should ideally gain organically over a period of years, fitting in some in the short term to beef up your application is better than ignoring the problem. If you do take on some physician shadowing or hospital volunteering, update the schools on these new developments. (See the later section "Sending a letter of update" for more information.)

✔ **Letters of recommendation:** In the time that's passed since you submitted your letters of recommendation, you may have taken a course or started a new activity from which you can secure an additional letter. I cover submitting extra letters in more detail in the later section "Knowing what to do if you're waitlisted," but you don't have to hold off until you get to the waitlist; you can also send letters to schools you're still under consideration at. (Just make sure you check with each school first to see if they accept additional letters.)

✔ **Interview:** If you suspect that your interview performance was a weak point, work on perfecting your skills in this area prior to your next interview. If you haven't already done a practice interview, do one now. If you did go through a mock interview previously, revisit the feedback you received and do a second interview with a different advisor or mentor. Also, make a list of questions you had difficulty with during the interview and develop more effective answers to them; they may be asked somewhere else. For more tips about interview preparation, check out Chapter 10.

✔ **School selection for submission:** If you receive a slew of pre-interview rejections early in the cycle, you may have aimed too high; consider adding schools that are more reachable to your list. Although applying early in the cycle is ideal, a last-minute addition that is in your range may give you a better chance of admission than your early applications to more-selective schools does. Such a midcourse adjustment may allow you to start med school in the fall instead of repeating the grind of applying for one more cycle. (See Chapter 5 if you need help with dates in the application cycle.)

What Now? Working Your Way off Waitlists

After waiting to receive secondaries, waiting for interview invitations, and waiting to hear back from the schools about their decisions, the results are finally in, and your status is . . . waitlisted. This anticlimactic response is frustrating and disappointing, especially when it comes after months of hard work on your part. However, you're still in the game as long as you haven't been rejected. So instead of passively hoping that you'll be offered a place in the class, continue to work toward gaining admission into a program you're interested in, as I explain in the following sections, until the cycle is over.

Distinguishing types of waitlists

To understand how and why waitlists (also known as *alternate lists*) are used, keep in mind that the goal of each school is to ensure that its class is full and is composed of high-quality students. If a school accepted only exactly enough applicants to fill the number of spots in the class, it would find itself with empty seats in the fall because applicants holding multiple acceptances may choose to attend another school. Therefore, schools usually offer acceptances to more students than they can actually accommodate as well as place a group of applicants on a waitlist to draw from when an accepted applicant declines to attend the school.

The details of how a waitlist is structured and used differ from school to school; however, you can categorize waitlists into two broad types: ranked and unranked.

✔ A *ranked waitlist* is ordered so that the applicant at the top of the list is offered the first spot that opens up, and the school moves down the list to the next person when another place becomes available.

> ✔ With an *unranked waitlist,* the school draws from a pool of applicants when a seat opens up in the class. The decision about which applicant within the pool to select may be based on factors such as application strength and the need to create a balanced class in terms of diversity and experiences.

For you as an applicant, the advantage to an unranked list is that actions you take after the interview are more likely to influence your chances of selection because the order in which applicants are selected from ranked lists is largely predetermined. Therefore, by keeping the school apprised of your activities and your ongoing interest in the program, you may be able to influence the committee's ultimate decision.

Knowing what to do if you're waitlisted

After you find out that you've been waitlisted, check the admissions page on the school's website or contact the admissions office to find out whether you may submit additional information, updates, or letters of interest. After you determine what information a school accepts, sending an additional letter of recommendation, an update about your recent activities, or an expression of your interest in the school may benefit your application.

Skip the sparkly paper or other gimmicks in your correspondence with the school. Your goal is to convey professionalism to demonstrate that you know how to present yourself in your interactions with patients and healthcare professionals in medical school.

Adding a letter of recommendation

If you've participated in a new activity since submitting your application, such as a summer research project, a shadowing experience, or a community service project, consider getting an additional letter of recommendation from someone affiliated with the activity. This is especially valuable if your letters of recommendation were a weak point in your application or if the additional letter adds a different perspective to your existing ones.

As always, though, only ask for a letter if you're confident it'll be a strong one; a weak one may hurt your application rather than help it. See Chapter 9 for more about letters of recommendation.

Sending a letter of update

A *letter of update* is a means of apprising the schools of your activities since you submitted your application. You can send a letter of update pre- or post-interview; a good time to submit one is after finding out that you've been waitlisted.

Like a thank-you letter, you can send a letter of intent by either regular mail or e-mail. Check with the admissions office about the school's preferred means of communicating, and make sure you include your applicant ID number to ensure that the information you send is matched to your file. If you send the letter via e-mail, attach it as a PDF file instead of typing the letter into the body of the e-mail. A PDF has a cleaner, more formal format.

Keep the letter to no more than one page by focusing on the important points; admissions officers, who must read thousands of pages of application materials, generally value concise communication. After stating who you are and the purpose of the letter, summarize each of your recent activities, giving details such as the organization or individual you worked with, the dates the activity took place, and a description of your duties. In addition to new endeavors, discuss increased responsibilities or new projects you took on within existing activities reflected in your original package. In addition to updating the school about your activity, make sure that you discuss why you're interested in the school. Showing that you're a good fit for a program may help you to be selected when a spot opens up. See Figure 11-1 for an example of what a letter of update entails.

Submitting a letter of intent or interest

Schools are looking for applicants who are enthusiastic about attending their programs, so letting a school know how interested you are and why may help your case when the committee needs to make a decision about selecting someone off the waitlist. The two types of letters expressing interest in a school are a letter of intent and a letter of interest:

- ✔ A *letter of intent* is a letter stating that the school is your first choice and that you intend to matriculate at the school if you're accepted. You should therefore send a letter of intent to only a single school. Figure 11-2 shows a sample letter of intent.

- ✔ For other schools you're highly interested in, you send a *letter of interest*. A letter of interest indicates that you're very interested in a school but doesn't go so far as to state that the school is your first choice or top choice.

The two types of letters have many similarities: Both should express in specific terms why you want to attend the school, why the school is a good fit for you, and how you can contribute to the program.

If you have significant updates to your activities, the best approach is to send a letter of update (described in the preceding section) and to mention within the letter that you're very interested in attending the school or even that it's your first choice (if applicable), creating a hybrid letter of update/letter of interest or intent. You may then send another letter later in the cycle that focuses only on your interest in/intent toward the school.

December 3, 2013

Office of Admissions
Physicians Medical College
122 Residency Road
Radiograph City, FL 79764

Dear Admissions Committee:

I am currently waitlisted for admission at Physicians Medical College (PMC) and am writing to provide an update of the activities I have undertaken since submitting my secondary application in July. Since returning to college at Top Premedical University (TPU) in September, I have become more deeply involved in ongoing activities as well as undertaken a new volunteer position, all of which have been personally enriching as well as valuable in my continued preparation for medical school.

During the summer term at TPU, I completed English 201, "Literature of the Renaissance," in fulfillment of PMC's English requirement. I received an A in the class, as reflected on the attached transcript. While taking the course, I also worked full time as a research assistant in Dr. Stanley Scientist's laboratory, continuing my participation in a project focusing on antibiotic resistance in *Streptococcus pyogenes*. In October, I travelled with other members of the lab to the annual American Society of Bacteriology conference in New Orleans, Louisiana, where I presented a poster describing my research. Explaining my research to visitors helped me examine my work critically and analyze my approach to each step of the project.

In addition to continuing my research, I have also expanded my clinical experiences by undertaking a volunteer position at New Hope Center for Rehabilitation Medicine in Kirksville, Oregon. After learning about the specialty of Physical Medicine and Rehabilitation (PM&R) during a panel discussion sponsored by my school's premedical club, I contacted one of the speakers, Harriet Healer, MD, about opportunities to explore the field. Dr. Healer invited me to apply as a volunteer at New Hope where she practices; each week since October, I have been assisting the center's healthcare team members in their work with patients as well as shadowing PM&R physicians. I will be continuing my involvement with the center until graduation.

In addition to these activities, I have resumed my role as a peer health educator on campus and have recently been offered the position of program assistant, for which I am currently training. In this capacity, I will be helping to develop and implement education campaigns for health issues commonly affecting college-age populations. I am eager to complement the work I do counseling individual students with such larger-scale efforts.

I am confident that PMC is the ideal school for me and hope to be given the opportunity to join next fall's entering class. Among the reasons I strongly desire to attend PMC is the integration of clinical experiences throughout the curriculum, which would allow me to develop my patient care skills through all four years of medical school. My interest in medicine has been fueled by my interactions with patients as a volunteer; I would also be eager to participate in the PMC Student Run Clinic as well as other community outreach efforts. When visiting the city to interview at PMC, I experienced the rich diversity of the area served by PMC Medical Center, and as a student at your school, I would develop the skills to effectively care for patients from a broad spectrum of backgrounds. Seeing the school's state-of-the-art facilities, witnessing a problem-based learning session, and hearing the students speak about the superb education they receive further confirmed to me that I would be very fortunate to attend PMC.

I appreciate your continued consideration of my application.

Regards,

Samantha Student

Samantha Student
AAMC ID # 22211133

Figure 11-1:
A letter
of update
keeps the
school
apprised of
your latest
activities.

Illustration by Wiley, Composition Services Graphics

January 15, 2014

Office of Admissions
Elite University School of Medicine
122 Internship Avenue
University Village, WA 89573

Dear Admissions Committee:

I was very happy to receive your letter offering me a space on the waitlist for admission at Elite University School of Medicine (EUSM) and hope that I will be admitted to next fall's entering class. If I am accepted, I fully intend to attend. The opportunity to pursue the primary care track, research opportunities in public health and policy, and educational philosophy of the school are exactly what I am seeking. Further, I firmly believe that through my background and interests, I could contribute to the EUSM medical community.

I am particularly drawn to the school for the opportunity to participate in the primary care track. I have volunteered for more than two years in the practice of Dr. Wanda Wellness, a family physician, as well as at two community clinics providing primary care and am deeply attracted to this field of medicine. At EUSM, I would benefit from the exceptional preparation for this career path offered by the primary care track. I am excited about the chance the track offers for students to participate in the care of several families on an ongoing basis during the last two years of medical school. The opportunity to be matched with a faculty advisor in the area of primary care and to take electives geared toward students planning a career in primary care would be very valuable to me. I would also greatly look forward to participating in the Primary Care Interest Group and to share my experiences and learn from other students and mentors with similar interests and goals.

During my interview visit to EUSM, I learned more about the research requirement that is part of the school's curriculum. This requirement would offer me the chance to further explore two areas of interest to me: public health and health policy. I am especially interested in the work conducted by Dr. George Genius on the use of the "medical home" approach within federally funded community clinics and in Dr. Robin Researcher's studies on programs to address childhood obesity in immigrant communities. Working with these faculty members, or any of the many other EUSM professors studying related fields, would allow me to contribute to research in the areas of public health and healthcare delivery and develop the tools to engage in research as a future physician.

Meeting EUSM faculty, staff, and students on interview day reinforced to me that the school has a close-knit, vibrant medical community and an environment in which I would thrive. I was deeply impressed by the enthusiasm of the medical students about the school and their obvious camaraderie as a group. However, most important to me is the extremely high caliber of the education offered by EUSM. I know that by attending EUSM, I would have the opportunity to learn from faculty who are leaders in their fields, to participate in cutting-edge research, and to develop into a physician equipped to offer the highest quality care to patients. For these reasons, EUSM is unequivocally my first choice for medical school.

I am excited about the prospect of becoming part of EUSM's medical school community and hope to hear from you soon.

Regards,

Ursula Undergraduate

Ursula Undergraduate
AAMC ID # 22211133

Figure 11-2:
A letter of intent lets a school know that it's your first choice.

Illustration by Wiley, Composition Services Graphics

Part III

Osteopathic Medical Schools, Dual-Degree Programs, and More

Five Things to Do Before You Apply to Osteopathic Medical Schools

- ✔ **Find out about the philosophy, principles, and development of osteopathic medicine.** DO schools look for applicants who have taken the time to look into osteopathic medicine and have made an informed decision about applying to their programs.

- ✔ **Understand the similarities and differences between MDs and DOs.** Both DOs and MDs work as primary care physicians or specialists; the major difference between them is that DOs are trained to perform *osteopathic manipulative medicine* (OMM), also known as *osteopathic manipulative treatment* (OMT). OMM is a hands-on method of diagnosing and treating musculoskeletal disorders that isn't taught in allopathic medical schools but is a required part of the curriculum at DO schools.

- ✔ **Shadow an osteopathic physician (and try to get a letter of recommendation from him or her).** Shadowing gives you firsthand contact with someone in the profession and helps make you a more competitive candidate for DO schools.

- ✔ **Become familiar with the American Association of Colleges of Osteopathic Medicine (AACOMAS) application.** It includes sections for biographical information; a personal statement; work experience; extracurricular, volunteer, and community service activities; awards, honors, and scholarships; MCAT information; and colleges and course work.

- ✔ **Determine how to convey your interest in osteopathic medicine through your personal statement, secondary applications, and/or interviews.** Application materials for osteopathic schools should be tailored to these programs and convey the reasons you want to attend a DO school.

Discover how to answer the question "Why do you want to be an osteopathic physician?" on your applications and during interviews at www.dummies.com/extras/gettingintomedicalschool.

In this part . . .

✔ Find out about osteopathic medical schools and how they're similar to and different from allopathic medical schools.

✔ Undertake the application process for DO schools with special tips for the personal statement; the work, volunteer, and extra-curricular activities sections; letters of recommendation; and interviews.

✔ Check out baccalaureate-MD, MD-PhD, and other dual-degree programs. Dual-degree programs provide benefits such as the opportunity to complete two degrees in a shorter time than earning them separately typically takes, a broader educational experience, and, if the second degree is a graduate degree, potentially increased career options.

✔ Consider international medical schools. These schools may be an option for students who have application portfolios that aren't competitive for acceptance to either an MD or DO U.S. medical school; are competitive for admission to a DO U.S. medical school but not to an MD one and strongly prefer to attend an MD school; or have personal reasons for wanting to attend school in another country.

Chapter 12

Applying to Osteopathic (DO) Medical Schools

Getting an MD isn't the only way to become a physician. In fact, many physicians bear the letters *DO,* for "Doctor of Osteopathic Medicine," after their names. However, because the majority of physicians in the United States are MDs (allopathic physicians), many premedical students know little about osteopathic medicine, leading them to overlook schools that may be good options for their medical education. Although the approaches, philosophies, and curriculums differ somewhat between allopathic and osteopathic medical schools, the similarity between the two is even more important: Graduates of both types of programs are eligible to obtain medical licensure in the United States and work as practicing physicians.

This chapter contains information both for applicants who are just starting to consider osteopathic medicine and for those who are already committed to taking this path. I begin with a discussion about the field of osteopathic medicine, including the ways in which it's the same as and different from allopathic medicine. Next, I cover topics such as writing your personal statement for DO schools and preparing for osteopathic medical school interviews to help you put forth a strong application package if you decide that DO programs are the right fit for you.

Understanding What Being an Osteopathic Physician Means

According to the American Association of Colleges of Osteopathic Medicine (AACOM), the United States is home to more than 60,000 licensed osteopathic physicians, and more than 20 percent of current medical students are osteopathic medical students. Despite the ever-growing presence of DOs, many people, including premedical students, are unsure of exactly what a DO is, sometimes confusing these doctors with chiropractors or other types of alternative practitioners.

First and foremost, DOs are physicians, and both MDs and DOs are eligible to practice medicine in every U.S. state. However, as the following sections describe, osteopathic medicine has some distinctive approaches and philosophies in addition to allopathic education. By finding out more about osteopathic medicine, you can determine whether an osteopathic school is a good option for you.

Perusing the principles and philosophy of osteopathic medicine

The *osteopathic* approach includes a holistic view of patient care that addresses the physical, psychological, social, and emotional aspects of health and emphasizes the interdependency among the various systems of the body in the prevention, diagnosis, and treatment of disease. Some of the principles that underlie the osteopathic approach were promoted by Dr. Andrew Taylor Still, who founded the institution that eventually became the first osteopathic medical school.

Today, osteopathic physicians practice medicine in much the same way as allopathic physicians. Both DOs and MDs work as primary care physicians or specialists, diagnosing and treating patients as well as providing preventive care. However, the major difference between allopathic and osteopathic physicians is that DOs are trained to perform *osteopathic manipulative medicine* (OMM), also known as *osteopathic manipulative treatment* (OMT). OMM is a hands-on method of diagnosing and treating musculoskeletal disorders that isn't taught in allopathic medical schools but is a required part of the curriculum at DO schools.

Osteopathic medical students study OMM in addition to the subjects that all medical students must learn, such as physiology, anatomy, pharmacology, and clinical skills. OMM is an extra technique that DOs use in patient care if they choose. They're still fully equipped to use other diagnostic and treatment methods just as allopathic physicians are.

Osteopathic medical training also typically emphasizes primary care and service to medically underserved communities. However, as an osteopathic physician you can pursue any specialty you choose, so becoming a DO isn't synonymous with committing to primary care. You should be aware, however, that obtaining a residency position can be more challenging in some specialties if you're an osteopathic medical student; check out the later section "Getting a license as an osteopathic physician and matching into a residency" for more details.

Comparing and contrasting allopathic and osteopathic medical educations

The basic structure of MD and DO schools is the same. Typically, students complete two years of preclinical studies and then two years of clinical rotations, at which point they're awarded their degrees. After medical school, graduates of DO schools proceed through residency training, and perhaps a fellowship, before becoming attending physicians. (See Chapter 2 for a description of the steps of medical education and training).

Although most of the medical school curriculum is the same for both DO and MD students, as described in the preceding section, only osteopathic medical students study OMM. Another difference is that unlike most allopathic medical schools, many osteopathic medical schools don't have their own teaching hospitals. Students at these schools may need to travel to complete their clinical rotations at other institutions with which the school has an affiliation or agreement. In some cases, students may need to relocate during part or all of their clinical years because rotation sites are distant from the medical school.

At some osteopathic medical schools, rotations take place mostly at community hospitals or smaller teaching hospitals rather than at large teaching institutions. As a result, students may have the opportunity to work primarily with an attending physician instead of being lowest on a hierarchy that includes interns, residents, and fellows. The disadvantage is that the range of cases you see may be narrower than at a larger facility. You also may not receive as much exposure to the role of a medical resident if you're working primarily with the attending rather than as part of a larger team.

When you're exploring osteopathic medical schools, make sure you find out the location and type of facilities where students do their clinical rotations so that you can weigh this information as you make your decision.

Exploring osteopathic medicine

If you're considering applying to osteopathic medical schools, you need to go out and explore the profession in depth for yourself to determine whether it's right for you. Because medicine is dominated by MDs in terms of sheer numbers, finding out about osteopathic medicine takes some extra effort. To get started, check out the AACOM site at www.aacom.org. There, you can find information about osteopathic medicine as well as links to articles and other resources about osteopathic medicine and OMM. The American Osteopathic Association (AOA) site — www.osteopathic.org — is another useful resource for students interested in becoming DOs.

Shadowing an osteopathic physician gives you firsthand contact with someone in the profession and helps make you a more competitive candidate for DO schools. In some areas of the country, DOs are relatively uncommon, so finding a DO to shadow may take some perseverance. However, if you ask around, you may be surprised to find that you already know one or more DOs. One applicant I worked with only realized that her longtime family physician was a DO after she happened to look at his diploma on the wall! That quick bit of research led to a conversation with her physician about the osteopathic profession as well as to contacts with several of her doctor's osteopathic colleagues, whom she later shadowed.

In addition to checking with every physician you know, ask your premedical advisor, other premedical students, and anyone else remotely related to medicine if they know a DO they can put you in contact with. State and local osteopathic medical organizations, as well as osteopathic medical schools, also are good resources for leads about volunteer and shadowing opportunities with osteopathic physicians. The AOA website offers a database to help you "Find a DO" at www.osteopathic.org/osteopathic-health/find-a-do/Pages/default.aspx.

Like MDs, DOs practice in specialties as well as in primary care, so plan to volunteer or shadow with DOs in several different fields to get a broad view of the profession. Try to include different practice settings such as hospitals, community clinics, and private practice so that you can observe the responsibilities of a DO in various clinical environments. Check out Chapter 2 for tips about making the most of a physician shadowing experience.

Getting a license as an osteopathic physician and matching into a residency

All 50 U.S. states grant medical licenses to osteopathic physicians. Like graduates of allopathic schools, osteopathic medical school graduates must pass a series of licensure examinations as well as complete one or more years of residency training per the requirements of the state medical board in order to obtain a medical license.

The Comprehensive Osteopathic Licensing Examination of the United States (COMLEX-USA) is analogous to the United States Medical Licensing Examination (USMLE) I describe in Chapter 2. The COMLEX has three levels:

- Level 1 covers the basic sciences and is usually taken after the second year of medical school.

- Level 2 consists of two parts: Level 2-Cognitive Evaluation (CE) and Level 2-Performance Evaluation (PE). These levels are usually taken during the fourth year of medical school.

- Level 3 tests knowledge in the clinical sciences and is typically taken after the first year of residency.

COMLEX Level 1, Level 2-CE, and Level 3 are computer-based tests. Level 2-PE is a clinical skills test. DO schools usually require their students to take the COMLEX, but some DO students choose to take the USMLE as well in order to be more competitive for certain allopathic residency programs.

More information about the COMLEX-USA is available at the National Board of Osteopathic Medical Examiners site at www.nbome.org.

Although osteopathic physicians are eligible for medical licensure throughout the United States and in many foreign countries, some foreign countries don't recognize osteopathic physicians (or do but grant them only limited practice rights). This lack of recognition can present a problem for students who want to practice in a foreign country at some point in their medical careers, although there's a global trend toward increasing practice rights for osteopathic physicians. If you envision practicing internationally and are considering osteopathic schools, research the policies pertaining to osteopathic physicians in the country in which you're interested.

Osteopathic medical school graduates have two options for residency training: AOA-accredited residency programs and Accreditation Council for Graduate Medical Education (ACGME) accredited residency programs. To apply for an AOA-accredited (osteopathic) residency program, fourth-year DO students participate in the AOA Intern/Resident Registration Program, also known as the AOA Match. Because DO residency programs don't have enough places to accommodate DO graduates, many osteopathic students choose to participate in the National Resident Matching Program (NRMP) match to apply for ACGME-accredited (allopathic) residencies.

Some allopathic residency programs favor graduates of MD schools, so if you're an osteopathic student applying to MD residencies, focus particularly on programs that have a history of accepting DOs into their programs. You can make yourself a more competitive applicant by working hard to distinguish yourself during medical school through your grades, letters of recommendation, board scores, and by doing rotations at institutions with residency programs you're interested in to make connections there.

Note that changes are underway regarding accreditation of residency and fellowship programs. Currently, some programs are AOA-accredited, others are ACGME-accredited, and still others are dually accredited. The AOA and the ACGME are working toward a single accreditation system for all graduate medical education programs in the United States with a proposed implementation date of July 2015. If you're interested in osteopathic medicine, make sure you keep up with the changes by checking the AOA site listed in the preceding section on a regular basis.

Making the Decision to Apply to DO Schools

One of the decisions you need to make as a medical school applicant is whether to focus only on MD schools or DO schools or to include both types of programs on your list. For some applicants, whether a program leads to an MD or DO is of little importance; they apply to whichever schools provide them with the best chance of admission. For others, the distinction between DO and MD is critical, and they strongly prefer one type over the other. By exploring both allopathic and osteopathic medicine and evaluating your educational preferences and career goals, you can determine whether you're a better fit at one type of program or another.

If you plan to apply to osteopathic schools, you need to ensure that you're a strong candidate for these programs by demonstrating a genuine interest in osteopathic medicine and an understanding of its underlying principles and philosophy. DO schools are looking for applicants who have taken the time to look into osteopathic medicine and have made an informed decision about applying to their programs.

The following sections help you consider the osteopathic route and set yourself up to be a strong applicant for DO schools if you choose to take it.

Determining whether osteopathic medicine is right for you

Premedical students have different reasons for applying to osteopathic medical schools. Some have been exposed to osteopathic medicine early on, decided they like the osteopathic approach to medicine, and planned from the outset to apply to DO schools along with, or rather than, MD schools. However, other premedical students start out focused solely on allopathic schools but realize they may not be competitive for admission to these schools and investigate DO schools as an alternative. These students may have little familiarity with osteopathic medicine and sometimes decide to apply to DO schools at the last minute after minimal investigation of the profession.

Although a hasty decision can have a happy ending, doing your research long before you plan to apply is much less risky; you can assess whether osteopathic programs are a good fit before jumping into the admissions process. Some questions to ask yourself as you decide whether to pursue admission to DO schools are

- ✔ Have I thoroughly researched osteopathic medical education? Do I believe I would be happy at an osteopathic medical school?

- ✔ Do I understand how MDs and DOs are the same and different?

- ✔ Have I spoken with osteopathic physicians to understand potential benefits and drawbacks to being a DO?

Students interested in primary care are sometimes more comfortable pursuing osteopathic degrees knowing that attaining a residency in these specialties is less competitive and that DO schools tend to emphasize primary care.

The decision to apply to DO schools isn't one that you make in a rush. If you think there's even a small chance that you're interested in applying to DO schools, start investigating them at least a year before you plan to apply. As you look into osteopathic medicine, keep an open mind, consider what you want from a medical education and career, and then make the choice that's best for you.

Becoming a strong DO applicant

Applicants who show that they've thoughtfully explored osteopathic medicine and whose goals and interests in medicine align with what DO schools offer are most competitive for osteopathic programs. Schools can usually tell when an applicant has applied to DO programs only as an afterthought, because his clinical experiences, his letters of recommendation, and other elements of his application reflect that he's had minimal or even no exposure to osteopathic medicine.

Some of the ways in which you can make yourself a strong candidate for admission to an osteopathic school are by doing the following:

- ✔ **Shadowing or volunteering in settings with osteopathic physicians:** Not only does spending time with DOs allow you to determine whether you're a good fit for osteopathic medicine, but it also demonstrates to DO schools that you've invested time and effort in exploring the field.

- ✔ **Obtaining a letter of recommendation from a DO:** A very small number of osteopathic medical schools require a letter of recommendation from an osteopathic physician. Even for schools that don't require a DO letter, having such a recommendation is an asset to your application.

- ✔ **Doing community service in underserved areas:** As I note in the earlier section "Perusing the principles and philosophy of osteopathic medicine," many DO schools are committed to training physicians who will work in rural or other underserved areas. Students who volunteer in underserved areas demonstrate a commitment to serving those in need.

- ✔ **Writing a personal statement and secondary applications that reflect a specific interest in osteopathic medicine:** Application materials for osteopathic schools should be tailored to these programs and convey the reasons you want to attend a DO school. (For tips about writing a personal statement for DO schools, check out the later section "Creating a compelling personal statement for DO schools.")

Taking these steps helps make you competitive for admission to an osteopathic school; however, like allopathic schools, osteopathic schools also evaluate your academic record and MCAT scores when making admissions decisions. As Chapter 2 indicates, data from the AACOM placed the average MCAT score of DO students entering med school in 2011 at just over 26.5 and the average GPA slightly below 3.5. The most competitive applicants for DO schools present a well-rounded application that demonstrates academic preparation, exploration of the field, and excellent interpersonal skills.

Undertaking Applications for Osteopathic Medical Schools

The application process to osteopathic medical schools is similar to that for allopathic schools, and much of the guidance I give in Part II of this book for primary applications, secondary applications, and interviews applies to both MD and DO applicants. However, as an applicant to osteopathic medical school, you also need to understand the details of the application process to

DO schools and make sure that your application materials and preparation for interviews are directed toward these programs. Your goal as you compile your application is to show DO schools that you have the background, motivation, and preparation needed to make a great osteopathic medical student.

Getting an overview of the AACOMAS application

As Chapter 8 describes, you can use three different primary application services. Most osteopathic medical schools use the American Association of Colleges of Osteopathic Medicine Application Service (AACOMAS). However, like allopathic public medical schools in Texas, the Texas College of Osteopathic Medicine uses the Texas Medical and Dental School Application Service (TMDSAS) as its primary application.

The AACOMAS application includes sections for

- Biographical information
- A personal statement
- Work experience
- Extracurricular, volunteer, and community service activities
- Awards, honors, and scholarships
- MCAT information
- Colleges and course work

The AACOMAS application may be submitted beginning in early June, and you should aim to complete your application as close to then as possible. Most osteopathic medical schools use *rolling admissions,* which means they evaluate applications as they receive them. The timeline in Chapter 5 gives you guidance about scheduling tasks related to your application so that you can complete the process while many seats in the class are still available.

If you're also planning to apply to MD schools, you fill out the American Medical College Application Service (AMCAS) application as well. One way to handle the deluge of work that comes with filling out multiple primary applications is to handle the one for the group of schools (DO or MD) that's most important to you first. The basic information the various primary applications ask for is the same, so the second primary goes more quickly than the first, but you should modify your personal statement in terms of both content and length for each to tailor it to the particular application.

Creating a compelling personal statement for DO schools

Instead of simply discussing your interest in medicine in general, an effective personal statement for osteopathic schools demonstrates that you're familiar with osteopathic medicine and are an excellent fit for the profession. Chapter 8 provides strategies for writing a strong personal statement for both MD and DO schools. In addition, here are some examples of specific topics and themes to include in the osteopathic personal statement:

- ✔ Experiences with osteopathic medicine, such as physician shadowing or volunteering

- ✔ An interest in caring for patients holistically, in preventive care and maintaining wellness, and/or in other aspects of the osteopathic approach to medicine

- ✔ A desire to work with underserved populations or an interest in primary care

- ✔ Personal qualities or experiences that make you suited to practice osteopathic medicine

This list gives some ideas to get you thinking; however, you should discuss elements from your own background in the personal statement, tying them in with your interest osteopathic medicine. Don't just try to write what you think the committee wants to hear. If you profess an interest in primary care, for example, but don't have the experiences to back up that claim, your personal statement may well come across as weak. You may even end up in an awkward position during the interview if you're asked to discuss your supposed passion for primary care in more detail. The best personal statements are reflections of the individual who writes them, so stick to discussing only what you can support and would be happy to elaborate on in an interview setting.

If you use your AMCAS statement as the foundation for your AACOMAS one, make sure that you do more than simply cut back the length (the AACOMAS statement is 4,500 characters, including spaces, compared with 5,300 characters, including spaces, for AMCAS). If you don't say a word about osteopathic medicine in your statement, DO schools may wonder how interested in the profession you really are. You can draw from your AMCAS statement when discussing your interest in medicine, but modify it by weaving in themes related to osteopathic medicine and your reasons for applying to DO schools.

Checking out a sample DO personal statement

Take a look at the following sample personal statement for an example of a statement that will leave the committee convinced that this applicant is a great candidate for a seat at its osteopathic medical school:

> *As a kid, I tried all the usual sports: soccer, baseball, basketball. I enjoyed each for a while, especially the camaraderie of being part of a team, but nothing really clicked until I discovered running. I loved the simplicity of it; no balls, bats, or nets stood between me and the sport. Watching a physician performing OMM, I was instantly reminded of the pureness of running; OMM was a technique that required only the use of a physician's hands. However, while my goal as a runner was to shave a few minutes off my best time, this doctor's aim was to improve his patient's quality of life. Observing the physician working to alleviate the patient's chronic back pain, I felt the same "This is it" certainty about osteopathic medicine that I did when I slipped on my shoes for my first cross country race.*

> *I am especially drawn to osteopathic medicine for the "whole patient" approach to care practiced by DOs, which I first observed during a summer internship program after my freshman year. Each two-week block, premedical students rotated through a different department of the hospital, shadowing physicians and doing volunteer work. Over the course of the summer I helped check patients into the emergency room, observed in the operating room, and accompanied ward teams on rounds. By the last block, all that remained was obstetrics and gynecology, a field I was eager to experience. I was fortunate to be matched with Dr. Harris, an osteopathic ob-gyn. Dr. Harris allowed me to accompany her both in the hospital and in her practice, giving me a behind-the-scenes view of her job. To my surprise, watching the doctor interact with her patients in her office impacted me as much as the drama of the delivery room. Prenatal visits were not just a matter of going through a checklist of questions to make sure that the mother and baby were physically well. Dr. Harris also inquired about family members and hobbies, stress levels, and sleep habits in a way that encouraged patients to communicate openly with her. Although she was a specialist, her approach was anything but narrow. Her example resonated with me, confirming my decision to pursue an osteopathic medical education.*

> *Community service experiences complemented my clinical exposure, helping me understand both the satisfactions and challenges of serving others. For the past three years, I have volunteered at the Central Mission Shelter as a tutor for clients living in transitional housing. Although most of my tutees are children, one of the most memorable students I worked with was Ana, a 22-year-old mother struggling to pass her GED test. Coming from a background that included poverty and domestic violence, she seemed to expect defeat as the end result of her efforts. Over months of working with her,*

I learned that listening to her fears and celebrating small victories was a vital part of the lesson plan, and slowly we made progress. When Ana called me with the news she had passed, I was thrilled to hear the happiness and confidence in her voice. I know that as a physician I would receive the same deep gratification from helping my patients maintain and improve their health that I did from assisting Ana in achieving this success.

I also appreciate that medicine allows its practitioners to develop relationships with others in the context of a field grounded in science. After trying to choose between biochemistry and history for a major, my decision to pursue both allowed me to meld the sciences and humanities in my education. As I juggled classes in two very different disciplines, I sometimes questioned the wisdom of my decision, but I made it work: I found an on-campus job to eliminate the commute time my previous position required, and I cut out extracurricular activities that weren't truly important to me. As a result of my unusual mix of majors, I received an education that taught me to view issues from multiple perspectives and developed discipline and time management skills that will be invaluable as I take on the challenge of medical school.

Throughout college, I have continued to run almost every morning. I miss the breathless chats with my high-school teammates during my treks, but running alone allows me to relax and let my thoughts drift. During these moments, I often consider the future. With great enthusiasm, I envision becoming an osteopathic physician so I may someday provide holistic, compassionate, high-quality care to a diverse group of patients.

Analyzing the example

By starting off with an anecdote about observing OMM, this applicant makes it clear from the outset that he has a specific interest in osteopathic medicine. Using running as an analogy allows him to inject one of his interests into the first paragraph, making the discussion more personal. He goes on to demonstrate that he's explored medicine through a summer internship, focusing on his interactions with an osteopathic physician in order to illustrate why he's chosen to apply to DO schools.

After establishing his interest in osteopathic medicine in the first half of the statement, he spends the second half showing how his nonclinical experiences have helped prepare him for medical school and shaped him as an individual. He uses the discussion of volunteering in the shelter in the third paragraph to show that when he commits to a cause, he sticks with it, and that he understands that helping others isn't always easy or quick. He then reveals his ability to handle a heavy workload in the paragraph about his double major by mentioning that he balances school with a job. The mention of his major also serves to remind the committee that he offers something different as an applicant because he has both a liberal arts and a science background. In the last paragraph, he returns to the topic of running, this time using it as a device to conclude the essay with a look toward the future and his enthusiastic vision of himself as an osteopathic physician.

Completing the work, volunteer, and extracurricular activities sections

Coupled with the personal statement, the sections on the AACOMAS application in which you list employment, volunteer, and extracurricular activities allow the committee to understand what you offer as an applicant. For each entry, you provide the name of the organization and your position title, dates of involvement, hours per week, and total hours. In addition, you have 750 characters, including spaces, in which to describe the activity. Well-crafted descriptions tell the committee how you've spent your time outside of academics as well as how your experiences have prepared you for osteopathic medical school. When writing the descriptions, make sure you do the following:

- ✔ Clearly and concisely convey your responsibilities for a particular position or activity.

- ✔ Give some context about the activity, such as the type of clinical setting or the mission of an organization you volunteer with.

- ✔ Briefly reflect on what you learned or gained from an experience, especially if it contributed to your understanding of osteopathic medicine or motivation to become an osteopathic physician.

- ✔ Make it clear when an experience involved interaction with a DO. For example, instead of referring to an osteopathic physician as "Dr. Samuel Smith," say "Samuel Smith, DO" or "Dr. Samuel Smith, an osteopathic physician" the first time you refer to the doctor by name.

As you're writing each description, think about the how the activity adds to your overall application portfolio. Does it show how you've investigated osteopathic medicine? Or that you've demonstrated leadership skills or another personal quality? Doing so allows you to determine which aspects of an activity to focus on in the very limited space you're given for each one.

Mastering the interview at osteopathic schools

Preparing for an osteopathic medical school interview requires that you be ready not only to tackle typical interview questions such as "Why do you want to be a physician?" but also to handle questions about topics related to osteopathic medicine. Along with the common questions asked by both MD and DO schools (refer to Chapter 10 for a list), questions you may encounter during osteopathic medical school interviews include the following:

✔ Why are you interested in osteopathic medicine?

✔ How have you explored osteopathic medicine?

✔ What makes osteopathic medicine different from allopathic medicine?

✔ What do you know about the history of osteopathic medicine?

✔ What are some of the principles of osteopathic medicine?

✔ What is osteopathic manipulative medicine?

To get ready for questions designed to determine how familiar you are with osteopathic medicine, do some reading about the history of osteopathic medicine, its tenets, and what it means to be a DO today. You don't have to become an expert on osteopathic medicine, but make sure that you know enough to discuss these topics intelligently with an interviewer and that you can clearly articulate your reasons for applying to DO schools. If you're in contact with an osteopathic physician, see whether he's willing to do a practice interview with you and ask him to focus especially on questions specific to osteopathic medicine.

Applicants applying to both allopathic and osteopathic medical schools are sometimes concerned about how to respond if asked whether they've applied to any MD programs; they're afraid DO schools won't take them seriously if they reveal that they're also looking at allopathic schools. However, many successful applicants apply to both types of schools; interest in MD schools doesn't discount you as a candidate for osteopathic programs. If faced with this question, answer honestly and then discuss what you're looking for in an individual medical school. Many factors that attract students to particular institutions, such as a collaborative learning environment, a focus on problem-based learning (see Chapter 7), or a reputation for good teaching aren't exclusive to DO or MD schools. If you happen to be applying solely to DO schools, let your interviewers know that if possible, but if you're casting a wide net, don't worry. DO schools are aware that most applicants' priority is becoming a physician; the particular type, MD or DO, is secondary.

Although preparing for DO-centric questions is important, don't neglect to prepare for questions about issues in medicine, your background and experiences, and other likely general interview questions. Your interviewer may only ask a quick question or two about osteopathic medicine, and you still need to be ready for all the other types of questions he may throw at you.

Chapter 13

Exploring Dual-Degree Programs

- -

- -

*D*ual-degree, joint degree, and *combined degree* programs all refer to pro-grams that allow students to earn both a medical degree (MD or DO) as well as a bachelor's or graduate degree through an integrated program. Dual-degree programs provide benefits such as the opportunity to complete the two degrees in a shorter time than earning them separately typically takes, a broader educational experience, and, if the second degree is a graduate degree, potentially increased career options.

Note: The discussion of baccalaureate-MD programs in the first part of this chapter is geared toward high-school students considering a career in medi-cine. Premedical students who have already started college should head to the second half of the chapter, where I describe other types of dual degree programs: MD-PhD, MD-Master of Public Health (MD-MPH), MD-Master of Business Administration (MD-MBA), and a combined medical and law degree (MD-JD). With an idea of what's out there and what getting admitted takes, you can determine whether you're suited to a program that leads to an MD or DO plus more.

 If you're interested in a program that offers early admission to medical school but aren't ready to commit before entering college, Early Assurance/Early Acceptance Programs offered by some schools may be a good option. You can apply to these programs during your first, your second, or sometimes early in your third year of college for assured admission to a medical school after you finish your undergraduate studies.

Considering a Baccalaureate-MD Program

Most students interested in medicine follow the traditional route of applying to medical school during or after their undergraduate studies. However, if you're still in high school and already sure you want to be a physician, you also have the option of pursuing your baccalaureate and medical degrees through a combined baccalaureate-MD (bacc-MD) program. Acceptance into a bacc-MD program means you've secured not only a seat in an undergraduate institution but also provisional acceptance into a medical school. Attending a bacc-MD program can take some of the uncertainty out of being a premedical student and may shave a year or two off the usual eight-year time frame required to earn both a bachelor's degree and an MD.

Either option — applying to college and medical school separately or going through a bacc-MD program — will ultimately get you to the same place. However, for some students a bacc-MD is the preferred choice. In the following sections, I introduce you to bacc-MD programs, describe how to apply, and discuss what makes applicants competitive for admission to these highly selective programs.

Some osteopathic medical schools offer bacc-DO programs. Check out the *Osteopathic Medical College Information Book* from the American Association of Colleges of Osteopathic Medicine (AACOM) for a list. For a list of bacc-MD programs, see the Medical School Admission Requirements (MSAR) guide.

Examining the mechanics of a bacc-MD program

Baccalaureate-MD programs last from six to eight years. The first two to four years usually focus on undergraduate course work, although in some programs elements of the medical school curriculum are integrated throughout the program. Accelerated (six- or seven-year) programs are year-round and/or allow some of the medical school course work to count toward undergraduate requirements, letting you complete what is normally eight years of academic work in six or seven years. The pace isn't quite as intense in an eight-year program because students spend four years in their undergraduate studies and four years in medical school, which is the same amount of time earning each degree alone takes. Eight-year programs therefore provide a more typical premedical student experience and generally give greater latitude in course choices compared with shorter combined programs.

Signing on to a bacc-MD program doesn't necessarily mean you're at the same institution for your entire education. In fact, the undergraduate and medical school components of the program often take place at different institutions. One factor to consider when choosing a bacc-MD program is whether you prefer to move on to a new place to attend medical school or settle in at one institution for the long haul.

When you're accepted to a bacc-MD program, your admission to the medical school may be provisional. The school guarantees a seat for you in its affiliated med school as long as you hold up your end of the bargain. For example, you may be required to maintain a minimum GPA during the undergraduate component of the program and/or achieve a certain minimum score on the Medical College Admission Test (MCAT). The criteria for advancement vary significantly among programs, and some don't require students to take the MCAT at all.

Recognizing the advantages

Bacc-MD programs are highly selective because they offer some significant benefits when compared with the usual path from high school to med school. These perks may include the following:

- ✔ **The opportunity to complete college and medical school in fewer than eight years:** Six- and seven-year programs save participants one or two years of time as well as cut down on educational costs.

- ✔ **A reserved seat in medical school:** As noted in the previous section, to matriculate into the medical school portion of a joint program, you may have to meet particular requirements as an undergraduate. However, your place is still more assured than that of your peers who are several years from even applying for admission to med school.

- ✔ **The luxury of needing only a minimum score on the MCAT or avoiding the test completely:** The possibility of skipping the MCAT is a major draw for some students. Studying for the MCAT can be a major drain on your time, and not having to take it frees you up to pursue other interests and eliminates one of the biggest stressors premedical students face. Some bacc-MD programs that do require the MCAT set the bar relatively low, requiring that students score only in the high 20s to advance to med school. (A typical score for traditional med school acceptance is more like a 31.) Note that the minimum MCAT score for bacc-MD programs varies, though; for some, you need a 30 or even slightly higher. You need to hit whatever mark the school sets, but doing so may require much less time spent studying and worrying about doing your absolute best just to be competitive.

✔ **Freedom from worrying about how your choices for classes and activities will look to med school admissions committees:** You can pursue your interests knowing that you won't have every grade, activity, and choice of class picked over by admissions officers in a few years' time. You still need to do well in your courses to prepare for medical school (and to meet any GPA requirements set by your program), but going from a 3.7 to a 3.6 doesn't create a crisis the way it may seem to for your premed friends.

✔ **Early clinical exposure and access to specific volunteer, research, and other activities for students in the program:** Some programs integrate patient contact into the program as early as the first semester. In addition, many bacc-MD programs offer medically related volunteer positions, seminars, workshops, and/or research opportunities for their students.

Determining the drawbacks

When considering bacc-MD programs, you can easily get swept up by the thought of skipping the MCAT or cutting a year or two off the time you spend in school. However, having a realistic view of combined programs is critical so that you can make the best decision for the long run. Here are some of the potential drawbacks of bacc-MD programs:

✔ **Fewer options for classes and majors at some programs:** Some programs have limitations on the major you may pursue or leave little leeway for you to make your own choices regarding course selections. Accelerated programs in particular may require you to follow a fairly strict schedule so that you can complete your undergraduate studies in less than four years.

✔ **Complications if you decide to leave the program before completing your undergraduate degree:** Six- or seven-year programs may not award the undergraduate degree until after the first or second year of medical school because they count some preclinical medical school courses toward completion of a BA or BS. This situation means that if you decide you don't want to complete the entire program, extracting yourself may be more complicated than at an eight-year program. You have to determine which classes count as undergraduate credits and what additional courses you may need to take to get a bachelor's degree at your current institution or another one.

✔ **Strict rules about where you can apply to med school:** At some programs, a student forfeits provisional admission to the program's med school if she decides to apply to other medical schools. This policy puts a bacc-MD student who realizes that she may prefer another medical school that isn't part of the combined program in a tough position: Stick with the school that's the sure thing, knowing that it's not ideal for her, or relinquish her reserved seat to take her chances as an applicant. Before committing to a bacc-MD program, check its policy to find out whether you can hold onto your guaranteed seat if you decide to apply to outside med schools.

✔ **A compromise in the undergraduate institution or medical school that you attend:** Finding the perfect college or med school is hard enough, so it's no surprise that going to a program that combines the two may require you to compromise on one or the other. For some students, reaping the benefits of a bacc-MD is worth giving up a little in terms of school choice. However, if you're having serious doubts about either the undergrad or med school affiliated with the program, you may be better off attending the college of your choice and applying to medical schools on the regular timetable I outline in Chapter 5.

When you enter a bacc-MD program, there's the risk that you won't hit the benchmark GPA and/or MCAT score that may be required to advance into the medical school portion of the program. If you choose a college primarily because it's part of a bacc-MD program rather than because you truly want to attend the school and then you don't end up advancing to the medical school component, you've compromised on your choice of college without receiving the hoped-for reward. Weigh the risks and benefits carefully as you consider bacc-MD programs to minimize the chance that you'll have regrets if you don't end up going all the way through the program.

Applying to Baccalaureate-MD Programs

To gain admission to a bacc-MD program, you need to do two things: Build a strong application portfolio during high school and present your application package effectively. In the next sections, I familiarize you with the steps to take to make yourself a competitive applicant as well as when and how to put together a strong application so that you give yourself the best chance of becoming a dual-degree student.

Discovering how to be a strong contender for bacc-MD programs

Applying to a bacc-MD program means you're trying for admission to a college as well as to a medical school, so the factors that bacc-MD programs look for are a combination of what undergraduate programs and medical schools seek in their future students.

A strong academic record and superb test scores are essential to be a competitive applicant. Admissions committees consider both how rigorous your high-school classes were and how well you performed in them. Take the most difficult courses you can handle, such as Advanced Placement or International

Baccalaureate classes, and focus especially on building a strong foundation in the sciences. You need to be able to not only manage your rigorous course load but also excel in your classes. The minimum GPA required to apply is typically a 3.5 (unweighted), but for many programs, you need a significantly higher GPA to be competitive.

For the SAT, the minimum score required for application to some programs is 1200 total for the critical reading and math sections; for others it's 1300 or even higher. Some schools have a SAT minimum score that includes the writing section as well and/or require SAT subject tests in math or science. Some programs accept the ACT and often set the minimum score for it at 30. Upon checking a school's admission statistics, you may find that the test scores for accepted applicants are much higher than the minimum needed to apply.

Bacc-MD committees also consider nonquantitative factors when making admissions decisions. By exploring medicine through clinical experiences you can assure the committee (and yourself!) that your decision to become a physician is an informed one. You can obtain clinical experience during high school by volunteering in hospitals and clinics and shadowing physicians. Clinical or *basic* (lab) research experiences are valuable as well. (Chapter 4 has tips on gaining clinical and research experience.)

Programs seek students who demonstrate maturity, integrity, commitment to service, excellent communication skills, flexibility, and other qualities that are desirable in a future medical student and physician. Therefore, letters of recommendation should not only attest to your achievements but also describe your personal traits and character. Pick teachers, counselors, and other evaluators who know you well enough to discuss you as a person, not just as a student. Your application essays and interview also help schools get to know who you are and whether you'd be a good fit for the program.

Surveying the bacc-MD application process

The application process for bacc-MD programs typically requires you to submit these items:

- ✔ The *Common Application* (a standardized college application that's filled out by a student one time and can be submitted to multiple schools) or other application for the undergraduate institution
- ✔ A supplemental application for the baccalaureate-MD program
- ✔ High-school transcripts
- ✔ Standardized test scores (SAT or ACT)
- ✔ Letters of recommendation

Many programs don't consider an applicant for admission to the bacc-MD program until she's accepted into the undergraduate institution. At some schools, applicants don't even receive the bacc-MD supplemental application until they've been offered admission to the undergraduate institution.

A bacc-MD committee reviews applications from individuals who have been accepted into the undergraduate program, and a small number of applicants are invited to visit for an interview. (See the later section "Interviewing for bacc-MD programs" for more information.) Following the interview, the committee makes a decision about whether to admit, deny, or waitlist the applicant. (This general outline of the admissions process applies to many programs, but each bacc-MD has its own process.)

Handling supplemental essay questions

As a combined program applicant, you have to write the typical college application essays as well as craft responses for essay prompts on the bacc-MD supplemental application. These prompts often address topics such as

- ✔ Your reasons for wanting to participate in a baccalaureate-MD program
- ✔ The nature of your interest in a particular institution
- ✔ Why you've chosen to pursue a career in medicine
- ✔ Your exposure to the medical profession

Other supplemental questions may not be directly related to medicine or the program but instead focus on topics such as your extracurricular activities, challenges you've faced, or your strengths and weaknesses. Many of the tips in Chapter 8 about writing a strong medical school personal statement also apply to creating compelling essays for bacc-MD programs.

Interviewing for bacc-MD programs

After you've been offered an interview for a bacc-MD program, you're much closer to admission, but you still face stiff competition from other highly qualified applicants. Use the interview as an opportunity to stand out by conveying your interest in medicine and suitability for the program as well demonstrating good interpersonal skills.

You may be interviewed by members of a medical school admissions committee or joint baccalaureate-MD committee depending on how the school structures its admissions process. Either way, the interview usually takes place at the medical school rather than at the undergraduate campus. During interview day, you can expect to take a tour of the campus, learn more about the program, and interview with one or more committee members.

Wear professional attire to the interview and treat every moment from the time you step on the campus until the time you leave as part of the interview process. You want to make the best impression possible with your whole visit. (Chapter 10 provides details about dressing for success as well as general tips about interviewing.)

A bacc-MD interview lies somewhere between a college interview and one for medical school in terms of the types of questions asked. You can expect to be asked about your extracurricular activities and academic experiences in high school the way a regular college applicant would, but you also face questions related to your interest in medicine. Common baccalaureate-MD interview topics include

- ✔ Why are you interested in a baccalaureate-MD program?
- ✔ What motivates you to become a physician?
- ✔ Why did you apply to our particular program?
- ✔ Describe your involvement in clinical, community service, and leadership experiences.
- ✔ What would you contribute to the program if admitted?
- ✔ What qualities do you have that make you suited to the program?
- ✔ What careers other than medicine have you considered?

You're evaluated not only on the content of your responses but also on your communication skills, personality, professionalism, and other qualities. Programs want to be confident that the students they select can succeed academically and work effectively as part of a team as they interact with patients, fellow students, physicians, and other professionals. Your performance on the interview can help to demonstrate that you're both book smart and people smart.

Getting to Know MD-PhD Programs

Does your ideal job include going back and forth from lab bench to patient bedside? If so, you may be suited to a career as a physician-scientist, combining medicine with scientific inquiry.

The road to becoming a physician-scientist is a long one, but in the end you'll be equipped to pursue both your passion for medicine and desire to do research. One increasingly common way to get the credentials needed for a career as physician-scientist is by completing a joint MD-PhD program.

Obtaining both an MD and a PhD isn't absolutely required in order to become a physician-scientist, but it's become more common in recent years. However, a physician without a PhD may find landing a career position involving research more difficult when she's competing against the growing number of MD-PhDs. For those who opt to get both degrees, a combined program offers certain advantages, such as the ability to obtain the two degrees in less time and the opportunity for financial support during both the medical school and graduate school components at most programs.

After completing their educations and training in both medicine and research, physician-scientists often find positions in academic institutions or in industry and spend a significant amount of their time doing research. The balance between research and other duties varies among physician-scientists and may fluctuate at different points in a single person's career. Because physician-scientists frequently work in teaching institutions, they often divide their time among doing research; caring for patients; and teaching medical students, graduate students, residents, and/or fellows. The following sections introduce the physician-scientist's education and highlight some considerations for those thinking about this field.

Describing MD-PhD programs

MD-PhD programs are typically seven to eight years long. At most MD-PhD programs, students spend the first two years in medical school completing the preclinical curriculum alongside their peers in the regular MD program. While the rest the class moves on to the third year of med school, combined degree students enter the graduate school phase of their education. They spend the next three or four years doing research toward their doctoral thesis under the supervision of a faculty member. Some programs integrate clinical experiences into the graduate school phase to make the eventual transition back to medical school smoother.

After the research project is complete, students return to medical school for two years of clinical rotations. Students graduate with both MD and PhD degrees and then go on to residency, often followed by a fellowship.

Typically, MD-PhD students do laboratory rotations during the summers before and after their first year of medical school. By spending time in different laboratories, a student can determine where she wants to spend her graduate school years doing a research project for her PhD thesis. During the school year and/or summers, MD-PhD students may be required to attend seminars, retreats, or other events to discuss topics relevant to them as future physician-scientists in addition to their regular medical school courses.

What is an MSTP program?

You may hear of MD-PhD programs referred to as *MSTP* programs. MSTP stands for *Medical Scientist Training Program,* a designation given to programs that receive funding from the National Institute of General Medical Sciences (NIGMS) arm of the National Institutes of Health (NIH). There's a prestige factor attached to MSTP programs, but many non-MSTP MD-PhD programs are also excellent. MSTP programs usually cover a student's tuition for her entire education as well as offer a stipend for living expenses. Find out more about MSTP programs at www.nigms.nih.gov/ training/instpredoc/predocover view-mstp.htm.

Many MD-PhD programs provide students with both tuition and a stipend for living expenses. MD-PhD programs that aren't funded by the National Institutes of Health (NIH) support their students through institutional funds, faculty grants, and other means. The amount of funding offered by programs varies, so find out exactly what's being offered before you commit to a program. (For info on NIH-funded programs, check out the nearby sidebar.)

More information about MD-PhD programs and a list of programs is available at the Association of American Medical Colleges (AAMC) site: www.aamc. org/students/research/mdphd/.

Carefully considering MD-PhD programs

Students who are dedicated to a career as a physician-scientist, have strong academic and research backgrounds, and strongly believe that they need both degrees to achieve their career goals should consider MD-PhD programs. If you simply can't see yourself doing without either degree or you view the extra years of education as an opportunity rather than a burden, delve deeper into exploring the joint-degree option.

After looking at the amount of training required becoming a physician-scientist, though, some students decide to pursue either medicine or research rather than both. As you investigate your career options, make sure you speak directly with physician-scientists as well as explore both clinical medicine and research before making your decision. Students sometimes have a change of heart partway through an MD-PhD program and switch to either an MD- or PhD-only track. However, by exploring both your interests thoroughly before you enter a combined program, you can minimize the likelihood of having to change course later on.

The financial incentives offered to MD-PhD students are significant; however, they shouldn't be the driving force in the decision to apply. If the high cost of medical school has you tempted to talk yourself into doing an MD-PhD, stop and regroup. Financial motivation probably won't be enough to sustain you through the three or four research years planted halfway through medical school. In the long run, you may be better off finishing your education more quickly by getting an MD alone so that you're out making an attending physician's pay, even if you incur some debt along the way. Only pursue an MD-PhD if it's the path you truly want to follow, not as a means of subsidizing your medical degree. (See Chapter 18 for information about how to pay for medical school.)

Admission to MD-PhD programs is extremely competitive, so your decision-making process should involve a realistic assessment of your odds of admission. (The following section has details about admissions requirements.) If you aren't a strong applicant for an MD-PhD program, determine whether you're passionate enough about this path to work on improving your credentials or whether you prefer to apply to a single-degree program that may give you a better shot at acceptance.

Note: Some MD-PhD programs accept applications from first- and second-year medical students at their institutions. This policy provides an additional pathway to enter an MD-PhD program for students who didn't apply prior to medical school or who applied but weren't accepted. Whether this option is available at a particular institution may depend on whether spaces open up within the program.

Navigating the MD-PhD Admissions Process

The application process to MD-PhD programs is similar to that for medical school alone but with a few extra hoops to jump through, such as additional application essays and a more extensive interview process. However, that's understandable when you consider that you're being evaluated for admission to both graduate and medical school; the schools want to know as much as possible about you. You'll be part of the institution for at least the next seven years, so you and the program have to determine that you're a good fit for each other. The following sections take you through the application process, from deciding whether you're even competitive to tackling the application, essays, and interview.

Figuring out whether you're a competitive MD-PhD applicant

Some of the major factors that admissions committees consider when evaluate MD-PhD applicants are as follows:

- **Academic record and MCAT scores:** According to the AAMC, for 2012 matriculants into MD-PhD programs the mean GPA was 3.8 and the mean MCAT score was 34.5.

- **Research experiences:** Getting into an MD-PhD program requires you to have substantial research experience. In particular, programs look for students who have worked on their own projects and whose research is hypothesis driven. Being an author on a publication relating to your research isn't required, but it's an asset.

- **Motivation for entering a dual-degree program:** MD-PhD programs want to know that you have compelling reasons for desiring both an MD and a PhD.

- **Letters of recommendation, especially from research mentors:** Your research supervisors can attest to how you approach a research problem and your critical thinking skills, dedication, and ability to function effectively as a member of a research team.

- **Clinical experience:** Research experience is more important than clinical experience for MD-PhD programs, but schools also look for evidence that you've investigated patient care and spent time in clinical settings.

- **Personal qualities:** Maturity, integrity, and excellent communication skills are among the characteristics that are important in both clinical and research settings. Letters of recommendation, the interview, and your essays allow committees to determine whether you have the non-academic qualities that are important for a future physician-scientist.

Going through the application process for MD-PhD programs

At most schools, the basic steps for applying to either the regular MD or the MD-PhD program are the same:

1. **Submit an American Medical College Application Service (AMCAS) application.**

   On the application, you designate whether you're applying to the regular MD program or the MD-PhD program at a particular institution.

2. **Submit a secondary (supplemental) application.**

3. **Go through an interview process.**

Chapters 8 through 10 discuss these steps in detail, and most of the information there applies to MD-PhD applicants as well as those aiming for admission to medical school only. Like regular MD programs, MD-PhD programs require that you take the MCAT.

The major differences in the application requirements for MD-PhD programs are

> ✔ **Two additional essays (the MD-PhD essay and the significant research experience essay) on the AMCAS application**
>
> ✔ **A requirement for one or more letters of recommendation from researchers who have supervised an MD-PhD applicant's work**
>
> ✔ **A more extensive interview process for MD-PhD programs than for regular MD programs**

Keep reading for details on the extra essays and the rigorous interview process.

At some programs, the medical school admissions committee reviews your application before sending it to the MD-PhD admissions committee for evaluation. At other schools, MD-PhD applications are handled by a separate committee throughout the process.

Gearing up for additional application essays

MD-PhD applicants must write a total of three application essays for the AMCAS application: the personal statement, MD-PhD essay, and significant research experience essay. Together, these essays should convince the committee that you're dedicated to a career as a physician-scientist, that you understand what it means to be both a physician and a researcher, and that you have the characteristics to be successful in the program and beyond.

The personal statement is the same as the one you write for traditional med school admission; I cover it in Chapter 8. The MD-PhD essay provides you with the opportunity to explain to programs why you want to pursue a dual-degree program. The length limit is relatively short: 3,000 characters, including spaces, so you need to focus on only a few important points. As you're writing the MD-PhD essay, ask yourself, "What can an MD and a PhD together provide me with that either degree alone can't?" MD-PhD programs often look for students whose focus is on *translational research*, a term that refers to basic science investigation translating into applications in medicine. Think about how going from bench to bedside and back will give you a unique perspective that will allow you to turn findings in the lab into advances in the diagnosis and treatment of patients.

The significant research experience essay allows 10,000 characters, including spaces, for you to discuss your research background. In this section, you're required to provide basic information, such as the name of your research supervisor and the institution where you conducted the research. You also describe each experience, making sure that you not only explain each project but also discuss the scope of your responsibilities. Having this space to dedicate to your research means that you don't need to try to cram all the details about your research experiences into the other two essays, freeing you up to use those areas in part to discuss other topics that give greater breadth to your application portfolio.

You may discuss your interest in research in the personal statement as well, but that shouldn't be the only focus of the statement. Your application may be evaluated both by members of the medical school and by MD-PhD admissions committees, and med school admissions committee members in particular are going to be looking for evidence of your interest in medicine, not just research.

Interviewing for MD-PhD programs

If your application is very competitive for an MD-PhD program, you'll be invited to interview at the school. During the interview process, the admissions committee can discern more about your motivation for wanting to earn dual degrees, discuss the details of your research experiences with you, and determine whether you'd fit in as a member of that MD-PhD community. Your mission is to use the interview to demonstrate that you'd be an asset to the program and that you're qualified to spend your career at the cusp of scientific inquiry and medical practice.

Getting an overview of the interview visit

MD-PhD interview visits usually last for two days and involve the following:

- **Four to eight interviews with admissions committee members:** At some programs, you interview with the members of the medical school admissions committee one day and with the members of the MD-PhD committee the next.

- **Informal interviews/meetings with faculty members whose research you've expressed interest in:** Prior to an MD-PhD interview, you may be asked to select which faculty members you want to meet with during your interview visit.

- **Social events with faculty and students:** These stops may include meet and greets with faculty members, evenings out with students in the program, and other activities designed to help you get to know the MD-PhD community in a more relaxed setting.

- **A campus tour, talks by members of the admissions office or faculty, and/or the chance to sit in on a medical school class**

One notable difference between interviews for regular MD and MD-PhD programs is that for the latter, the program sometimes pays for at least some of your interview expenses. Some programs reimburse visiting students for their hotel rooms and provide most of their meals; others also pick up the tab for plane tickets. Programs may also offer to cover certain expenses for a revisit later on if you've been offered admission and are making a decision about where to attend.

Preparing for an MD-PhD interview

To get ready for an MD-PhD interview, you should take the steps outlined in Chapter 10 as well as a few additional ones. Most importantly, you need to know your research very well. Be ready to explain the question your work was attempting to answer, your approach to the problem, and the results and potential implications of your findings. You should also expect to be challenged about issues such as why you used a particular approach or how you solved challenges that arose. The committee members know you don't have a graduate degree yet, but they expect you to be able to discuss your research and related topics in detail.

In addition to brushing up on the details of research you've done you should also spend time reading up on the work of faculty members with whom you know you have an interview or meeting.

Although important, research certainly isn't the only topic your interviewers cover. Chapter 10 provides a list of questions that may be asked at either a regular MD or an MD-PhD interview. Here are some additional topics commonly addressed during an MD-PhD interview:

- ✔ Why are you interested in an MD-PhD program?
- ✔ What is the role of a physician-scientist?
- ✔ If you had to choose between an MD and a PhD, which degree would you select?
- ✔ What areas of research interest you?
- ✔ What are your career goals as a physician-scientist?
- ✔ Which scientific journals do you read?
- ✔ Describe a journal article you've read recently.

To make sure you're a good match at the program, use the interview visit to gather information. When it's your turn to ask questions during your encounters (formal, informal, or social) at the school, you may want to ask questions such as

- ✔ How are research experiences integrated into the medical school portion of the program?

✔ What patient contact, if any, do students have during their graduate school years?

✔ Why did you choose this program?

Eyeing Other Types of Dual-Degree Programs

In an era where the practice of medicine demands skills drawn from multiple disciplines, dual degrees with varied fields have become increasingly popular. In addition to the baccalaureate-MD and MD-PhD programs I introduce earlier in the chapter, a variety of other options exist, including those that combine medical degrees with a master's degree or law degree.

MD-MPH and MD-MBA programs are among the most common types of MD-master's programs. Both are typically five years long; often the majority of the work toward the master's degree comes during a one-year period after the second year of medical school. Students may choose to pursue a combined MD-master's program in order to prepare for a career in public health, healthcare administration, or healthcare policy. Others obtain a second degree in order to gain a broader perspective on the practice of medicine or to be able to deliver healthcare to their patients more effectively.

Applicants for MD-MPH or MD-MBA programs are usually considered by the medical school admissions committee first and, if admitted, evaluated for admission to the master's program. Some schools don't accept applications for the MPH or MBA portion until a student is in the first or second year of medical school.

MD-JD programs lead to degrees in both law and medicine. Programs are typically six years, one year shorter than the seven you'd need to complete both an MD and JD separately. The application process for these programs can be very intensive, requiring you to take the MCAT as well as the Law School Admission Test (LSAT) and go through the entire admissions process at both the institution's medical school and law school. Some MD-JDs practice medicine and law concurrently, devoting part of their time to each profession, while others integrate their skillsets through a single position such as medical malpractice attorney or healthcare administrator.

The option to combine a medical degree with a graduate degree isn't limited to MDs. Some osteopathic medical schools offer dual-degree programs including DO-PhD, DO-MPH, and DO-MBA. Check out the list of osteopathic dual-degree programs in the *Osteopathic Medical College Information Book* as well as the websites for individual osteopathic medical schools.

Chapter 14

Investigating International Medical Schools

In This Chapter

▶ Deciding to attend an international school

▶ Making sure you thoroughly examine a potential international school

▶ Introducing popular international study locations

▶ Revealing the obstacles of licensure and residency matching for international graduates

Schools outside the United States are options for those who want to become physicians but who are unable to gain entry to a U.S. medical school or who have other reasons for desiring to study internationally. However, variability in the quality of education among international schools, potential difficulty in getting into a U.S. residency training program, and other issues associated with attending school abroad make this path one that you should only undertake after careful consideration.

In this chapter, I focus on researching international schools, discuss some of the details about medical education in the more popular international locations, and describe the process international graduates go through to become licensed to practice medicine in the United States.

Schools in the specific countries I discuss throughout this chapter aren't the only options for international medical schools. Students from the United States also attend programs in Mexico, Israel, Italy, and numerous other countries. Some of these programs approach medical education in a similar way as U.S. schools; others require fluency in a foreign language or have significant differences in curriculum structure when compared with U.S. institutions. The particular country you focus on may be guided in part by your comfort with the culture, a language you speak, or familiarity with the country. However, when considering a school in any foreign country, your first priority should to be the quality of education offered and whether you'll be qualified to obtain a U.S. medical license at the end of your medical training.

Considering Reasons to Apply Internationally

For some students, an international medical school is the only means to realize their goal of practicing medicine. They may have GPAs and/or Medical College Admission Test (MCAT) scores that aren't competitive for U.S. medical schools and may have tried to be admitted to a U.S. school without success. However, not all international applicants lack other options; some choose to attend an international school for reasons such as having a tie to another country or a personal desire to study and live abroad. This section discusses reasons students may have for making the decision to apply internationally, as well as some of the potential pitfalls of being an international medical student.

The surest route to practicing medicine in the United States is to graduate from a U.S. medical school. However, for students who are determined to become physicians but can't obtain a place in a U.S. school, an international program may allow them to realize their dream of practicing medicine. Students for whom international schools may be a potential option include those who

- Have application portfolios that aren't competitive for acceptance to either an allopathic (MD) or osteopathic (DO) U.S. medical school. These students prefer to move forward with their medical training more quickly than would be possible if they took time to strengthen their credentials for U.S schools. Some applicants are particularly concerned that they may invest time and money into attempting to remediate their academic records, raising their MCAT scores, and reapplying to U.S. schools and still not be successful in gaining admission to a school in the United States.

- Are competitive for admission to an osteopathic U.S. medical school but not to an allopathic one and strongly prefer to attend an allopathic school. Flip to Chapter 12 for info about the osteopathic option.

- Have personal reasons for wanting to attend school in another country. Some applicants have dual citizenship or have family members in another country and want to attend school there. Although most U.S. students who attend an international medical school plan to return to the U.S. to practice, a small number intend to practice in another country and prefer to obtain their medical educations there.

The success of students who study internationally varies as much as the reasons they chose for studying abroad do. Some international students receive high-quality educations, thrive on living in another country, and match into residencies in their specialties of choice. Others receive substandard educations and/or are unable to obtain residencies in the specialties they desire — or in some cases, any residency at all — and are unable to become licensed in the United States. To minimize your odds of a negative outcome, you must do meticulous research and assess your own potential for success in medical school prior to making the decision to apply internationally.

Selecting International Schools

You should carefully investigate any med school programs you're considering; however, meticulous research is especially important if you're interested in international schools. Allopathic medical schools in the United States and Canada are accredited by the Liaison Committee on Medical Education (LCME), which ensures that schools meet specific standards for everything from faculty qualifications and curriculum to facilities and student services. U.S. osteopathic schools are accredited by the Commission on Osteopathic College Accreditation (COCA).

An international school may be accredited by its home country, but that doesn't mean that country has standards for medical education that match those of the United States. Therefore, if you're considering attending medical school abroad with the intent of returning to the United States to practice, you need to ask more questions and do deeper research than you would for a U.S. school. Most important is to determine which schools provide the credentials you need to eventually become licensed to practice medicine in the United States. If you graduate from an accredited U.S. medical school, you can be confident that state medical boards in the U.S. will recognize your degree. The same isn't true of every international school.

Beyond these basics, you need to figure out what various international schools offer in terms of preclinical curriculum, clinical rotations, facilities, financial aid, and many other factors. Some of these considerations are items that you'd need to address when choosing a school in the United States, while others, such as what language instruction is conducted in, are concerns that only apply to international schools. Knowing where to look for information as well as what questions to ask allow you to determine whether attending an international school is right for you and which program is the best choice.

Researching international schools

By gathering information from different sources regarding international schools, you can get a broad perspective of a school's strengths and weaknesses. Here are some sources to start with:

- ✔ The *International Medical Education Directory* (IMED): International medical students and graduates must receive certification from the Educational Commission for Foreign Medical Graduates (ECFMG) in order to enter a residency program and become licensed to practice medicine in the United States. To meet ECFMG requirements, you must be a graduate of a school listed in the IMED. Check the IMED (`https://imed.faimer.org`) to make sure that the schools you're considering are listed. (Flip to the later section "Residency Training and Licensure for IMGs" for more about the medical licensure process.)

- ✔ The *WHO World Directory of Medical Schools:* The World Health Organization (WHO) collects data submitted by individual countries, which it uses to compile a list of medical schools. Inclusion in this directory indicates that a medical school has been recognized by a country; however, note that the WHO doesn't accredit or approve schools. The WHO World Directory of Medical Schools is located in the AVICENNA database maintained by the University of Copenhagen at `avicenna.ku.dk/database/medicine`.

- ✔ Individual schools: Carefully read the websites and other informational materials provided by individual schools and then speak with a representative to ask additional questions that you have about the program. (The following section provides a list of questions to include.) Also, ask that the rep put you in contact with alumni who are practicing medicine in the United States as well as U.S. students attending the program. These individuals can give you a firsthand view of what being a student/graduate of the program is like.

You may have more difficulty gathering information about programs in countries that have fewer U.S. students and alumni than you do for ones in more "popular" countries (such as the ones I address later in the chapter), but persevere until you have good evidence that a school is going to serve its purpose for you.

Visit an international med school you're considering at some point before you commit to attending it. Many international schools conduct interviews by phone or video conferencing or do regional interviews in the United States. Although that approach saves you money and time during the interview process, you don't get to see the school as part of your interview experience. I've had multiple students relate stories of arriving on a Caribbean island to start med school and immediately realizing that they wouldn't be happy living in the area or that the school's facilities were smaller or shoddier than expected. Some stayed and stuck it out; others started the program but left within weeks or months. For the cost of a plane ticket and accommodations, you can avoid the potential difficulty and wasted tuition of starting a program that you don't finish because you're unhappy with the school or the living conditions.

Asking the right questions

To gather the information you need about an international medical school, you must know what questions to ask. Among the critical questions you want to obtain answers to are the following:

✔ When was the school established?

✔ What language are classes conducted in?

✔ What are the qualifications of the faculty?

✔ Do clinical rotations take place in the U.S. or abroad? At which facilities?

✔ What percentage of students who matriculate into the program graduate?

✔ What's the school's passing rate on the United States Medical Licensing Examination (USMLE)? What's the average score on the USMLE Step 1? On the USLME Step 2 Clinical Knowledge?

✔ What percentage of students entering the National Resident Matching Program (NRMP) matched into a residency spot?

✔ Is the list of residency programs that graduates from the past several years have entered available for me to see?

✔ What assistance does the school give to students who don't match into a residency?

✔ What support services are available to students?

✔ Will I be eligible to do a residency and obtain licensure in the United States with a degree from this school?

✔ Which state medical boards have approved the school?

✔ Will I be eligible for U.S. federal financial aid if I attend this school?

✔ What are the living conditions in the area?

✔ Can you connect me with alumni and students from the school?

I provide more guidance on what kinds of answers you should be looking for on these topics throughout the chapter.

Contemplating Caribbean Medical Schools

Caribbean medical schools are popular choices among U.S. students who attend an international program. The admissions requirements for Caribbean schools vary, but overall, gaining admission to these schools is much easier than it is for U.S. medical schools. For this reason, a Caribbean school may offer a route to becoming a physician for students whose academic records, MCATs, or other factors make them noncompetitive for U.S. schools. Some of the more established Caribbean schools report average MCAT scores of 26 to 27 and average GPAs of 3.3 to 3.4. Other Caribbean schools have average numbers that are significantly lower or don't require the MCAT at all.

Some students are also attracted to Caribbean schools because the application process is quicker than for U.S. schools. You have to apply to each school separately because no centralized application service exists for Caribbean schools. However, the applications aren't typically as long and involved as they are for U.S. schools; you may be able to start med school within a few months of submitting your application. Additionally, Caribbean schools have more options for start dates. Unlike U.S. schools, which accept students for fall entry only, some Caribbean schools admit new students for the spring and summer terms as well. This greater flexibility may be especially attractive to students who have applied to medical school multiple times and are eager to start their medical education as soon as possible.

Caribbean schools typically conduct classes in English and structure their programs the same way many U.S. medical schools do: two preclinical years followed by two clinical years. One advantage some Caribbean schools offer over many other international programs is that students spend only the preclinical years outside the United States. For these programs, after two years of medical school in the Caribbean, students do clinical rotations at U.S. hospitals with which the school has an affiliation. In addition to cutting down on the amount of time you live outside the U.S., doing clinical rotations at U.S. institutions provides benefits in terms of securing a residency position. During your rotations, you have the chance to get letters of recommendation from U.S. attending physicians as well as to make connections at the hospital's residency training program.

You may have to move frequently during your clinical years if you're a Caribbean medical student rotating in the United States because the hospitals your school has agreements with may be scattered throughout the country. All that relocating can be difficult, especially for students with families. To give students the option of staying in a single location for most of their third year, some Caribbean schools have established affiliations with a hospital or group of hospitals in one geographic area. Make sure you ask about the locations of rotations and how often students typically need to move during the clinical years.

Among the best-known, most-reputable Caribbean schools are a group sometimes known as the Big Four: Ross University, St. George's University, American University of the Caribbean, and Saba University School of Medicine. You can find many other Caribbean schools that encompass a wide range of quality of education, reputation, and success of their graduates.

Although living on a Caribbean island may sound like paradise, some students have a difficult time adjusting to their new environment. Depending on the island on which the school is located, you may have far fewer options than you're used to having for everything from grocery shopping to healthcare. You may miss the amenities that come with living in the United States or simply feel homesick living in a foreign country with a different culture and customs. You can't know for sure ahead of time exactly how you'll feel after you relocate, but if you're having significant trepidation about the idea of moving to the Caribbean for medical school, you may want to rethink the viability of attending school outside the United States.

Courting Canadian Medical Schools

Canadian medical schools offer a medical education similar to that of U.S. medical schools in terms of structure and quality. In fact, a major benefit Canadian schools offer over other international medical schools is that Canadian schools are accredited by the LCME, the same agency that accredits U.S. medical schools. (See the earlier section "Selecting International Medical Schools" for more about LCME accreditation.) If you attend a Canadian medical school, for the purposes of applying to residency programs and getting a U.S. medical license, you won't be considered an International Medical Graduate (IMG). That means that you don't have to take any special steps such as getting ECFMG certification before applying to residency or becoming licensed. You'll also be viewed the same way as your counterparts who attend similarly ranked U.S. schools when vying for residency positions. Canadian medical schools therefore offer an opportunity for students from the United States to obtain their medical educations in a different country without confronting the drawbacks of being an international medical graduate.

This description may make Canadian medical schools sound like a perfect option; however, like U.S. medical schools, medical schools in Canada are highly competitive in terms of admission. Some applicants enter the U.S. admission cycle thinking that they'll apply to Canadian schools as a backup in case they don't get into a U.S. school. The reality, though, is that Canadian schools are at least as selective as U.S. schools.

Canadian schools should be considered an alternative to U.S. schools for highly qualified applicants, not as a fallback plan. Apply to Canadian schools if you have a genuine desire to attend medical school in Canada, but check out the other options mentioned in this chapter if you're seeking schools that are easier to get into than U.S. schools.

Only a small number of Canadian medical schools consider applications from individuals who aren't citizens or permanent residents of Canada. Some schools that admit non-Canadian applicants are McMaster University, McGill University Faculty of Medicine, and University of Toronto. To gain admission as an international applicant requires a very strong application portfolio. If you decide to throw your hat into the ring for Canadian schools, note that most have school-specific applications, although schools located in the province of Ontario use the Ontario Medical School Application Service (OMSAS).

Mulling Medical Schools in the United Kingdom, Ireland, and Australia

U.S. students choosing to obtain their medical degrees abroad sometimes opt for schools in the United Kingdom, Ireland, or Australia. Because these are English-speaking countries, you don't encounter a huge language barrier, and U.S. students may feel comfortable in these countries because the living conditions and cultures are relatively similar to that of the United States.

Medical schools in the United Kingdom, Ireland, and Australia may be either undergraduate entry or graduate entry.

- *Undergraduate entry* courses are intended for students coming out of high school and are five to six years long.

- *Graduate entry* programs are similar to U.S. medical schools in that they're intended for students who have completed their undergraduate studies prior to matriculation. Graduate entry programs are sometimes tailored specifically to international students because the traditional pathway to medical school in some of these countries is through an undergraduate program following high school.

Some medical schools in these countries accept MCAT scores; others require another admissions test such as the UK Clinical Aptitude Test (UKCAT) or the Graduate Medical School Admissions Test (GAMSAT). Check with each school regarding its specific admissions requirements such as course work, GPA, and admission tests.

The Atlantic Bridge program provides a centralized application through which U.S. and Canadian students can apply to six Irish medical schools. Information is available at www.atlanticbridge.com/

Noting Financial Considerations for International Medical Students

Paying for medical school is an issue on the minds of both U.S. and international medical students. If you need financial aid to pay for medical school, make sure you check to see whether the schools you're considering are eligible for participation in the Direct Loan Program. (For a description of this program and other forms of financial aid, see Chapter 18.) The U.S. Department of Education National Committee on Foreign Medical Education and Accreditation (NCFMEA) determines whether the standards a country uses to accredit its medical schools are comparable to those used by accrediting agencies for U.S. medical schools. Only if a country is determined by the NCFMEA to meet this criteria of comparable standards can schools accredited by that country be eligible to apply for participation in the Direct Loan Program.

The NCFMEA page at the U.S. Department of Education's site at www2. ed.gov/about/bdscomm/list/ncfmea.html provides more details for students trying to determine which schools are eligible for participation in the Direct Loan Program. If the school you plan to attend doesn't participate in the Direct Loan Program, you may need to rely on private educational loans to pay for most of your medical school and living expenses.

As an international student, you may be eligible for some scholarships, but others are restricted to students of U.S. schools only, so check the requirements carefully for any scholarship program you're considering applying to. Like U.S. schools, some international schools offer institutional aid such as scholarships and grants, but others don't or do but restrict institutional aid to citizens of their own country. Work with the financial aid office at your future school and do your own research to make sure you have a solid plan for financing your medical education before you matriculate.

Incurring debt may be necessary in order for you to attend medical school internationally. However, be aware that some students end up in the very difficult position of carrying significant medical school debt and not being able to practice medicine because they were unable to finish their degrees, couldn't pass their licensure exams, or couldn't obtain a residency position. If you're considering an international medical school because you faced academic difficulty in college and may not be competitive for admission to a U.S. school, you need to develop a plan for how you'll build the study skills required to succeed in completing medical school abroad and navigate your way through exams, residency, and licensure so you'll be able to practice medicine in the end.

Tackling Licensure Guidelines and Residency Training for IMGs

Even before you enter an international medical school, you should be thinking beyond graduation to what you'll have to do to achieve your ultimate goal of practicing medicine in the United States. As described in Chapter 2, obtaining a U.S. medical license requires more than just having a medical degree. In addition, you must also pass all sections of the United States Medical Licensing Examination (USMLE) and complete one or more years of residency training (specific requirements are established by each state's medical board). International students must receive ECFMG certification prior to applying for residency programs, a process mentioned briefly earlier in this chapter and described in more detail in the following sections.

As a student at an international school, you face a particular challenge in matching into a residency. Despite this obstacle, many IMGs are successful in getting into residency training and become licensed physicians providing primary or specialty care in the United States. The following sections familiarize you with some of the issues facing international students and graduates applying for residency programs or licensure in the United States.

Understanding licensure challenges for IMGs

According to data from the National Board of Medical Examiners (NBME), the Step 1 passing rate in 2011 for first-time examinees from allopathic U.S. and Canadian schools was 94 percent. For international graduates taking the test for the first time, the passing rate was only 73 percent. Although this disparity is concerning for students contemplating attending an international school, note that this data doesn't separate U.S. citizens and permanent residents (U.S. IMGs) from other international graduates. Non-U.S. IMGs may face additional obstacles to passing the exam, such as experiencing language barriers or having been out of medical school for years and therefore not being as fresh on the material as a U.S. IMG following the typical timeline, and their scores may negatively skew the results.

Because a good score on the USMLE Step 1 makes you much more competitive for residency programs, make sure that you find out not only about a school's passing rate but also about the average score for its students on this part of the examination. (See "Asking the right questions" earlier in this chapter for a list of other questions to ask when you're looking into international schools.)

ECFMG certification is also required in order for graduates of international medical schools to be eligible to train in an Accreditation Council for Graduate Medical Education (ACGME) accredited residency program. To become ECFMG certified, an IMG must provide documentation showing that he has

✔ Passed the USMLE Step 1, Step 2 CK, and Step 2 CS

✔ Graduated from a medical school listed in the *International Medical Education Directory* (IMED)

✔ Been granted credit for at least four credit years by a school included in the IMED

More information about ECFMG certification as well as other services provided by the ECFMG for medical students and graduates of international schools is available at www.ecfmg.org.

In some states, only students and graduates of approved medical schools are eligible to participate in residency training or to obtain licensure in the state. Check with the individual state boards to discover which schools are on the approved list for a state as well as to find out about the state's specific licensure process.

Landing a residency

One of the biggest concerns international medical students have is whether they'll be able to get into a residency program, which is required in order to become licensed to practice medicine in the United States. To obtain a residency position, you apply to residency programs along with students at U.S. medical schools and take part in the National Resident Matching Program (NRMP) during your fourth year of medical school. (Flip to Chapter 2 for more details about the match.)

Being a student at an international school can place an applicant at a major disadvantage to students attending U.S. medical schools, and match rates are significantly lower for students and graduates from international medical schools than for their U.S.-educated counterparts. For this reason, you absolutely must check the track record of any international school you're interested in to find out its graduates' success in obtaining residencies. You should also plan to apply broadly and strategically to residency programs and be aware matching into more-competitive specialties may be extremely difficult if you attend an international school.

Some residency programs are more open to IMGs than others. When you're arranging for elective rotations in the specialty you're considering pursuing, focus especially on institutions that have programs with a history of training IMGs. This way, you can make connections at programs that you have a chance of matching into rather than at ones that don't seriously consider applications from international graduates. Check to see which programs past graduates at your school have been accepted to and speak with your school for guidance about which programs are most accessible for IMGs.

The difficulty of obtaining a residency is likely to become greater as U.S. medical schools continue to increase in size and number without a corresponding increase in the number of residency positions. (Chapter 2 discusses the growth of the number of seats in U.S. medical schools in recent years.)

The "Data and Reports" section of the NRMP site (www.nrmp.org) provides statistics about the results of the main residency match, including the number of residency positions offered through the NRMP in specific specialties as well as the percentage of students from various categories (for example, U.S. students, U.S. IMGs, and non-U.S. IMGs) who matched. Spending some time going through this information allows you to make a more informed decision about attending medical school internationally. Keep in mind, however, that your individual chances may be greater or lower than average because success in getting a residency depends on myriad factors in addition to the school you attended, such as your performance in medical school and your score on the USMLE Step 1.

Part IV
Nontraditional Applicants, Reapplicants, and Disadvantaged Applicants

Five Steps to Take Before You Reapply to Medical School

- **Evaluate your application to identify weaknesses.** The timeline for your reapplication strategy may be relatively short or stretch over one or more years depending on the reasons you were rejected initially.

- **Retake the MCAT and/or strengthen your academic record if your numbers weren't competitive.** A too-low MCAT score can doom even an otherwise-superb application, and if either your overall or science GPA isn't up to par, getting admitted to medical school is going to be extremely difficult or even impossible.

- **Add new clinical or research experiences to your portfolio.** By doing so upon reapplication, you have strong evidence of your exploration of the medical field.

- **Revamp your personal statement.** Do a significant amount of fresh writing, and emphasize your achievements and growth since the last time you applied; be sure to discuss how they've further motivated or prepared you for a medical career.

- **Revisit your list of schools to ensure it's realistic.** If you were very selective about your school list the last time you applied, consider rethinking your approach to increase your odds of admission. You may also want to consider osteopathic schools (if you focused on MD schools before) to see whether they'd be a good fit for you.

Contemplate making a career change to become a physician in an article at www.dummies.com/extras/gettingintomedicalschool.

In this part . . .

- Address issues facing nontraditional applicants, such as the difficulty of returning to school, finding a peer group, and facing stereotypes.

- Improve your odds of admission as a reapplicant by bettering your GPA, upping your MCAT scores, revisiting your list of schools, and updating your personal statement and letters of recommendation.

- Look at a variety of opportunities for minority and disadvantaged applicants.

- Take on the medical school application process with a disability.

Chapter 15

Doing Things Differently: Nontraditional Applicants

Not every future physician goes straight from high school to college to medical school with only a summer break between each step. Some applicants take a windier road to medicine and may have pursued other careers, established families, and gained life experience before considering a career as a physician. These applicants bring maturity, experience, and determination to their premedical aspirations; however, they also face challenges such as returning to school after many years, juggling outside responsibilities along with their studies, and feeling like the odd one out among the mostly younger students in their classes.

In this chapter, I provide tips for nontraditional applicants as they make the switch to medicine, complete their premedical course work, and prepare for the application process. Finally, I address obstacles facing nontraditional premedical and medical students.

Getting an Overview of Nontraditional Applicants

The term *nontraditional applicant* encompasses a broad range of people that defy a single description (see the nearby sidebar for details). However, nontraditional applicants fall roughly into several groups:

- ✔ **Career changers:** *Career changers* are established professionals who are making the switch to medicine after pursuing another career. Career changers are from fields as diverse as engineering, teaching, and art. Those who come from a science field are usually a step ahead in making the change to premed because they've already completed some or even all of the core science courses needed for entry to medical school, whereas those coming from nonscience backgrounds may be starting from scratch.

- ✔ **Late deciders:** Some students don't begin to consider medicine as a career until their last year or two of college. By then, they may not be able to fit some or even any of the premedical classes into their schedule and graduate on time. Instead of delaying graduation to accommodate two years' worth of science classes, such a student may opt to graduate as planned and then go back to school fairly soon after as a post-bac student to take her premedical course work.

- ✔ **New/reentry students:** Applicants in this group may have spent time working, serving in the military, and/or raising a family before attending college. Some of these students didn't have the opportunity to attend college at all earlier in life and are now beginning college as freshmen. Others started college following high school but left before completing their degrees and are now returning to school with renewed focus as a premedical student.

Members of each group face particular advantages and challenges. Recent graduates may have an easier time returning to school because they're still in student mode. Although they haven't had the chance to spend significant time in the workforce earning income as older nontraditional students have, they also generally don't have the level of financial obligations that many older students have. Professionals with a degree in the sciences have the benefit of having already completed some premedical course work; however, if their grades in these courses were low, they may need to take additional classes to raise their science GPAs, whereas someone who hasn't attended college previously is starting with a fresh slate. I discuss the challenges of nontraditional applicants in more detail later in the chapter.

The evolving definition of "nontraditional"

According to a 2011 AAMC survey, half of incoming medical students took one or more gap years between college and medical school. Now that taking time off before med school is so common, students who take a year or two to work, take additional course work, and/or volunteer prior to medical school aren't generally considered nontraditional based on that alone. Although there's no hard-and-fast definition that determines who is considered a nontraditional applicant, some examples of applicants who are more likely to be viewed as nontraditional are those who have taken three or more years between college and medical school, are switching to medicine from another career, or have served in the military. Also, even a student who goes straight to medical school following college may be considered nontraditional if she didn't go directly from high school to college but instead spent time working, serving in the military, raising a family, or doing something else before starting her undergraduate studies.

Completing or Updating Premedical Course Work

Preparing academically for medical school as a nontraditional student can range from starting from scratch with the prerequisite course work to jumping straight into more-advanced science courses to further strengthen an already-solid science foundation. The ultimate goal is to gain the credentials you need to get into and succeed in med school, but you can accomplish that goal in a lot of different, equally valid ways. The way you approach your premedical course work largely depends on your previous background. As I indicate in the preceding section, some nontraditional applicants switch to the premedical track with most or all of their prerequisite course work already completed, while others have yet to take a single science class. However, even those nontraditional applicants who already hold a science degree may benefit from taking additional courses in order to refresh their knowledge of core science subjects or gain recent academic experience before applying to med school. The following sections run the gamut from getting in all your course work now to beefing up a decent existing record.

Doing the prerequisite course work required for medical school

A nontraditional student who hasn't completed her bachelor's degree needs to attend college as an undergraduate to obtain her prerequisite course work and get her degree; in this way, she's similar to a traditional applicant. However, those who already have a bachelor's degree but lack the core science classes have several options for obtaining these requirements:

- ✔ **Attend a premedical post-baccalaureate program designed for career changers.** These programs are tailored to applicants who already hold a college degree but have completed very few or none of the courses required for admission to medical school. (Check out Chapter 3 for details about career-changer post-bac programs.)

- ✔ **Take the needed courses independently.** By taking classes on your own as a post-bac through a local college or university, you incur lower costs than you would by participating in a structured program. However, be aware that you may face difficulty obtaining classes and lack the advising and peer support formal post-bacs offer.

- ✔ **Obtain a second bachelor's degree.** Instead of attending a post-bac program to complete their prerequisites, some applicants choose to obtain a second bachelor's degree in a science discipline. For example, if you hold a bachelor's degree in sociology and then decide you want to become a physician, you may opt to go back to college to get a bachelor's in biology, biochemistry, or another science. This route takes longer than doing a post-bac but can be a good choice for those with low GPAs in their first bachelor's degrees.

Medical schools typically prefer that prerequisite course work be completed at a four-year institution rather than at a community college, and some med schools don't even accept community college courses for prereqs. Therefore, I recommend taking your prerequisites at a four-year school. However, if you do decide to take your prereqs at a community college, supplement those classes with upper-level science courses at a four-year institution to demonstrate your ability to excel in more-advanced science classes. (For more discussion about the issue of taking prerequisites at a community college, turn to Chapter 3).

Updating your academic experiences

Some nontraditional students have already completed many or all of the prerequisite courses earlier in life either because they had an interest in medicine as an undergraduate student or earned a bachelor's degree in a science field in preparation for another career. However, even if you completed all your prereqs previously, you may still benefit from taking additional classes as a post-bac student. In particular, consider taking more science courses if you

- ✓ **Completed premedical course work more than three years ago:** Although most med schools don't place an expiration date on prerequisite course work, they usually like to see that an applicant has successfully completed science classes recently so that she won't be diving back into the classroom cold as a first-year medical student. Taking some upper-level science classes strengthens your academic foundation prior to med school and proves to the schools that you've still got what it takes to tackle tough classes.

- ✓ **Performed poorly as an undergraduate student:** Even if you finished all the prerequisites years ago, if you received a string of Bs and Cs for them, you'll need some additional work to make yourself competitive for medical school. Many students who weren't highly motivated or who had poor study habits when attending college immediately after high school are far more successful when they return to the classroom later as a nontraditional student because they now have greater maturity and focus. Students who have taken the basic prerequisites for medical school and need to improve their academic record may benefit from the academic record enhancer post-bac or special master's programs described in Chapter 16.

- ✓ **Took only the minimum required premedical courses:** Any applicant, traditional or nontraditional, is better off taking at least a few courses beyond the bare minimum required for entry to medical school. Taking upper-level science courses relevant to medical school more fully prepares you for the intense load of science classes you'll face in med school and assures admissions committees of your aptitude in academics. (Flip to Chapter 3 for a rundown of recommended courses.)

Another benefit of taking additional classes before applying to medical school as a nontraditional student is the opportunity they provide to obtain a letter of recommendation from a faculty member with whom you've had recent contact. As I describe in the later section "Lining up letters of recommendation," getting faculty letters can be especially challenging for applicants who've been out of college for a significant amount of time.

Undertaking the Application Process

The key to succeeding in the medical school admissions process as a non-traditional applicant is to create a compelling application package that highlights the life experiences, skills, and qualities you've developed as a result of traversing a longer, less direct path to medicine. However, although your unique experiences may give you an edge in some ways over more typical applicants, you also face certain pitfalls when it comes to applying. The following sections show you how to take advantage of the benefits of being a nontraditional applicant and to overcome obstacles you may confront as you fill out your primary application, obtain letters of recommendation, and go through the interview process.

Telling your story in the personal statement

As an older applicant, you've had more experiences, both professional and personal, than an applicant fresh out of college. For this reason, you may find tackling the personal statement especially challenging because the approximately one page of space allotted may be woefully insufficient to fit in everything you want to discuss. Your breadth and depth of experiences provide you with a rich store of material to choose from and allow you to craft a statement that will help to set you apart as long as you choose wisely and don't attempt to stuff too much into your statement. Therefore, in addition to the general guidelines for writing the personal statement provided in Chapter 8, keep these additional tips in mind:

✔ **Don't dedicate the entire essay to elaborating on your past career.** Mentioning your current or previous profession in the context of how you came to make the switch to medicine or what skills you'll bring to the medical field is appropriate. However, if a discussion of your experiences outside of medicine dominates the essay, you'll have little room in which to talk about why you want to be a physician, how you've explored the medical field, and what you have to contribute to it. If you're worried you won't have space to do your professional achievements justice in the personal statement, remember that you also have the work and activities section of the application in which to discuss your employment history.

✔ **Be clear about the timing and chronology of events.** If you have a complicated history that includes taking breaks from college, attending several institutions, travelling for extended periods, or holding jobs in various fields, giving the reader a good road map to follow about the order and timing of particular events is critical. Your story may be perfectly clear to you but confusing and disjointed to a committee member who hasn't memorized the rest of your application.

✔ **Address why you're making the switch to medicine.** Simply stating what you like about medicine isn't enough to convince the committee that you're committed to your new path. You should also address how and why you made the decision to change, perhaps drastically, your career plan. Leaving a career and returning to school at a later stage in life takes a lot of sacrifice, so make sure the committee understands how strong your motivation is to enter medicine and why you're dedicated to becoming a doctor despite the literal and figurative costs.

✔ **Highlight the elements of your background that will make you a good medical student and future physician.** Many of the skills you gained during your years of working and living life are apt to transfer to medicine. For example, you may have honed your communication skills as a team member in the workplace or developed excellent time management techniques by juggling a full-time job with your premedical classes as a returning student.

Using the work and activities section effectively

Medical schools strive for diversity in their student bodies, and one advantage that nontraditional applicants have is that they bring something different to the class through their background and life experiences. The work and activities list gives you the opportunity to showcase the range of your experiences during the years from after high school up until your application. Older applicants tend to have diverse, robust lists that help them stand out on this section of the application.

As I note in Chapter 8, the American Medical College Application Service (AMCAS) application limits the number of activities you can include to 15. Nontraditional applicants may have far more entries than the spaces allowed because of the extra years they've had to accrue experiences, so being selective is imperative. Full-time employment, clinical experiences, research, community service, and activities demonstrating leadership are among the most important. Also include any activities that are especially unique or that you pursued in depth, and emphasize more recent activities when it comes down to choosing among entries.

Note that you have the option to select three activities as "most meaningful" and additional space in which to describe these, so consider using one of these slots for current or recent full-time employment. This approach allows you a designated space in which to address what you gained from your time in the workforce and how the skills you've acquired are transferrable to a medical career.

Lining up letters of recommendation

Obtaining letters of recommendation can be one of the greatest trials for nontraditional applicants, especially for those who finished their undergraduate studies more than a few years previously. Asking for a letter from a faculty member with whom you haven't spoken in several years can be awkward, and more importantly, may result in a weak letter. Therefore, in addition to taking the steps outlined in Chapter 9 to obtain a strong set of letters of recommendation, as a nontraditional applicant you should also do the following:

- ✔ **Check with your undergraduate institution to determine whether it provides premedical committee letters for alumni.** Med schools prefer you use a premedical committee letter over submitting individual letters if you have access to a committee. In addition, some post-baccalaureate programs have premedical committees, so make sure you check into this option as well if you're enrolled in a post-bac. You can read about committee letters in Chapter 9.

- ✔ **Find out whether the medical schools you're applying to have different letter requirements or options for nontraditional applicants.** For example, some med schools require students who've attended a graduate program to submit at least one letter from graduate school and one from undergraduate. Others allow applicants who finished their undergraduate studies longer than a specific number of years ago (for example, five) to submit a letter from a supervisor from their employment in place of one of the faculty letters.

- ✔ **Take a science class or two in order to obtain a recent letter from a science faculty member.** One or two science faculty letters are required by many schools, so if you completed your prerequisite course work several years ago, taking additional sciences classes close to when you apply not only gives you some recent experience in the classroom but may also provide you with a faculty contact from whom to request a letter.

Looking at interview tips for the nontraditional applicant

Interview performance is an area in which nontraditional applicants frequently excel. Many nontraditional applicants have been interviewed on multiple occasions for jobs or even have experience on the other side of the table as an interviewer. In addition, with time and experience often comes greater composure, not to mention more anecdotes and stories to make the responses interesting. Because of these factors, the interview can be a chance for a nontraditional applicant to truly shine. (See Chapter 10 for more information about med school interviews.)

Although nontraditional applicants have good reason to be confident about the interview process, be aware that schools may have particular concerns about older applicants that may be addressed during the interview. For example, an interviewer may ask questions to determine whether you'll be comfortable starting over as the low man on the totem pole as a first-year medical student after leaving a successful career behind. If the issue of your ability to readjust to being a student or to take direction from others arises, be ready to give specific examples demonstrating your flexibility and willingness to learn, such as by pointing out volunteer experiences that required you to perform basic tasks under the supervision of medical staff. Approaching the interview with the right mix of confidence and deference also helps make the case that you know when to lead and when to follow.

Another area that med schools may question you about is your ability to manage the multiple responsibilities that often come with being a nontraditional student. For example, you may be asked about your marital status or whether you have children; these questions are inappropriate, but schools occasionally ask them anyway. If you find yourself in that situation, you can decline to answer. Another option is to consider addressing the spirit of the question rather than what's literally being asked. The intent behind these questions is usually to find out whether you'll be able to focus on medical school given the other demands in your life. Therefore, in response to these questions, you may simply state that you're adept at balancing your professional life with your personal life and then give examples of your ability to multitask that don't reveal details about your personal life.

If you mention in your personal statement or elsewhere in your application that you have a family, the topic may come up during the interview. In this case, discussing the topic is completely appropriate. Emphasizing that your family is a source of support lets you present the fact that you're a spouse and/or parent as a strength, not a weakness. Med school is stressful, and the built-in support system your family provides can help you to be more productive.

Considering Challenges Facing Nontraditional Applicants

As much as you may want to realize your dream of practicing medicine, the reality of what becoming a physician takes may be daunting. Like any medical student, you'll have to make major sacrifices in time and money to go through medical school and residency; however, as a nontraditional applicant, you may be facing additional concerns relating to family responsibilities and financial obligations as well as the idea of being surrounded mostly by peers who are different from you in terms of age and life experience. However, despite the logistical barriers nontraditional applicants face, many decide to pursue their dream of becoming a physician and make it work. In this section, I address some of the common concerns nontraditional applicants have as they adjust to being a student again, work to balance family life with med school, and try to connect with others in similar situations.

Like anyone else contemplating a career in medicine, nontraditional applicants should thoroughly research the profession, shadow physicians, and volunteer in clinical settings to make sure that they have a realistic view of the job and are confident that it's the right one for them. If upon careful consideration you opt to go ahead with applying to medical school, know that although you'll have some additional obstacles as an older applicant, you'll also be armed with the maturity, perspective, and clarity that come with experience.

Returning to school

If you've been out of school for more than a couple of years, you probably take the freedom from homework assignments and examinations for granted. However, upon returning to school as a premedical student, you'll have to readjust to getting ready for examinations, paying tuition, and spending many evenings and weekends studying. Taking the following steps can help smooth your transition to the life of a student:

✓ **Ease back into your studies.** Med schools look for students who have demonstrated their ability to manage multiple science classes at once; however, this fact doesn't mean that you have to dive into a full load of science classes your first semester as a premedical student. Upon your return, you may find that the material comes naturally to you or discover that it's going to take more work than you anticipated. Even if you have a strong science background, you may take a semester to get back into the rhythm of school. Career changers who completed non-science majors as undergraduates may be surprised at how much time is involved in a full load of science course work.

✔ **Cut back on outside commitments.** Getting into medical school requires very strong grades in the sciences, so before you take your first class, free yourself from as many commitments as you can. If you continue to work full time and/or have a family, most of your time will already be accounted for, so extract yourself from clubs, organizations, committees, and anything else nonessential to your academic success or financial survival.

✔ **Connect with other premedical students.** If you enroll in a structured post-bac program, you'll have lots of fellow premeds with whom to study and trade tips about applying to med school. However, if you're taking your prerequisites on a part-time basis at a local college, you'll need to make a greater effort to find others in your position. Seek out a few students to form a study group, and try to build a network of premeds as you progress through your classes. That way, you have some company as you take on the challenges posed by tough premedical courses, taking the MCAT, and applying to med school.

Facing stereotypes

When you announce your plans to apply to medical school, you'll receive varying levels of support for your decision among the people in your life; some will applaud your determination, and others will simply think you're crazy to give up a great job, go back to school, and possibly rack up a lot of debt. Some of the most pervasive questions you face as a nontraditional student pertain to why you want to go through all the work of becoming a doctor "at your age," especially if you already have a good career. Of course, you don't have to justify your choice to anyone, but facing doubts or even outright criticism is difficult when you're trying to take on something as challenging as getting into medical school.

Therefore, find a network of people who understand what you're trying to achieve, such as others who are going through career changes themselves (even if they aren't switching to medicine in particular). Team up with other returning students you meet through class or check out online forums for nontraditional premedical students for support. The National Society for Nontraditional Premedical and Medical Students, Inc., offers information and forums for nontraditional applicants. The organization's site is oldpremeds.org/.

Older applicants may also face doubt that they have the stamina to last through years of school and residency training or to function during the long nights on call and hours on end of standing in the OR. However, older med students are actually the ones who seem complain the least about the hours involved, perhaps because such students made a very well-informed and deliberate decision to become a doctor and have the maturity to understand that nobody, especially overworked residents on the ward team, likes whining.

The image of the typical med student as an early-twentysomething can actually work in the favor of an older med student because some patients feel more comfortable with someone who looks like she didn't graduate from college last week. You may even find yourself being mistaken for a resident or attending physician — which is something you need to quickly correct by clearly identifying yourself as a medical student to patients, however flattered you may be. Overall, being the exception means you may have to correct misconceptions and do some educating and explaining along the way to becoming a doctor, but with medical schools more diverse than ever, being a nontraditional student is getting easier all the time.

Lacking a peer group as a medical student

Nontraditional students may feel a bit out of place when they enter medical school and find themselves immersed in a group of students who are mostly younger than they are and who are at a different stage of life. This situation can be especially difficult for nontraditional students who are single and may have the added concern of wondering how they're going to find a partner when almost all of their time is spent with people outside of their age range. As an older student without the instant peer group (and dating pool) that younger med students have, you need to put in extra effort to cultivate a social life. Keeping these tips in mind can help you avoid isolation and find a group you're comfortable with:

- ✔ **Plan a get-together with the other nontraditional students in your class.** You can probably find at least a few other students in your class in the same position as you, so set up a time to meet for coffee or lunch. You may find that they're feeling a bit lost, too, and end up making your outings a regular event.

- ✔ **Keep in contact with people from your previous life.** Going to med school doesn't mean you have to drop off the radar completely. Make sure that you keep the connection with your family and old friends even if you've had to relocate a long way from them to attend med school. Even at a distance, good friends and family can provide a listening ear or a pep talk when you need it.

- ✔ **Connect with students in other graduate degree programs.** Students in other graduate programs will share some of the same concerns but have slightly different perspectives, and you may feel less stress or competition with them. By joining activities on the wider university campus, such as sports or organizations that aren't just directed at medical students, you can meet students outside of the medical school.

- ✔ **Participate in activities outside of campus.** You'll be extremely busy as a med student, but carving out time to participate in at least one hobby or interest unrelated to medicine is still possible. Taking a salsa class, joining a hiking club, or becoming a volunteer with a local organization helps you meet people in the larger community so that you're not limited to people you go to school with to meet your social needs.

Finally, don't discount younger students as potential friends. Whether you're going through med school at 22 or at 40, you're dealing with many of the same experiences, from dissecting a cadaver to being stuck holding a retractor for four hours while you're half asleep. No one is going to be able to understand those events quite like someone living through the same thing.

Medical students who are married or in a relationship may feel less motivated to seek out friendships in the class because they have a partner to confide in, turn to, and spend their free time with. However, the stress of med school can affect both the person going through it and her significant other, and building friendships within med school also gives your partner a chance to meet a counterpart when you get together as couples or in a group.

Balancing family life with medical school

If you're married or in a serious relationship during medical school and/or have children, you may find yourself facing competing priorities as you try to juggle school with family life. Even the most understanding partner may struggle at times with the long hours you spend away from home, the stress your absence puts on the family, and the financial burden of medical school. You may feel that you don't have the time to do justice to your studies or your family obligations; however, when things are at their most difficult, remember that you aren't the first person to go through medical school with a family and that it can be done.

Certain times during medical school are particularly challenging, such as when you're on a rotation with a lot of nights on call. However, you also have windows of time during which your schedule isn't quite as intense, particularly the summer after your first year (which is time off at most schools) and when you're on some of the easier elective rotations during your fourth year. During those months, you can spend extra time with your family, catch up with things around the house, and give your spouse a break from watching the kids.

If you're a medical student who's also a parent, having reliable childcare with a backup plan is essential, especially during your third and fourth years when you're on clinical rotations. Your schedule during the first two years may be somewhat flexible depending on the number of hours of lectures each week and whether attendance is mandatory. However, for rotations, you have a set schedule of when you need to be in the hospital or clinic.

Chapter 16

Try, Try Again: Reapplicants

A pplicants who complete the admissions cycle without receiving an acceptance are left wondering "What next?" or "Will I ever get the chance to become a physician?" Although some angst at the end of an unsuccessful cycle is understandable, a setback doesn't have to mean an end to your dream of becoming a doctor. By determining why you weren't accepted, tackling the issues that prevented you from getting an offer, and moving forward with a stronger application, you may still be able to get a place in a medical school class, even if the timetable ends up being a bit longer than you had planned.

Figuring out what went wrong and how to correct it can be challenging, so this chapter provides you with guidance for addressing these issues and strategies for application timing, school selection, and updating your application before reapplying.

Timing Your Next Application

After you've been denied admission to medical school, you need to regroup and decide whether to reapply immediately or sit out a cycle or more before trying again. Because medical training takes so long to complete, you may be eager to get started with medical school as soon as possible; however, reapplying immediately isn't always the best strategy. How long you should wait before applying again depends on the reasons you were rejected initially and the amount of time you need to address those areas. In the following sections, I describe situations when you can consider reapplying immediately and note when you may want to hold off for a year or more.

Note that a third application is discouraged at some schools. Even schools that are more amenable to those who apply multiple times may look at a third-time applicant more critically than a first- or second-time candidate. Therefore, don't waste a try by reapplying before you're truly ready.

At many schools, MCAT scores are only valid for three years. Therefore, check with the schools you plan to apply to regarding their policies on MCAT scores so that you know how long your current scores are good for before you make a decision about when to reapply.

Reapplying immediately

If you don't have an acceptance in hand by January of your senior year, start thinking about whether to reapply immediately or sit out a cycle if you don't eventually receive an offer of admission. Planning for the worst case scenario gives you sufficient time to improve your application and get ready for the new cycle instead of scrambling to retake the MCAT, add activities to your resume, or rewrite your personal statement in time to submit a new, improved application when June rolls around.

In fact, you should continue to build your application portfolio throughout the summer and fall of the year that you apply regardless of your competitiveness because you can use those additional experiences to strengthen your candidacy during secondary applications, interviews, and through update letters for the current cycle. In the event you end up having to reapply, your efforts will have given you a head start on strengthening your application.

After you've received a rejection, seek feedback from the admissions offices at the schools you were denied admission to, and speak with your premedical advisor as well. Along with these outside assessments, take a critical look at each aspect of your application yourself and develop a plan to correct your weaknesses. The timeline for your reapplication strategy may be relatively short or stretch over one or more years depending on the reasons you were rejected initially. If you were unsuccessful in the previous cycle for one of the following reasons, you can reasonably consider reapplying immediately:

- ✔ **A late application:** As I describe in Chapter 5, applying early is essential with *rolling admissions* (where schools review files as soon as they're complete). If you submitted your primary application relatively late in the cycle or lagged on completing secondaries, you may increase your chances of admission simply by submitting earlier the next time.

- ✔ **A list of schools that was too short or unrealistic:** You may be a competitive applicant for *a* school, just not the particular schools you aimed for last time. Revamping your list (with the help of Chapter 7) may allow you to snag an acceptance the next round without major changes to your application portfolio.

✔ **A GPA that is slightly too low:** If your GPA was only marginally below what is competitive for medical school admission (see Chapter 2), a single year of good grades may be enough to propel you into the "accepted" pool. If you applied at the end of your junior year initially, by the time the next cycle opens at the end of your senior year you'll have another year's worth of grades to add to your application.

✔ **A low MCAT score:** If you can raise your score in time for the new cycle, you may be positioned to reapply quickly and with a significantly improved chance of acceptance. Chapter 6 and the later section "Taking Action When the MCAT Is the Issue" provide tips for determining whether and when to retake the MCAT.

Waiting a year or more

If reapplying right away won't give you sufficient time to correct the short-comings in your application, hold off on reapplying until you're more strongly positioned. For example, if your GPA is significantly below the average for accepted applicants (see Chapter 2), you may need to complete additional courses after graduation as a post-baccalaureate or graduate student in order to become competitive. (See the next section for information about post-bac programs.) In addition, preparing for the MCAT again may preclude you from jumping back into the applicant pool right away, especially if you need to strengthen your foundation in the sciences before attempting the test again.

Taking extra time can also allow you to develop your clinical and/or research experiences in greater depth. Adding a *gap year* can give you the chance to work or volunteer extensively in a clinical or research setting. For example, working as an emergency room scribe, volunteering in a clinic, or performing biomedical research during a gap year provides you with valuable hands-on experience and further demonstrates your commitment to a career in medicine. (See the later section "Adding to Your Clinical, Research, and Other Experiences" to find out more about adding to your activities before reapplying.)

Improving the Numbers: Applicants with Low GPAs

If either your overall or science GPA isn't up to par, getting admitted to medical school is going to be extremely difficult or even impossible. (See Chapter 2 for statistics about applicants and matriculants to medical school.) Even a strong MCAT score and extensive extracurricular activities may not be enough to compensate for a weak GPA, so if your grades are keeping you from reaching your goal of becoming a doctor, make a plan to tackle this issue head-on.

For students who initially apply to medical school at the end of their junior year but aren't accepted, senior year provides more opportunities to get great grades and increase their GPAs before reapplying. However, if a single year of good grades isn't enough to bump you into the competitive range, or if you've already finished college, taking courses after graduation as a post-baccalaureate or graduate student may be necessary.

The term *post-baccalaureate program* (or *post-bac*) refers to two distinct types of programs, which causes some confusion:

- ✔ **Career changers:** Post-bacs for career changers are intended for individuals who have graduated from college but haven't completed the prerequisite courses needed for medical school. Students in career changer programs may be recent college graduates with nonscience degrees or working professionals who graduated many years ago and pursued another career before switching to premedicine. I discuss these programs in Chapter 3.

- ✔ **Academic record enhancers:** *Academic record enhancers* allow med school applicants who've already completed their core science courses a chance to strengthen their academic records. These programs offer a second chance for applicants who didn't perform well in their science courses during college. Some programs include only undergraduate-level courses, while others consist of graduate-level work and lead to a master's degree. The latter are often referred to as special master's programs or SMPs.

As a reapplicant trying to strengthen your academic record, you may decide to participate in a formal academic record enhancer or to take classes on your own outside of a structured program. The length, cost, and benefits of different types of programs and the do-it-yourself route vary considerably. The following sections explore each type to help you find the best fit for you.

You can find a list of post-bac programs, including SMPs, at the American Association of Medical Colleges searchable database at `services.aamc.org/postbac/`. The admissions cycle for many post-bac programs opens in January of the year you plan to enter the program, although some schools accept applications as early as September. Deadlines for submitting an application typically fall between March and June, but the date differs for each school. Admission to many post-baccalaureate programs is done on a rolling basis, so apply early.

To apply, you typically have to submit your transcripts, a personal statement, a resume or other list of activities, and letters of recommendation. For most programs, you also need to provide standardized test scores — usually the MCAT, although some programs accept Graduate Record Examination (GRE) scores instead. Applicants may be notified of their admission status in less than a month for some programs, while other programs take several months to reach a decision.

Considering post-baccalaureate programs with undergraduate-level course work

Some post-baccalaureate programs focus exclusively on undergraduate courses. The emphasis is usually on upper-level courses such as physiology, anatomy, molecular biology, and other classes recommended but not necessarily required for medical school. However, students may also have the opportunity to repeat core science courses that they performed poorly in as an undergraduate before they move on to more-advanced courses. Because these classes are undergraduate level, they're factored in as part of the undergraduate overall and science GPAs when your GPAs are calculated as part of the primary application. (Check out Chapter 8 for details about the types of GPAs generated on the primary application.)

Post-bac programs range from full-time, highly-structured programs that include academic advising, a committee letter of recommendation (see Chapter 9), and MCAT preparation to much more loosely organized setups that you can complete on a part-time basis and that offer little in the way of support services. Many structured programs provide a certificate of completion to those who complete a specific set of classes or number of units.

However, a drawback to some of the more highly structured programs is the cost. At private institutions, tuition for a one-year program may top $40,000. Further, the selectivity of the program varies significantly. At the most highly competitive programs, successful applicants have strong MCAT scores and GPAs of around 3.2. Some programs are less competitive and accept applicants with GPAs below 3.0 (although usually not below 2.75) and relatively low MCAT scores.

Surveying special master's programs

SMPs offer students the opportunity to strengthen their science backgrounds by taking courses at the graduate level and earning a master's degree. However, SMPs are different than a typical graduate program in a science discipline — hence, the designation "special." Most regular master's programs in fields such as biology, physiology, or related areas are research-focused, require a thesis, and are designed to prepare students for a career in that field of study. By contrast, SMPs are specifically tailored to students seeking to enter the health professions. They offer graduate-level course work that is similar to or the same as what students encounter in medical school. At some programs, SMP students even take classes right alongside medical students at the institution's medical school.

SMPs may take one or two years to complete and are usually full time. Like their counterparts offering undergraduate-level courses (see the preceding section), these programs may include premedical advising, a committee letter, and other support services.

Because SMP courses are graduate-level, the grades received for these classes aren't included in the undergraduate GPA on the primary application; rather, they go toward a separate graduate GPA. Strong performance in a graduate program can overcome a weak undergraduate GPA, but if your undergraduate science GPA is very low (such as below a 3.0), your best bet may be to focus on improving your undergraduate GPA directly rather than going on to an SMP. In fact, many SMPs require a minimum undergraduate GPA of 3.0 for admission. Students with undergraduate GPAs below that number may have trouble getting into one without some additional undergrad course work first.

Don't view an SMP as an easy fix for whatever academic difficulties you faced as an undergrad. These programs are quite challenging and designed to simulate the experience of medical school in order to throw you into the deep end, so to speak. Poor performance in an SMP is a great way to prove you're not ready for med school.

Taking classes independently

Strengthening your academic record doesn't necessarily require signing on as part of a structured program. Many applicants choose to take courses on their own by taking advantage of open enrollment or extension courses offered by a local university. A do-it-yourself academic record enhancer shares many of the same benefits as the DIY career-changers discussed in Chapter 3, including lower cost, convenience, and greater flexibility.

One major obstacle that you may face as an academic record enhancer student going it alone is finding available upper-level science classes through extension or other avenues. Students sometimes have to cobble together a schedule that involves attending classes at two colleges in order to find classes in subjects such as physiology, cell biology, genetics, or other advanced science subjects. Simply retaking core courses won't impress the medical schools and isn't worthwhile unless you originally received a C– or below in the course. Although the DIY option is usually far less expensive than a formal post-bac, its feasibility depends on the access you have to colleges or universities offering upper-level science courses to post-bac students.

Master of Public Health: A good option?

Some reapplicants wonder whether attaining a Master of Public Health (MPH) will help make them more competitive for medical school. These students may have an interest in public health or health policy and see pursuing such a degree as a way to delve into an area that they may be able to incorporate into their eventual career as a physician while enhancing their application at the same time.

Although this option can be a good one for students who have strong undergraduate GPAs and want to spend their gap year building their credentials in an area complementary to medicine, it's rarely the best choice for those who need to improve their academic standing in order to gain admission to medical school.

Many, and often most, of the courses that comprise a typical MPH are in disciplines such as health policy, environmental health, social and behavioral sciences, health administration, or other subjects that med schools don't count as science courses for the purposes of GPA calculations.

MPH curriculums vary, and some programs include a heavier emphasis on science, but make sure you investigate the individual programs carefully before committing to this route. If you need to improve your science GPA, the best bet is usually a post-bac or SMP intended for that purpose rather than an MPH, masters in health policy, or global health degree.

Taking Action When the MCAT Is the Issue

For some applicants, the MCAT, not their GPA, is the problem. Such applicants may enter an admissions cycle hoping that a good GPA, a solid list of extracurricular activities, and strong letters of recommendation are enough to help them overcome their low MCAT score. However, as Chapter 6 explains, the MCAT is critical in admissions; although other factors can somewhat compensate for a relatively weak MCAT score, a too-low score can doom even an otherwise-superb application. If you've assessed your application and determined that the MCAT is the problem, you should work to eliminate that roadblock to success before going forward with your application again.

Facing the problem

After going through the grueling process of preparing for and taking the MCAT, you may have walked out of the testing room vowing "never again." In fact, for some applicants the aversion to retaking the MCAT is so strong that they focus on improving other areas of their application even though they're fully aware that their MCAT score is the real problem. The most common scenario is that of an applicant with a good undergraduate GPA but poor MCAT score who, rather than retake the MCAT, completes a post-baccalaureate or SMP (described earlier in this chapter) in hopes that an even stronger academic record will convince the committee to give him a chance despite his subpar test score.

Although good performance in a post-bac program is an asset to an application, applicants with marginal GPAs are the ones who derive the greatest benefits from these programs, not those with already-competitive GPAs. For example, an applicant with a 3.7 overall GPA and 3.6 science GPA will get minimal benefit from a post-bac, whereas someone with a 3.3 overall GPA and a 3.2 in the sciences has much more to gain. The cost in time and money of post-bac programs can be great, and these resources are usually better invested in doing extended preparation for the MCAT for applicants who already have solid GPAs.

Trying to get around retaking the MCAT by working on other parts of your application may just delay the inevitable. If your MCAT needs improvement, you'll have to deal with that sooner or later, so it's better to address it early.

Retaking the MCAT

If the admissions cycle isn't going well for you and you realize that your MCAT score is the likely problem, start preparing to retake the test early so that you'll have your score available by the time the new cycle opens. Optimally, you want to be ready to retake by May of your senior year (close to the start of the new application cycle), which means that you should start studying again in March or even earlier, depending on the exact date of your test and how much work you need to do to get ready.

Although thinking about studying for the MCAT while you're in the midst of an application cycle is difficult, nailing the MCAT is especially important if it's your second (or third) try, so give yourself sufficient time to reprepare. When planning your new study schedule, keep in mind how much time has elapsed since you took your core science courses because you may need extra time to brush up on the fundamentals of physics or chemistry, especially if your recent course work has been mostly nonscience or focused on the biological sciences.

If you realize that your class schedule or other commitments won't allow you to dedicate sufficient time to MCAT studying, consider waiting a cycle before reapplying so that you aren't pressed to take the test before you're fully prepared.

For more details about when to retake the MCAT and how to prepare, check out Chapter 6.

Adding to Your Clinical, Research, and Other Experiences

In addition to addressing weaknesses in your GPA and/or MCAT score (covered earlier in this chapter), you should use the time you have between application cycles to continue to develop your clinical, research, and other experiences. Minimal exposure to clinical medicine, an overall thin resume, or a lack of in-depth involvement in community service and leadership activities are among the reasons you may be denied admission. If you're lacking significant shadowing or clinical volunteer experience, actively seek opportunities in those areas so that upon reapplication you have strong evidence of your exploration of the medical field. If you already have numerous clinical experiences on your application, seek out different specialties within medicine to explore or branch out into doing basic or clinical research. (Check out Chapter 4 for more information.)

Whatever area you participate in, get involved early, because a sudden flurry of activities dated a few months before your new application is much less valuable than evidence of an ongoing, organic commitment to your endeavors. As I note earlier in the chapter, if reapplying results in a gap year, you potentially have the opportunity to work in a clinical setting or research position on a full-time basis, which can provide a significant boost to your application portfolio. For ideas on how to make the most of a gap year, see Chapter 5.

Applicants who already have strong resumes sometimes rely on their previous experiences to carry them through the new application cycle and thus end involvement in their activities to focus on retaking the MCAT or improving their grades. However, stopping all volunteer work, physician shadowing, and other activities is a bad idea. Schools like to see evidence of continued involvement in activities, not that an applicant dropped everything upon submitting his application to medical school. Continue your work with existing organizations or seek out new opportunities as you gear up for another application cycle, no matter how robust your previous achievements are.

Revisiting Your School Options

On the first try, some applicants are extremely selective with their school choices, aiming only for schools that they view as prestigious or that are located somewhere they want to live. However, keep in mind that your ultimate goal is to become a physician, and the top-tier schools aren't the only ones that can help you to get there.

If you were very selective about your school list last time you applied, consider rethinking your approach for the new cycle in order to increase your odds of admission. If you applied to only a few schools or to schools for which you weren't really competitive, a longer or more realistic list will likely improve your chances of getting an acceptance. You may also want to consider investigating osteopathic schools prior to the next admissions cycle (if you focused on MD schools before) to see whether they'd be a good fit for you.

Applying to a broader range of schools

If you applied to a only a small number of schools the first time or compiled a list that was mostly based on wishful thinking, expanding your options for schools can go a long way in helping you get admitted on the next try. Although there are definitely differences between schools, and some schools are better than others, note that *any* U.S. medical school is a good one. Therefore, when developing your new list of schools, don't just ask yourself, "Where do I want go?" Instead, also pose the question, "Which schools do I have the best chance of being accepted to?" Although you shouldn't apply to a school you definitely don't want to attend, admission to medical school is so competitive that being too picky about location or other factors may delay or even prevent you from pursuing a career in medicine.

Chapter 7 provides guidance on developing a well-rounded list of schools. As you read the tips there, focus especially on the step-by-step guide to crafting a list of schools.

Considering osteopathic or international schools

At the outset, you may have had your sights set solely on allopathic (MD) U.S. medical schools. However, these schools aren't the only options for medical education. Osteopathic (DO) medical schools offer an education that is similar in most ways to that of allopathic medical schools; however, the average MCAT score of matriculants to DO schools is significantly lower than for MD schools (26 versus 31, per AACOM and AAMC statistics), making these programs a viable option for applicants whose main weakness is their MCAT score.

Before adding osteopathic schools to your list, though, make sure that you explore this route thoroughly by researching the field and shadowing osteopathic physicians (and doing so with an open mind). Although the similarities between osteopathic and allopathic medicine outweigh the differences, training as an osteopathic physician includes instruction in osteopathic manipulative medicine (OMM), which is unique to the osteopathic profession. Checking into osteopathic medicine and medical schools before proceeding ensures that you're a good fit for a DO school and you understand both the similarities and differences between allopathic and osteopathic physicians. (For information about applying to osteopathic schools, flip to Chapter 12.)

Another option for medical school that some applicants pursue is applying to international programs. Numerous medical schools outside the United States cater to U.S. students who plan to return to the States for residency training and to establish their medical practices. Schools in the Caribbean are especially popular, although programs in Europe, Australia, Mexico, Israel, and various other countries also accept students from the United States. (Note that Canadian medical schools should not be considered a back-up option for students having difficulty gaining admission to a U.S. school. Admission to Canadian schools is highly competitive, on par with U.S. med schools.)

If you do plan to apply to international schools, be aware that quality of education varies greatly at these institutions, and graduates of international schools can face challenges in attaining medical residency positions in the United States. Therefore, you should make the decision to attend school overseas only after very careful research and consideration. Chapter 14 provides help in assessing international programs and deciding whether to pursue this option.

Revising Your Personal Statement

After spending weeks or months perfecting your personal statement (see Chapter 8), you may be wondering whether you really need to rewrite it when you reapply. You may be tempted to simply reuse your previous statement, but don't give in. As a reapplicant, you really need to differentiate your current application from the previous one as much as you can. Some schools keep previous applications on file and compare the old and current applications.

You don't have to do away with all the material from your original version. For example, if your previous statement discusses an early experience you had within the medical field that inspired you to pursue the profession, you can still mention that activity in your new version. However, you should also do a significant amount of fresh writing and emphasize your achievements and growth since the last time you applied, discussing how they've further motivated or prepared you for a medical career.

Because the opening and closing of a piece of writing make the greatest impact on a reader, revamping those sections for your new personal statement is especially important. A statement that starts exactly the same as last year's essay sets the expectation that you won't be offering much new material this time around.

Some applicants choose to directly address the fact that they're reapplicants, discussing what they learned from the experience of applying previously and reflecting on how they've worked to improve their applications since they last applied. Others highlight new activities and discuss why they're stronger candidates for medical school than ever before without addressing outright that they're reapplying. Both approaches are acceptable; however, if you decide to talk about a past attempt, don't make it a major focus of the essay. The limited space you're allowed for the personal statement is better used to discuss your strengths and motivation for medicine than to dwell on a previous rejection.

Even if you don't mention that you're a reapplicant, the schools that you've applied to before will likely still have your old application on file and be aware that you're reapplying.

Updating Your Letters of Recommendation

Updating your letters of recommendation is another way to strengthen your candidacy for medical school. Exactly how you handle letters of recommendation as a reapplicant depends on whether you use a premedical committee letter or individual letters of recommendation.

✔ If you applied with a premedical committee letter previously, check with your premedical advisor to find out the committee's policy regarding reapplicants. Some schools make changes to the committee letter or include an addendum updating the letter, whereas others simply resubmit the previous version as it stands. As discussed in Chapter 9, medical schools prefer a committee letter if one is available, so you should work with your committee to obtain a letter for the new cycle instead of switching to individual letters if possible.

✔ If you're planning to submit individual letters of recommendation, you can use some of the same evaluators as before. If you've continued to interact with the writer in an academic or professional setting since the original letter was written, request that he update the letter. In some cases, the letter may be from a professor, a physician, or another individual with whom you're no longer in regular contact and who would not have new material to add to the letter. If the letter is a strong one, using it again is fine, especially if it's needed to fulfill a requirement for a particular type of letter, such as a science faculty letter. (Chapter 9 has more guidance on what constitutes a strong recommendation.)

In addition to updating letters from previous evaluators, obtain one or two new letters that reflect activities you've participated in since you last applied. Schools don't expect you to submit an entirely new application package after only a year, but fresh letters are a way of demonstrating that you have recent accomplishments and experiences to add to your previous ones. If more than a year has passed since you last applied, getting recent or updated letters to add to your portfolio is especially important for showing continued growth.

Chapter 17

Minority Applicants, Disadvantaged Applicants, and Applicants with Disabilities

....

In This Chapter

▶ Applying to medical school as an underrepresented minority or with disadvantaged status

▶ Exploring resources aimed at increasing diversity in medicine

▶ Going through the admissions process as an applicant with a disability

....

Despite efforts to increase diversity, some racial, ethnic, and cultural groups as well as individuals from socioeconomically disadvantaged backgrounds remain underrepresented in medicine. Recognizing the importance of a diverse physician workforce, medical schools and other organizations have developed outreach programs, scholarships, and support services aimed at making the medical profession more representative of the larger population. As a minority or disadvantaged student, taking advantage of these opportunities and programs can make gaining exposure to the medical profession, preparing for medical school, and paying for your education easier.

Applicants with disabilities are a group who not only face the usual challenges that come with applying to med school but also have unique concerns such as whether or when to disclose a disability, how to obtain accommodations, and how programs will perceive them. Despite potential obstacles to becoming a physician, many applicants with disabilities persevere and are successful in gaining acceptance to and completing medical school.

This chapter discusses some of the issues affecting applicants who are minorities in medicine, are socioeconomically disadvantaged, or have disabilities and provides an overview of resources available to help members of these groups succeed in their quests to become physicians.

Defining Underrepresented Minorities in Medicine

Sometimes applicants are unsure whether the racial or ethnic group they belong to is considered a minority in medicine because a group that's a minority within the U.S. population as a whole may be proportionally represented, or even overrepresented, within the medical profession. Various enrichment programs, scholarships, and support services for minorities in medicine have their own specific criteria for inclusion; however, the Association of American Medical Colleges (AAMC) defines *underrepresented in medicine* as "those racial and ethnic populations that are underrepresented in the medical profession relative to their numbers in the general population."

Another way to consider the issue of minority status in medicine is from a historical perspective. Some racial and ethnic groups historically underrepresented in the medical profession include the following:

- African American
- Hispanic/Latino
- Native American
- Native Hawaiian/Pacific Islander

Enrichment, scholarship, and other programs for minorities may focus on members of these groups or use other criteria for eligibility. You can read more about such opportunities in the later section "Surveying Resources for Minority and Disadvantaged Applicants."

Designating Yourself as Socioeconomically Disadvantaged

Socioeconomically disadvantaged applicants are another group that's underrepresented within medicine. Medical school cost, lack of exposure to the profession, limited educational opportunities, and other factors are barriers that prevent individuals from disadvantaged backgrounds from becoming doctors. Schools understand that an applicant's financial, social, and family situations impact her opportunities, and they take into account obstacles a student has faced when assessing an application.

Primary applications (see Chapter 8) include questions that help schools to better understand your background. Don't hesitate to provide this information; medical schools are sincerely interested in understanding the challenges that applicants may have faced.

Questions in the "Childhood Information" section of the Association of American Medical Colleges' AMCAS application address factors such as the following:

- ✔ Whether you grew up in a medically underserved area

- ✔ Where your primary childhood residency was (city, state, county, country, and type of area, such as urban or rural)

- ✔ Whether your family has received public assistance (food stamps, welfare, and so on)

- ✔ What your family income level is

- ✔ Whether you were employed before age 18 and whether you contributed to the support of your family

- ✔ How you paid for your post-secondary education (scholarship, loans, family, self)

Applicants are also asked whether they want to be considered disadvantaged. If you respond "yes" to this question, you have the opportunity to explain your disadvantaged status by completing a short essay (1,325 characters, including spaces). Here are some examples of topics you can include in this discussion:

- ✔ Living in an unsafe and/or impoverished neighborhood

- ✔ Residing in a rural area with limited access to healthcare

- ✔ Growing up in a family without sufficient financial resources

- ✔ Working to help support your family or yourself

- ✔ Being the first member of your family to attend college

- ✔ Facing cultural or language barriers

- ✔ Attending a low-performing school or suffering from other educational disadvantages

Make the explanation of your situation as specific as possible. For example, avoid vague statements such as "The high school I went to didn't provide a good education." A more effective description would be "The graduation rate at the high school I attended was less than 60 percent. Fights, disruptions during class, and other disciplinary problems were common. Few honors or other advanced courses were available, especially in science subjects."

Like AMCAS, the American Association of Colleges of Osteopathic Medicine Application Service (AACOMAS) allows applicants to self-designate disadvantaged status. Applicants may select the type of disadvantage (for example, economic); however, you don't get any space in which to give additional explanation.

Even if you choose not to designate yourself as disadvantaged, schools may still learn about obstacles you've faced through your responses in other areas of your application. For example, if you indicate in the work and activities section that you worked a significant number of hours during the school year, admissions committees will be aware that you had less time to devote to your studies or other activities. Or you may describe how you overcame hardships that you faced as part of the personal statement or in response to a question on a secondary application.

You may self-designate as disadvantaged, but the admissions committee may not agree that your situation was significant enough to merit any type of special consideration. The best approach to take when filling out the disadvantaged status section (or any part of the application) is to be clear and thorough. After that, it's in the hands of the committee to decide how to use the information you provide.

Surveying Resources for Minority and Disadvantaged Applicants

Lots of programs are in place to help minority and disadvantaged applicants prepare for, apply to, and pay for medical school. For example, individuals who self-identify as a member of a group that has been historically under-represented in medicine or who are economically disadvantaged and who are U.S. citizens/permanent residents can choose to be included in the Medical Minority Applicant Registry (Med-MAR) when they register for the Medical College Admission Test (MCAT). If you participate in the Med-MAR, medical schools receive your MCAT scores as well as other basic information about you and may contact you as part of their diversity outreach efforts. (Flip to Chapter 6 for the basics on the MCAT.) You can find more information about the Med-MAR at www.aamc.org/students/minorities/med-mar.

Some programs reach out to minority and disadvantaged students in high school or earlier; others are available to premedical students during college; still others focus on helping minority and disadvantaged students who are already in medical school. Premedical advisors, medical school diversity offices, and student organizations also act as sources of support for minority and disadvantaged students.

Whether you're a minority or disadvantaged student who's just starting to consider a career in medicine, in the midst of applying, or in med school, the subsequent sections introduce you to opportunities for academic support and financial aid as you make your way toward becoming a physician.

Examining enrichment programs

Enrichment programs are available for minority and disadvantaged applicants in all phases of premedical and medical education. The following are the major types of enrichment programs:

- **Summer programs for high school and college students interested in medicine:** These programs are often sponsored by medical schools and include some combination of science classes and laboratories, study skills workshops, MCAT preparation, shadowing experiences, and advising. One example is the Summer Medical and Dental Education Program (SMDEP), a free six-week program open to college freshmen and sophomores who are selected to participate based on factors that include minority or disadvantaged status. More information is available at www.smdep.org.

- **Preparation programs for incoming first-year medical students:** Some medical schools offer a summer course to help minority and disadvantaged students who are matriculating in the fall prepare academically and personally for medical school. Students usually get exposure to some of the first-year course work as well as learn about academic and other support services available during medical school. When you're researching programs for your list of medical schools (see Chapter 7), check to see which schools offer summer preparation programs for incoming students and what the courses include.

- **Post-baccalaureate programs:** Some post-baccalaureate programs are specifically aimed at helping disadvantaged applicants become more competitive for admission into medical school. These programs may be for first-time applicants or for reapplicants and may include science courses, MCAT preparation, personal statement help, assistance with study skills, advising, and exposure to physicians and medical students. (Check out Chapters 3 and 15 for a discussion of types of post-bacs and tips for locating programs.)

At this point, you may be wondering how to locate these great-sounding programs.

- Your high-school counselor or college premedical advisor is a good starting point; see Chapter 5 for details on getting help from a premedical advisor.

- Check for information on the AAMC and AACOM websites (www.aamc.org and www.aacom.org, respectively) and contact the diversity affairs offices at individual medical schools to see whether a given school sponsors enrichment programs.

✔ Consider joining the Minority Association of Premedical Students (MAPS), which is the undergraduate wing of the Student National Medical Association (SNMA), a student-run organization dedicated to helping underrepresented minority premedical and medical students and underserved communities. SNMA/MAPS supports various outreach activities as well as provides a means for minority students interested in medicine to connect with one another and with mentors. The MAPS site is www.snma.org/premedical.php.

Finding financial resources

Although the cost of a medical education is high, if medicine is the career you really want, it's achievable even if you're from a background with very limited financial means. In addition to the financial aid programs described in Chapter 18 that are available to all students, you also may be eligible to apply for scholarships and grants established to help minority and disadvantaged students become physicians.

Even before you start medical school, you may be worried about expenses; the costs associated with applying can run into the thousands, including a registration fee for the MCAT, primary and secondary application fees, and perhaps the cost of buying a suit and travelling to interviews. However, help is available: Both the AAMC and the AACOM have programs that reduce the costs involved in applying to medical school. Information about applying to these programs is available through the AAMC and AACOM:

✔ The AAMC's Fee Assistance Program (FAP) allows applicants with financial need to register for the MCAT at a reduced cost. (See Chapter 6 for details about MCAT registration.) In addition, AMCAS waives FAP applicants' primary application fees for up to 14 medical schools. Some medical schools waive their secondary application fees for FAP applicants as well.

✔ If you're a financially disadvantaged applicant interested in osteopathic schools, you can apply for a fee waiver through AACOMAS that is applied to up to three schools on the primary application. Individual DO schools waive secondary fees at their discretion.

Although these programs decrease the cost of applying, the real expenses begin after you start medical school. The cost of a medical education can be especially intimidating if you don't have family resources to rely on; however, many grants, scholarships, and loans are awarded based on need (check out Chapter 18 for financial aid information). Overall, students with the fewest financial resources have the greatest likelihood of qualifying for more desirable forms of financial aid such as grants and low-interest loans. In addition, disadvantaged and minority medical students have access to both school-based and outside scholarships. For example, the American Medical Association's Minority Scholars Award provides up to a $10,000 scholarship for selected minority students. Check with your school's financial aid office, diversity affairs office, or your premedical advisor to find out about scholarship opportunities that you're eligible to apply for.

Applying with a Disability

Having a disability doesn't necessarily preclude you from becoming a doctor. Although it takes extra perseverance, individuals with learning disabilities, hearing and visual impairments, and other disabilities have attained medical degrees and become practicing physicians. Physicians with disabilities contribute to the diversity of the profession and bring unique insights to the practice of medicine.

Because the physical, emotional, and cognitive demands of medical school are different from those of undergraduate education, even individuals who applied for college with a disability may not know what to expect from medical school admissions and the medical education itself. Applicants with disabilities go through the same admissions process as anyone else; however, in addition to the usual application-related tasks, they often need to deal with extra issues. These obstacles may include requesting accommodations on the MCAT, determining how to handle the disclosure of a disability, and working with medical schools to determine accommodations for both classroom and patient care settings. The type and severity of disabilities applicants have varies greatly, so your personal situation determines exactly how you deal with these issues; however, the following sections discuss some factors many applicants with disabilities need to consider as they apply to medical school.

Obtaining accommodations for the MCAT

Some test-takers require accommodations for the MCAT because of a disability or medical condition. For example, an examinee with a learning disability may receive extra time for the test or be given a private room in which to take the examination. As part of your request for accommodations, you need to supply documentation about your disability, such as an evaluation from a professional and evidence that you've received accommodations in the past.

Requesting accommodations doesn't necessarily mean you'll get them. If you're denied your request, you have the option of appealing the decision or providing additional evidence and asking that your case be reconsidered. You may also opt to take the MCAT without accommodations.

For some accommodations, such as extended time, the score report notes that the examination was taken under nonstandard conditions, although it doesn't disclose any information about the type of accommodations or your disability or condition.

The AAMC recommends that examinees request any necessary accommodations at least 60 days prior to their planned test date. Register for the test prior to applying for accommodations so that you have a seat already reserved for the date you want while you await a decision about receiving accommodations. (Flip to Chapter 6 for more details about registering for the MCAT).

Disclosing a disability

"Should I disclose my disability? If so, when?" are questions that weigh heavily on the minds of many applicants with disabilities. The major concern of these applicants is usually that revealing that they have a disability may negatively impact their chance of admission, despite legal protections provided by the Americans with Disabilities Act. Some applicants decide to play it safe (in their views) and wait until after they've received an acceptance to disclose a disability. As you decide which course to take with regard to disclosure, make sure that you consider not only the drawbacks of earlier disclosure but also the potential benefits. For example, you may want to discuss your disability on your personal statement in the context of how you became interested in medicine or to illustrate how you overcome obstacles.

Although you may choose not to disclose a disability until you have an acceptance in hand, remember that you'll eventually have to discuss your situation with the school administration if you require accommodations during medical school. In that case, you provide the school with documentation regarding your disability and work with the administration, and usually staff from the university's office for students with disabilities, to determine whether you can complete the medical school curriculum with reasonable accommodations and what type of accommodations you require. Note that each medical school has its own procedure for students to follow when requesting accommodations, so check with the schools to find out when and how to approach this process. Some schools specifically request that students wait until a decision has been made regarding their admission before requesting accommodations.

Examples of accommodations include the following:

- A sign language interpreter
- A note-taking service
- Modified equipment (such as an amplified stethoscope)
- Course materials written in larger font

With advances in technology, med students and physicians with disabilities have resources that weren't available to previous generations, making a disability less of a barrier to becoming a doctor now than ever before.

Part V
You're In! Getting Ready to Go

Five Tips for Succeeding in Medical School

- **Make a study schedule.** Although keeping up with your courses in medical school is difficult, catching up if you fall behind is even harder.

- **Stay organized.** You're inundated with information and materials as a med student, so developing a system right away to keep track of everything for your courses is crucial.

- **Develop a support network.** Build up relationships with classmates and other members of your medical school community and maintain contact with your family and friends.

- **Take care of your physical and emotional health.** Even though you're very busy, make it a priority to eat well, get exercise, and set aside time to relax and do the things you enjoy.

- **Know that you've got what it takes to succeed.** If the school didn't think you had the right stuff to become a physician, you wouldn't be here. Have this same confidence in yourself.

Select a specialty with the help of a free article at www.dummies.com/extras/gettingintomedicalschool.

In this part . . .

✔ Confront the costs of attending medical school and craft a budget to help you keep those costs under control.

✔ Investigate options for financial aid, such as federal loans, institutional aid, and service-based scholarships.

✔ Prepare for your first year by figuring out housing, transportation, and more.

✔ Succeed as a medical student by staying organized, building a support system, and taking care of yourself.

Chapter 18

Paying for Medical School

. . . .

In This Chapter

▶ Assessing the cost of attending medical school and developing a budget

▶ Investigating options for financial aid

▶ Understanding how to apply for financial aid

▶ Being aware of the pitfalls of working during medical school

. . . .

*A*fter "Will I get into medical school?", the most pressing question for a premedical student is often "How am I going to pay for it?" However, becoming a doctor doesn't require winning the lottery or having a trust fund. In fact, most medical students rely on some form of financial aid to pay for part or all of their education, taking advantage of one or more of the many options available in the form of loans, scholarships, and grants.

Even if you're just getting started thinking about a medical career, you can benefit from understanding how much attending med school really costs and examining potential ways to pay for it. In this chapter, I discuss how to determine the cost of your medical education and to develop a budget to follow during your med school years. Next, I cover the types of financial aid, including loans, school-based aid, and military and other service-based scholarship programs, as well as go over the basics of applying for aid.

Students who rely on financial aid to pay for a significant portion of medical school are understandably concerned about of incurring debt. However, medicine is a stable career and offers a much-higher-than-average income, even for the less lucrative specialties. Believe it or not, getting into medical school, not paying for it, is usually the hardest part of becoming a physician.

Confronting the Cost of Medical School

You're probably well aware that medical school is expensive but may be unsure of exactly what costs are involved. Although tuition is the largest and most obvious expense, it's far from the only one you face as you make your way through the next four years. In addition to tuition and fees, you need to pay for things like books, rent, utilities, food, health insurance, transportation, and other necessities. Regardless of whether you need financial aid, a solid financial plan starts with researching your expected expenses and formulating a detailed budget.

The following sections explore the costs involved in attending medical school, the process of compiling a budget, and the way medical school financial aid offices determine your financial need based on a standard student budget.

The prospect of paying for medical school can be especially daunting for students from low-income families and those who are first-generation college students. However, both the means to pay for medical school and the help to navigate the financial aid system are out there, so don't give up. If you're unfamiliar with the system, contact a financial aid officer at your prospective med school and let him know. He can guide you through the red tape involved and make sure that you are on track to get the financial support you need.

Understanding the cost of attendance

Tuition and fees for a single year of medical school are well over $40,000 at most private schools and top $50,000 at some. Even going to a public medical school doesn't mean your education will be inexpensive; tuition and fees for state residents at public schools typically run $20,000 to $30,000. No wonder future medical students often focus on tuition when considering the costs of attending medical school! However, books, supplies, health insurance, rent, and other living expenses add another $20,000 or so to the total amount you need to pay for each year of school. In fact, the total cost for a student's expenses, including education and living expenses, has an official name: *cost of attendance* (COA).

COA is different for each medical school and is part of what financial aid offices use to determine financial need in order to allocate need-based aid. (See the later section "Determining your eligibility for financial aid" for more about the relationship between COA and financial aid.) Differences for COA among schools are the product of differences in tuition and fees as well as variations in the cost of housing, transportation, and other items in the budget.

For example, rent is typically higher in major metropolitan areas and lower in rural ones. Conversely, clinical sites at a rural school may be spread farther apart, necessitating a car, while students at urban schools have access to less-expensive public transportation. (See Chapter 7 for more about comparing costs of medical schools.) Each school's financial aid office determines that school's COA based on the many factors particular to that program and the area in which it's located.

The COAs for students attending an individual medical school aren't necessarily exactly the same. Your COA may be somewhat different from another student's at your school because of additional *allowable* expenses added to the COA. For example, a student's COA may be adjusted to include an allocated amount for childcare expenses.

COA is also valuable to you as a future medical student as you compare the cost for different medical schools and make your own personal budget. You can find the estimated cost of attendance for most medical schools on their websites or (for allopathic schools) in the *Medical School Admission Requirements* (MSAR) online database available for purchase through the Association of American Medical Colleges (AAMC) site at `services.aamc.org/30/msar/home`. For osteopathic medical schools, see the *Osteopathic Medical College Information Book*, downloadable from the American Association of Colleges of Osteopathic Medicine (AACOM) site at `www.aacom.org`.

Putting together a budget

The cost of attendance that a school's financial office determines doesn't vary much from student to student; however, you may have extra expenses unique to your situation. For this reason, you also need to formulate a personal budget based on your expected costs. By drafting a budget, you can ensure that you have enough resources to pay your bills instead of counting on a budget for a typical student at your school only to realize that you're going to run short of funds before the end of the semester. No matter what your situation, mapping out a budget before you start medical school and sticking to it as closely as possible is the wisest approach.

During medical school, your costs fall into two main categories: education expenses and living expenses:

- ✔ Education expenses

  - Tuition and fees

  - Books and supplies

  - Medical instruments

  - Computer and other technology

  - Fees for licensure exams (USMLE or COMLEX)

  - Application fees and travel expenses related to applying to residency programs

✔ Living expenses

- Rent and utilities

- Health insurance

- Food

- Transportation

- Phone

- Personal expenses (clothing, entertainment, and so on)

The budget for each year of medical school is slightly different because of the way medical education is structured. For example, first-year students have to purchase medical instruments such as a stethoscope and otoscope, but they usually incur lower transportation costs than third-and fourth-year students, who have to travel to clinical rotations. Fees for licensure examinations are an expense that usually applies only to second- and fourth-year students. You can use the school's standard student budget (available on the school's website or by contacting the financial aid office) to help you determine how much to allocate for each budget category.

Figure 18-1 shows an example of a student budget for the first year of medical school. Note that this budget includes living expenses for the summer; however, schools calculate cost of attendance based only on the time that school is in session (typically 9 to 12 months depending on your year and whether you're in a summer session). Therefore, the amount of financial aid you receive won't factor in summer break after the first year, so if you don't plan to move home for the summer, you'll have to find a way to pay for your expenses during that time. This situation is one example of how a student's personal budget can differ from the budget estimated by the school.

The amount of financial aid you receive can't be higher than the COA. If your personal budget is higher than the cost of attendance determined by your school's financial office, check to see whether any of your additional expenses are considered allowable. For example, your base COA may not account for the fact that you need to buy a computer for school; however, the school may separately approve including that expense in your COA, which will raise your total COA. An increase in your COA allows you to receive more aid.

Because financial aid covers up to the cost of attendance only, you'll have to look for other options if your costs are higher than the ones the school estimates for you and you're depending on aid to pay for school. For example, the school may allocate $8,000 a year for rent when calculating your COA, a number that may only be feasible if you share an apartment with a roommate. If you decide that living alone is important to you and calculate the cost of renting a studio apartment to be $12,000 a year, you'll need to cut $4,000 from elsewhere in your budget to make up the difference. Other possibilities are getting help from family or seeking out a private loan that allows you to borrow above the COA. Or you may take another look at the numbers and decide you can put up with a roommate after all! In any case, by knowing what your true expenses will be, you can make an informed decision.

Annual Expenses

Education Expenses

Tuition	$ 41,000
Textbooks and supplies	$ 820
Instruments	$ 730
Computer and other technology	$ 700

Living Expenses

Rent and utilities	$ 10,500
Health insurance	$ 3,300
Food	$ 3,900
Transportation	$ 3,000
Phone	$ 720
Miscellaneous (clothing, personal items, recreation, etc.)	$ 4,080
Total	**$ 68,750**

Figure 18-1:
A sample budget for the first year of medical school.

Living Expenses Broken Down Per Month

Rent and utilities	$ 875
Health insurance	$ 275
Food	$ 325
Transportation	$ 250
Phone	$ 60
Miscellaneous (clothing, personal items, recreation, etc.)	$ 340
Total	**$ 2,125**

Illustration by Wiley, Composition Services Graphics

Determining your eligibility for aid

How much and what type of financial aid you receive depends on financial need. Financial need is determined by a formula that involves cost of attendance and expected family contribution (EFC). *Expected family contribution* is the amount that a student and/or his family are expected to pitch in to cover the cost of medical school.

The formula for determining financial need is as follows:

Cost of attendance – Expected family contribution = Financial need

For the purposes of most types of federal loans, graduate and professional students are considered to be independent from their parents. However, when determining the EFC for eligibility for institutional funds (including school-based grants, scholarships, and low-interest loans), medical schools usually factor in the income, assets, and benefits of the student, of his spouse (if applicable), *and* of his parents. A medical student may be married or have been self-supporting for many years prior to medical school, yet most schools still factor in parental contribution when determining EFC to determine need for institutional and certain other need-based funds. (Some schools make exceptions for students who are above a certain age or who are estranged from their parents, which allows these students to apply for institutional aid without providing their parents' financial information.) Schools include family contribution when determining need in order to ensure that funds go to students who have the fewest resources. (For more information about school-based aid see the later section "Institutional aid.")

Students who plan to pay for medical school themselves may be concerned about how they'll cover the amount designated as EFC if their parents won't be contributing money toward their medical educations. Don't worry, though; if this is your situation, you're not stuck. Many students don't receive the full EFC from their families for various reasons and use non-need-based federal loans (discussed in the later section "Federal Direct Loans") and private loans to cover the EFC.

Note that to receive federal aid you must be a U.S. citizen, national, or permanent resident or be a foreign citizen with asylum or other special status that confers eligibility. Policies regarding institutional aid vary by school, but many restrict certain or all types of school-based aid to U.S. citizens and permanent residents. Because of these policies, financial aid for international students attending U.S. medical schools is very limited.

Exploring Types of Aid

After your financial need has been determined, the school's financial aid office presents you with an award letter describing your financial aid package. If you submit your paperwork to the financial aid office by the priority deadline established by the school (often in March or early April) you're likely to receive your award letter by mid-May. Note, however, that the amount of time a financial aid office takes to process your application and send an award letter varies. Check with the school's financial aid office to find out the schedule.

Although a financial aid package may include scholarships and grants as well as loans, many medical students pay for the majority of their educations by borrowing money. In fact, more than 80 percent of medical students graduate with some level of debt. According to the AAMC, the average debt for medical students graduating in 2012 was $166,750, including undergraduate and other debt.

The following sections discuss some of the major types of financial aid available to medical students, including institutional, federal, service-based aid, and private educational loans.

Institutional aid

Many medical schools provide school-funded aid in the form of grants, scholarships, and loans. The amount and type of institutional aid varies significantly among schools. Schools with larger endowments and greater financial resources generally have the most-generous school-based aid packages. In fact, some private schools can actually be cheaper to attend than a public school because of the number and size of grants and scholarships awarded to students.

School-based grants and scholarships are often need-based. Unlike loans, grants and scholarships don't need to be paid back, so they're the best types of aid to have. Grants and scholarships may be "only" a few thousand dollars or may be much larger, covering a significant portion of the tuition.

In addition to need-based scholarships, many schools award a small number of merit-based scholarships. Students may be selected for these awards based on academic achievement (as demonstrated by GPA and MCAT scores), achievements in areas such as community service or leadership, or a desire to pursue a particular area (such as research or primary care). Some med schools award a few large merit scholarships that pay for most or all of tuition.

As part of institutional aid, some programs provide school-based loans to students with financial need. The terms of these loans are usually very favorable compared with other types of educational loans. For example, school-based loans usually have relatively low interests rates, and interest on the loan doesn't begin to accrue until after a student has graduated from medical school. Because this type of aid is very desirable, make sure you don't miss out on the opportunity to apply for it.

To qualify for institutional aid, you may need to provide your parents' financial information in addition to your own. As I discuss in the earlier section "Determining your eligibility for aid," schools usually determine need for institutional funds based on the financial situation of both the student and his family.

Federal Direct Loans

Direct Loans from the federal government are a major source of aid for many medical students. The lender for Direct Loans is the U.S. Department of Education, but the loans are serviced by outside companies that handle repayments, loan consolidation, and other issues. Direct Loans may be subsidized or unsubsidized; both types are also known as *Stafford loans.*

Because of a policy change effective July 1, 2012, graduate and professional students are no longer eligible for *Direct Subsidized Loans,* where the government pays the interest for a certain period. As a medical student, you can only take out a *Direct Unsubsidized Loan,* where the interest begins accruing immediately, even while you're in school.

In addition to Direct Unsubsidized Loans, medical students are eligible for *Direct PLUS loans,* another type of federal loan. Both Direct Unsubsidized Loans and Direct PLUS Loans are non-need-based, so your parents' income and assets don't affect whether you receive these loans. Both have fixed interest rates, meaning that the interest rate you're charged remains the same throughout the term of the loan. Table 18-1 compares some of the features of the two types of loans as of the 2012–2013 academic year.

Table 18-1	Features of Federal Direct Loans	
	Direct Unsubsidized Loan	**Direct PLUS Loan**
Interest rate	6.8%	7.9%
Origination fee	1%	4%
Annual loan limit	$40,500–$47,167[1]	Annual COA minus other aid
Aggregate loan limit	$224,000	None
Repayment grace or deferment period following graduation	6 months	6 months

[1]*The annual limit is different for each year of medical school. The annual loan limits in Table 18-1 represent the range of yearly limits.*

Direct PLUS Loans require borrowers to have good credit. A student with a bad credit history may need a cosigner to qualify for these loans.

Both loans have various options for repayment, which may include the following:

- ✔ **Deferment of loan payments during post-graduate education:** A minimum payment may still be required each month even with a deferral.

- ✔ **Extended repayment plans:** These plans allow you to take up to 25 years to repay the loan.

- ✔ **Graduated repayment:** Payments start out lower and then increase over time.

- ✔ **Income-contingent or income-based repayment:** These payment plans take your income into account when determining the amount of your monthly payments.

Check out the Federal Student Aid site at www.direct.ed.gov/ for more details on federal Direct Loans.

Other federal loans

Two other types of federal loans are federal Perkins loans and Primary Care Loans:

- ✔ *Perkins loans* are federally-funded loans administered by medical schools and awarded based on financial need. The annual limit for these loans is $8,000; the aggregate limit is $60,000, including any undergraduate loans. Interest is fixed at 5 percent and begins to accrue after the nine-month grace period following graduation has expired. Although the terms of these loans make them a good deal, the low annual limit means that they constitute only a small part of the financial aid packages for students with significant need. Scholarships, grants, and/or other types of loans have to make up the difference.

- ✔ *Primary Care Loans* are funded by the Department of Health and Human Services, with individual medical schools acting as lenders. Students may borrow up to the COA. The interest rate of the loan is fixed at 5 percent as of the 2012–2013 academic year, and interest doesn't begin to accrue until after the one-year grace period following graduation.

A major difference between Primary Care Loans and other types of federal loans is that they require a practice commitment following graduation. To be eligible for a Primary Care Loan, a student must agree to complete a residency in a primary care field (such as family medicine, pediatrics, internal medicine, or preventive medicine) and practice as a primary care physician for ten years — including time spent in residency — or until the loan is paid off (whichever comes first).

Unlike Direct Loans, these loans are need-based; even professional students have to submit parental financial income information to apply for these loans, with some exceptions.

Read about Perkins loans at `studentaid.ed.gov/types/loans/perkins`. For more information about Primary Care Loans, check out `www.hrsa.gov/loanscholarships/loans/primarycare.html`.

Private loans

Federal loans (described in the preceding two sections) usually have the best terms for students and are students' first choices. However, some students don't qualify for federal aid or they have other special circumstances and instead obtain *private* (alternative) educational loans. These loans are funded by private entities, and the interest rates, fees, terms, loan limits, and criteria for eligibility depend on the particular loan. Unlike federal loans, which have fixed interest rates, private loans often have variable interest rates that fluctuate based on market rates.

Private loans require a good credit history; applicants with poor credit records generally have to have a cosigner. If you're interested in private loans, check with your financial aid office for a list of lenders and check the terms carefully before you select one.

Service-based scholarships

Service-based scholarship programs are one means to graduate from school with little or no debt. These programs pay for some or all of a student's medical education and require a particular type and number of years of service in exchange. Service-based setups are a good fit for students who have a genuine interest in the type of service they'll be committing to, such as military service or work in a medically underserved area. Two major service scholarship programs are the Health Professions Scholarship Program (HPSP) through the military and the National Health Service Corps (NHSC) scholarship program.

Before undertaking any service-based program, make sure you determine whether the program fits your career interests. Having debt is stressful, but practicing primary care in a rural area when you're longing to be a cardiologist at an academic medical center can lead to a lot of angst as well. Take on any service commitment program only if you have good reason to think that you'll enjoy the setting you'll be working in and the specialty you'll be practicing.

Health Professions Scholarship Program

HPSP scholarships offered through the Army, Navy, or Air Force are very comprehensive. They pay the full amount of your medical school tuition, books, fees, and other educational expenses in addition to providing a monthly stipend of around $2,000. You may also receive a signing bonus.

In this program, you participate in various types of training with the military, such as officer training, during some of your breaks in medical school, but you focus mostly on your medical education. After graduating from medical school, most scholarship holders enter a military residency for post-graduate training, although some exceptions allow graduates to complete a civilian residency. After you finish your residency, you must to complete your active duty service obligation to the military: one year of active duty for each year that the military paid for your medical education, with a minimum three-year commitment. If you received your scholarship for all four years of medical school, you owe the military four years of active duty after residency. You also owe the same number of years of inactive duty in the reserve following active duty.

To find out more about the HPSP, contact a recruiter for the specific branch of the armed forces you're interested in.

National Health Service Corps scholarship program

The *NHSC scholarship program* is offered through the National Health Service Corps with the goal of increasing the number of primary care providers in medically underserved areas. The NHSC scholarship pays for the medical education of students interested in careers in primary care; in exchange, the student must commit to working as a physician in an area designated as a Health Professional Shortage Area (HPSA) approved by the NHSC. This scholarship is extensive and includes tuition, other education costs, and a living stipend for up to four years of medical school. After completing medical school and residency, you're required to practice medicine in a shortage area until your obligation is fulfilled. The commitment is one year of practice for each year of school that the scholarship has paid for, with a minimum service commitment of two years.

In addition to scholarships, the National Health Service Corps also offers loan repayment programs. For example, through the NHSC's "Students to Service" program, fourth-year medical students planning to go into primary care receive up to $120,000 in loan repayment for working as a physician in a medically underserved area for a minimum of three years full time or six years half time.

Head to `nhsc.hrsa.gov/index.html` to look into NHSC scholarship and loan repayment programs further.

Applying for Financial Aid

Applying for financial aid of any type means entering a complex world of forms, policies, regulations, and interest rates. The starting point for all this craziness is the Free Application for Federal Student Aid (FAFSA), a document you're familiar with if you applied for financial aid as an undergraduate student. The information you enter on the FAFSA is transmitted to the financial aid offices of the medical schools that you select and is used to determine your EFC and financial need (see the earlier section "Determining your eligibility for aid" for more info).

The FAFSA is available online at `www.fafsa.ed.gov/` and may be submitted as early as January. The deadline for submission is different for each school, but don't wait until the last minute to send your FAFSA; delaying means waiting longer to find out what your financial aid package is as well as potentially missing out on particular types of aid.

Along with other information regarding your background and financial situation, you need to submit tax information to complete the FAFSA. The easiest way to submit your tax info is by uploading it automatically onto the FAFSA with the IRS Data Retrieval Tool (DRT). If you fill out the FAFSA online, you can opt to answer questions within the application that determine your eligibility to use the DRT. If you're eligible, you'll be provided with a link to access the DRT.

Even if you're not sure which medical school you'll be attending, you can still proceed with filling out the FAFSA by designating the federal school codes for medical schools you've been accepted to and are still under consideration at. You must submit a new FAFSA each academic year in order to receive financial aid. In addition, some medical schools require their own supplemental applications in addition to the FAFSA, especially if you want to apply for institutional aid.

Keep in close contact with the financial aid office throughout the process of applying for financial aid. Medical school financial aid officers are experts on the process of applying for aid and are there to help you along the way. Financial aid officers can also provide you with information about outside grants and scholarships you may be eligible to apply for, help you attain an emergency loan if an unexpected expense arises, and provide counseling about budgeting, debt management, and loan repayment.

Working during Medical School

Holding a job (even a part-time one) as a medical student is extremely difficult. Although you may have worked as an undergraduate student, med school takes things to a whole new level of busyness. Because med school is so time-consuming, med student employment is generally only feasible the summer after the first year. That summer may be the only one during which you have a relatively long break; during that time, you may be able to find a research position with a stipend or other temporary employment if you choose. After the first two years of medical school, clinical rotations begin and working is impossible; you spend enough hours on the wards or at the clinic to at least equal a full-time job, and often much more than that.

Any money that you're able to earn during med school can help decrease how much debt you accrue, but your real job is being a medical student. If working even a few hours a week interferes with that, then you're better off not working. If you do take on some work, it should be very part time, such as 4 or 6 hours per week, and have flexible hours.

Chapter 19

Starting Medical School

• •

In This Chapter

▶ Using the summer to recharge and prepare for medical school

▶ Figuring out where you'll live and how you'll get to school

▶ Beginning medical school on the right foot

▶ Building a foundation for success as a medical student

• •

After you've celebrated your offer of admission and taken a break to recover from the application process, you're ready to dive into preparing to start med school in the fall. Embarking on this new phase of your life requires you to address the academic, logistical, and personal aspects of being a medical student. Finding housing, figuring out transportation, and taking care of other details related to relocating are a major part of your preparation if you're moving in order to attend school. However, whether you're going to med school across the street or on the other side of the country, you still need to develop strategies for handling the workload and new environment you'll encounter. Because med school is a big step up in difficulty from undergraduate studies, even the strongest student should put some forethought into the adjustment to first year, strategies for academic success, and resources available to her if she encounters difficulties.

This chapter walks you through the practical aspects of starting your first year of medical school and provides tips for addressing the academic and personal challenges that you may confront as a med student.

Enjoying the Summer Before: A Time of Relaxation and Preparation

Relish your summer. The months between the end of your undergraduate studies and the first day of medical school are a much-needed respite from academics and the application process, so taking this time to recharge is important. I'm not saying that you shouldn't take a summer job to earn some money before becoming a full-time student again or that you can't crack a book to brush up on academics. Just make sure that you also set aside time to spend with friends, travel, or otherwise take advantage of the fact that you're in a rare phase between the many steps on the long road to becoming a physician. Make it your goal for the summer to achieve a balance between preparing for medical school and simply relaxing and enjoying the fact that you've made it this far.

The decision about whether to do any pre-studying over the summer in order to get a head start on the material very much depends on your individual situation. I don't recommend turning the summer into a mini med school prep course or spending hours a day studying; however, if you've taken a *gap year* (or more) off between graduating from college and going to medical school, some light review of physiology, biochemistry, or other relevant subjects may make you feel more comfortable. (You can read more about considering a gap year in Chapter 5.) If you do decide to hit the books over the summer, check out the curriculum at your future med school to determine which topics are most useful to focus on as you work to get back up to speed.

Even those students who go directly from college to med school can benefit from familiarizing themselves with anatomy before their first semester, especially because many students haven't taken that subject previously. The best approach is to buy an anatomy atlas and spend some time perusing it to become familiar with some of the structures and terminology involved. As someone who didn't take anatomy prior to med school, I can attest that my life would've been easier during my first year if I'd learned the basics before setting foot on campus. Everything turned out fine, but starting from square one meant many extra hours and late nights of studying!

Along with addressing your academic preparation for med school, use the summer to finalize your plan to pay for your education and to get your personal finances in order. If you have any credit card or other consumer debt, try to eliminate it before you start school because those payments aren't factored into your student budget in determining aid. (Refer to Chapter 18 for information about financial aid). Working over the summer can help you to meet that goal or give you a cushion for emergencies or a little extra spending money.

Ideally, you already know where you'll be attending school by the time summer hits and can plan accordingly, but if you're still waitlisted at a school you prefer to attend over the one(s) you've been accepted at, don't give up your efforts to secure a desired spot. Continue to keep in touch with schools where you're waitlisted over the summer by sending a letter of update or letter of interest/intent (discussed in Chapter 11). Proceed with your plans to attend a school you've got an acceptance in hand for, but keep in mind that things may change even up to the last minute if another school comes through with an offer.

Nailing Down Logistics and More

For most students, attending medical school requires relocating to a new area — finding a place to live, figuring out the best way to get around your new area, and dealing with many other details. Students who continued to live at home during college may be on their own for the first time during medical school; others have been on their own for years. Either way, heading off to a new place takes a lot of planning. The following sections give you tips about managing the big issues (such as deciding where to live) as well as the small ones (figuring out the best route to campus) so that by the time school starts, you're set up and ready to go.

Housing

The biggest logistical issue you need to take care of is finding a place to live. The major options you have for housing as a medical student are these:

✔ **University-owned housing:** Many medical schools offer various forms of housing for graduate/professional students, including both single students and those who are married and/or have families. These possibilities range from on-campus dormitory-style rooms or suites to off-campus apartments. University housing is usually low cost relative to the area and convenient to campus. However, the supply may be very limited, making a place difficult to obtain.

✔ **Renting a privately-owned apartment or room in a house:** Renting an apartment, condo, or part of a house is a very popular choice for medical students. This option provides the most flexibility in terms of location and type of housing. Depending on your financial situation and preference, you may elect to live alone or share housing with one or more roommates.

If you need help finding a roommate, contact your medical school to see whether it has a mechanism for connecting incoming students who are looking for housing with one another. Also check to see whether a class page has been established at any social networking sites so that you can contact your fellow students directly. Take the time to choose the right roommate for your lifestyle as a medical student. You'll need a lot of quiet time to study, so look for someone who whose habits won't interfere with your ability to accomplish what you need to.

✔ **Purchasing a house or a condominium:** Buying a home requires significant financial resources, so this option is limited primarily to nontraditional students whose spouses are employed or to students whose families are purchasing a place for or with them. Owning a home offers the advantage of stability as well as the potential to build equity, but it also can be a burden if you need to relocate for residency training, especially if the housing market declines during the years you're in med school.

Figuring out where you're going to live is especially challenging if you're moving to a city you're unfamiliar with because you don't know the going rates for rent or nuances of different areas. To get an insider's view of what neighborhoods are good bets, see whether your med school can put you in touch with some current students so that you can get their take on the pros and cons of different neighborhoods. In particular, ask about the safety, affordability, and convenience to campus of areas you're considering. Your quality of life and productivity in medical school depend in part on your living situation, so do your research before signing a lease.

Transportation

Your transportation needs as a medical student depend on whether your school is located in an urban, suburban, or rural area; where you live in relation to the school; and where you are in your program. If the school is in an urban area with a good public transportation system, you may be able to use that as a means to travel to and from campus and perhaps even to clinical sites. However, if the school is situated in an area with limited public transportation (such as the suburbs or a rural area), owning a car may be necessary.

The mode of transportation you use may change during medical school based on your year in the program.

- ✔ At most medical schools, the first two years (the *preclinical years*) are spent doing primarily nonclinical activities such as attending lectures and labs. If you have on-campus housing or live nearby, you may not need a car for the preclinical years because you spend most of your time on campus.

- ✔ However, the situation changes significantly during the third and fourth years (the *clinical years*), when you rotate to different hospitals and clinics located varying distances from the main campus. For example, my clinical rotations ranged from 5 minutes away on foot to 45 minutes by car.

Although a car is often necessary for the clinical years, try to avoid being saddled with car payments during med school. When you're a medical student on a tight budget, that extra expense may be very difficult to meet. If you don't have a car already, one way to keep costs down is to look for a used car in good condition instead of splurging on a new one. If you do have car payments, even small ones, make sure you account for these in your budget. (See Chapter 18 for info on making a budget.)

Other considerations

After medical school starts, you get busy with classes and seemingly nonstop studying and don't want to waste time running errands that you could've completed earlier. Plan to move in at least a week before orientation for medical school begins — two is even better — in order to tackle the many details involved in getting set up in a new place.

Here's a list of some of things to knock off your to-do list before the first day of school:

- **Buy any miscellaneous items you need for your household.** A desk lamp, microwave, or coffee maker may not be essential to survival (well, maybe the coffee maker is), but if you're going to get them at some point, do it before you're knee-deep in schoolwork.

- **Shop for clothing and other gear appropriate to the climate.** If you're moving to a state with a much different climate from the one you came from, you may have some serious shopping to do. Buying the gear you need after you've arrived in your new location is usually best because the local stores stock items tailored to the region's climate. In fact, you may not even know what you need and may have to ask some of your fellow med students who are locals what basics to stock up on. Start out with a few necessities and then build up your wardrobe of cold- or warm-weather attire after you get an idea of what the weather is like during each season in your new area.

- **Determine the best route to campus.** To avoid worrying about being late for the first day of med school or having to get up early to figure out where you're going, take a trip to the campus at the same time of day that class starts. Your planned route may turn out to be a nightmare in rush hour traffic, or you may find that the bus you thought you'd take frequently runs late. Work out these kinks without the pressure of needing to be somewhere hanging over you.

- **Get to know the area.** Find the nearest grocery store and the cheapest gas station, locate a laundromat, and look for fun places to go for when you have some down time. If you have some free days, do a few of the touristy things that you may not have a chance for later in the year but want to check out. One of the benefits to moving to a new place is having fresh places to explore.

Another way to spend some of your time before school starts is getting together with some of the other first years. Meet up for coffee or dinner, or see some of the sights the area offers. Walking into orientation already knowing a few people makes the experience of starting med school more comfortable.

You can't plan for every eventuality, so you'll undoubtedly have some odds and ends to address during the first couple weeks of school as you settle in. However, taking care of as many details in advance as you can leaves you with that much less to do when the work involved in being a med student kicks in. By arriving early and familiarizing yourself with the area, you also get a head start on feeling at home in the community you'll be spending the next four years with.

Getting Off to a Good Start

The only way to fully understand what being a med student is like is to experience it. You learn more information in a shorter time than you would've imagined is possible and also go through many firsts, such as performing a physical examination on an actual patient, scrubbing into surgery, and spending the night on call in the hospital. The learning curve for being a medical student is steep and often requires on-the-job training; however, you can do some things to help start off strong and lay a solid foundation for the rest of your education. Doing well in med school requires being organized but flexible as well as having a strong support system.

Staying organized

Students who got by with a fly-by-the-seat-of-their-pants approach to academics as undergraduates may find themselves overwhelmed by the more intense demands of medical school. The number, difficulty, and pace of the courses you take as a med student are much greater than what you've likely encountered previously in your academic career. Cramming simply doesn't work when you're juggling anatomy, biochemistry, introduction to clinical medicine, and a couple of other classes, for example, as well as possibly spending days with a physician *preceptor* in her practice and doing other required activities. Keeping up with the course load in med school requires that you prioritize and stay organized. These tips can help you approach your academic responsibilities effectively:

- ✔ **Make a study schedule.** Having a plan helps you allocate your time realistically and feel less stressed about getting everything done. At first, your schedule creates a very general guideline to follow, but within a couple of weeks, you know which classes require a greater investment of time and can fine-tune your plan accordingly.

- ✔ **Find out from second-year students which textbooks you really need.** Frequently, the number of textbooks required and recommended for a course is greater than what you actually have time to read. Ask your peers who are farther along what materials are most important and then focus on those. This strategy also saves you money if you end up not buying every book listed in the syllabus. You can usually access textbooks in the library, so if you just need to use a particular one occasionally, you don't necessarily have to purchase it.

✔ **Don't fall behind.** The pace that classes move at is so rapid that catching up if you get even a few days behind can be difficult. You're also likely to absorb the information better if you do some studying almost every day rather than taking multiple days off and then doing a study marathon to catch up.

✔ **Develop a system to keep track of class materials.** Even in the age of electronics, you quickly accumulate papers of all types for your courses. For example, some students prefer to take handwritten notes because the act of writing helps them to retain information or because writing causes less eyestrain than using a laptop in class. Along with such notes, you may have printed handouts, copies of slides, and various other printed materials for your classes.

File everything in binders or folders immediately so that you don't have to waste time searching for something when you need it. Do the same for electronic information related to courses by creating (and using) a folder for each class on your computer. Even a few minutes saved each day adds up and may give you an extra hour of precious leisure time by the end of the week.

You may find that the study system you used in college doesn't translate to medical school. Be prepared for some trial and error as you find the best way to approach your classes, and be open to adapting your approach instead of being stuck on doing things a certain way because that worked for you as an undergraduate. Medical school is a whole new game!

Building a support system

Getting through medical school is a lot easier and more enjoyable if you have a strong support system. Even students who like med school overall and are happy with their career choice still go through tough periods and need someone to turn to. If you're attending medical school in or near your hometown or where you went to college, you may already have family members and friends nearby. However, being a med student is a unique experience, so building a network of peers and mentors who are in the midst of/have been through the same thing is also important. If you do relocate to an area where you know few or no people, finding a group to provide support and friendship is even more crucial.

Forming friendships

Your classmates are the most obvious place to look to form friendships, but don't expect these relationships to materialize without your putting in some effort. During orientation week, you get to know some of your fellow students before everyone becomes preoccupied with school, so make a point to reach out early on to people you want to know better. Some of the more socially driven members of the class usually take the initiative to organize group outings, and taking part in these events gives you the opportunity to spend time with your classmates in a context outside of school. If no one else is stepping up to get things going, take on the task yourself. Even if you don't find people you click with at first, don't give up. Eventually, you're likely to find a group that you fit in well with and may even end up meeting people in med school who are destined to become your lifelong friends.

Because much of your time revolves around studying after classes get underway, many friendships are built through meeting to do things like review drug interactions or biochemical pathways. Studying with a group at least occasionally gives you a change of pace and allows you to mix in some socialization with work.

Students in the years ahead of you are an excellent source of friendship and support as well. Some schools match each first-year student with a second-year who acts as a big sibling in navigating through med school. The trials of first year are fresh in the minds of second-year students, so they can tell you what to expect at each stage as they make their way through med school one step ahead of you.

Taking advantage of school resources

If you need help with something and aren't sure where to go, the student affairs office is a good place to start. A medical school's student affairs office provides guidance for academic and student life issues such as scheduling rotations, arranging for electives, and finding research opportunities. It can also provide support and connect a student to resources if she's having academic or personal difficulties. The student affairs office often organizes and runs orientation, so you'll probably meet the staff during that event.

Another source of guidance to you as a med student is your faculty advisor. At some schools, advisors are assigned at the beginning of first year, whereas others wait until the clinical years to provide an advisor. Advisors function as mentors, helping students to forge their paths professionally through discussions about topics such as which electives to choose, activities to pursue, and specialty to select. If your advisor is an attending physician, she's been through every step of the medical education process, so she can help you see the big picture even when you're caught up in the details of passing the next exam.

Although many support services are available at most medical schools, students may wait until they're struggling very significantly to get help — or not get help at all. Med schools are filled with independent-minded high achievers who are used to succeeding at everything they attempt and who may be uncomfortable asking for assistance. However, problems are much easier to solve when they're smaller, so act early if you're having difficulty academically or otherwise. Although you may not be aware of it, many of your fellow students are facing their own challenges of one type or another. Most people find it easier to seek assistance from someone they already have a working relationship, so take a few minutes to drop by the student affairs office occasionally to check out what it offers or just chat with the staff. Meet with your advisor on a regular basis even if you don't need help with a specific issue.

Most, if not all, med schools have a mechanism through which students can receive confidential counseling for mental health issues. If you're having a tough time coping with med school or have other emotional or personal issues that you prefer not to share with the school's faculty or staff, you can get assistance while maintaining your privacy by going through the counseling service.

Redefining Success as You Progress through Medical School

Defining what constitutes success in medical school is a bit different for every student. For some, success is almost exclusively about academic performance; others place a higher priority on achieving a work-life balance even if it means they don't graduate at the top of the class.

At the outset of medical school, you may not know exactly what you want to get from your education (other than your medical degree), but as you progress you get a better idea of what your goals are and what you are and aren't willing to sacrifice to achieve them. Doing well so that you keep your options open when it comes time to apply for residency programs is important, but not everyone needs or wants to go to a top program in one of the most competitive specialties.

Throughout medical school, constantly reassess your interests, goals, and quality of life and realize that your idea of success may change over time or be different from someone else's. Whether you're a future neurosurgeon aiming for the top grades and board scores necessary for this highly competitive field or are an aspiring primary care physician willing to forgo some study time to participate in community outreach, you can benefit from doing the following:

✔ **Taking care of your physical health:** When you're extremely busy, you may resort to fast food and snacks rather than regular meals, lose out on sleep, and skip exercising. This approach may work in the short term, but in the long term, you're better off taking care of yourself physically. The time you set aside to work out a few days a week or to make nutritious meals will likely be more than paid back in productivity through more energy and better overall health.

✔ **Maintaining your emotional well-being:** Medical school is very stressful at times, so you need to address not only your physical health but also your emotional health. Spending time with friends, having outside interests, and taking regular breaks from studying are important.

✔ **Realizing that medicine presents more information than one person can ever learn:** Like many med students, you may be very detail oriented and become frustrated that you just can't learn all the material thoroughly no matter how much time you spend studying. Medicine is a vast field, so the ability to prioritize information is one skill that's important to develop during med school. Learn the most important information first and well. If you have time after that, layer on more details. *Tip:* Often, the information presented in lecture is the highest priority for a class and should be focused on before anything else.

✔ **Keeping things in perspective:** Making it into med school means that you've passed through one of the biggest obstacles to becoming a physician. Med school and residency are a lot of work, but after you've secured a spot in med school, the chances that you'll finish the program and become a practicing physician one day are excellent. One less-than-stellar exam score or a rotation that didn't go ideally won't be the end of your medical career.

Part VI
The Part of Tens

Check out an additional Part of Tens list all about avoiding ten pitfalls of the application process at www.dummies.com/extras/gettingintomedicalschool.

In this part . . .

- ✔ Take stock of ten things to know about medical school. It'll be difficult yet fun!

- ✔ Decode ten terms used in medicine that aren't found in your textbooks.

Chapter 20

Ten Things to Know about Medical School

As a medical student, you have days when you wonder why you got yourself into this field in the first place and others when you actually find med school fun. When you start first year, you may doubt that you can possibly learn all the information you need to, and then, before you know it, you're off to do your clinical rotations as a third year. As you enter the realm of patient care, you feel like you've stepped into a separate world complete with its own language, rules, and hierarchy. To help you get ready to take on the challenge of med school, I use this chapter to give you a glimpse of what the experience is really like and arm you with strategies for surviving, and even enjoying, the next four years.

Your School Wants You to Succeed

Many students who start out as premedical in college switch tracks when they come up against the reality of classes like organic chemistry and physics. Even those who survive the prerequisite science courses may not do well enough in them to be admitted to med school or score competitively on the MCAT.

The result of premeds having to jump through so many hoops to be admitted to medical school is that the weeding out gets done before med school, not during it. Schools screen applicants very carefully in order to select individuals who are likely to succeed in medical school and who they believe will make good doctors. After students have started med school, the school's goal is for them to graduate, not to try to eliminate them from the program. Schools have support services in place for students who are struggling, and some even allow students a second chance by giving them the opportunity to repeat a year if needed. (See Chapter 19 for more about finding support in med school.)

It's Difficult

The fact that med school is difficult isn't an earth-shattering revelation, yet many students are still surprised by just how overwhelming the workload is. As an undergraduate, you probably had one or two nonscience classes each semester that you could neglect (to some degree) in order to focus on your science classes. However, your schedule during the first two years of medical school is almost entirely filled with intense courses like anatomy, physiology, neuroscience, biochemistry, and pharmacology. On top of all that, you're learning the basics of conducting a physical examination and taking a patient history in preparation for your clinical rotations. You may also be spending time working with a physician *preceptor* in her practice or learning in other clinical settings if your school integrates clinical exposure into the first two years of the program.

The *clinical* years (years three and four) are easier than the *preclinical* ones (years one and two) in some ways and harder in others. As a third- and fourth-year student, you spend almost all your time on the wards and in clinics with actual patients, which most med students find to be a big improvement over sitting in a classroom. However, even if you're no longer attending lectures, you're still absorbing vast amounts of information as you not only gain a knowledge base for each specialty, but also become familiar with the clinical aspects of the field. The learning curve during the clinical years is steep, because many of the things you're doing are going to be new to you. Even holding a retractor can be nerve-wracking when you've never done it before and the attending and senior resident are inches away watching your every move.

When you do feel overwhelmed, keep in mind that you've undergone intense scrutiny before achieving a place in med school. If you've made it this far, you have good reason to believe you've got what it takes to get through.

It's Fun

Medical school and *fun* are words that may not seem to belong together. However, despite the notorious workload associated with being a med student, going through med school can actually be an enjoyable experience (except maybe at exam time and on overnight call). During the clinical years, you get to work with patients, be part of the medical team, scrub in for surgeries, and see and do many of the things that attracted you to medicine in the first place. Even the first two years at most med schools involve some clinical experiences, and the course work is focused on subjects relevant to medicine. Overall, the tangible progress you make toward becoming a physician is exciting.

The social aspect of med school is another positive part of the experience. The foundations for many lifelong friendships, as well as a few marriages, are built during these years. Being surrounded by people who share your interests and are going through the same experience as you are creates a sense of belonging. Even studying can be reasonably enjoyable if you form a study group and build in some breaks to chat or make a coffee run. During clinical rotations, you sometimes luck out and have a good friend on the same service as you. Beyond the friendships you make with your classmates, you also have the opportunity to meet many different and interesting people — from residents and attendings to patients and their families.

You Start at the Bottom of the Hierarchy

Medicine is a tradition-bound profession. Even in an era when the lowest employee on the totem pole calls the CEO by her first name at some companies, you can plan on addressing all your attendings as "Doctor." However, hierarchy isn't just about honoring tradition; in medicine, you face the very real fact that you're dealing with emergencies and that sometimes things need to happen quickly. During these times, someone needs to call the shots, so establishing a chain of command has a practical purpose as well. By knowing who's who among the various players, you can walk into med school feeling less like a newbie. Here's a rundown from the top of the hierarchy at a teaching institution:

- The attending physician
- The fellows
- The residents
- The medical students

Seniority within each category matters as well. For example, a fourth-year resident is senior to a third-year resident, and a second-year fellow is a step up from a first-year fellow. As a third-year med student, you start out at the bottom of the hierarchy and advance one step each year.

During your clinical clerkships, you work closely with the interns (first-year residents) and junior residents on a day-to-day basis. If you can make life easier for either of these groups, do so. After you finish any tasks related to caring for the patients you've been assigned, ask the other members of the team whether you can do anything to help them out, such as looking up test results or gathering supplies they may need to do a procedure. The more-senior residents, chief resident, and the attending physician are responsible for a lot of the teaching you receive, and when it comes to getting recommendations for residency, you need to approach your attendings (who may seek input about your performance from other members of your team). The amount of interaction you have with the more senior members of the team varies a lot by program and specific rotation. If you're at a big teaching hospital, there are more layers between you and the attending; if you're at a community hospital without a residency program or fellowship program, you work directly with the attending.

Eat and Sleep When You Can

When you're on clinical rotations, even things that most people take for granted, like eating and sleeping, can present a challenge. This situation is especially true for surgery, when you may be trapped in the OR for hours, and ob-gyn, when a busy night in labor and delivery may keep your team on the go all night. Therefore, if you have the chance to eat, take it. The same goes for sleeping, going to the bathroom, or any other necessity. If the resident tells you to grab lunch or dinner, go do it even if you aren't quite ready to eat and would rather wait an hour. In an hour, you may be in the midst of a new admission or scrubbed in with the team for an emergency surgery. As for sleep, if you're on call overnight and things are very busy, you may not get the opportunity to even lie down. When you have the chance to rest, take it.

A final word of wisdom: Always go to the restroom before you go into the OR. You never know how long a surgery will take. Even a simple procedure can turn into a marathon if complications arise, and you don't want to have to deal with asking to scrub out if nature calls.

Nurses Can Make Your Life Easier — or Harder

Besides being the right thing to do, being polite and respectful to every member of the hospital staff, not just physicians, makes your life on the medical wards easier. You may notice an interesting pattern: The residents and med students who are respectful of nurses tend to have their sleep disrupted less frequently than the ones who are rude or dismissive to the nursing staff. The latter get paged for every little question or status update about their patients regardless of whether it's really necessary.

Nurses may not have medical degrees, but they're the ones spending most of the day with the patients and are often more experienced than the med students and even the residents. The input they provide about patients is valuable, so take their suggestions seriously. Nurses also know the ins and outs of the hospital, can fill you in on quirks of the system, and know how to get things done quickly (and where everything is). If you get to know the nurses, they may share their wisdom with you, which is good for both you and your patients.

You Change Your Mind about Your Specialty Many Times

You may enter medical school determined to be a pediatrician and emerge from it as a future trauma surgeon. Or perhaps you envision yourself as a psychiatrist someday but end up pursuing family practice. Even if you have a clear vision of what you want out of your career when you matriculate into med school, exposure to the various specialties may very well change your mind. Reading about a field, or even shadowing someone in it, isn't the same as being immersed in a specialty the way you are during your clinical rotations.

A minority of students fall in love with a field early on and never waver from their choices, but for most med students, the decision about what specialty to pick isn't quite so easy. Some find themselves with a new favorite every rotation: When they're on ob-gyn, they start planning a career delivering babies; during internal medicine, they're ready to commit to cardiology or gastroenterology. Others like certain aspects of several specialties but have a tough time pinning down a final choice.

Your third year required rotations expose you to the major specialties, while elective rotations and subinternships allow you to investigate more-specialized fields and to take a deeper look at some of the areas you've already encountered. In addition, talking to attendings about what their specialties are like provides you with the perspective of people who are out of training and are practicing. Finally, even if you have a favorite specialty when you start out, approach every rotation with an open mind; you may just find your niche in a field you hadn't even considered before.

Sometimes You Wonder Why You Went

When you're sitting in the library night after night or feeling groggy after a rough night on call, you may start to question your decision to become a doctor. Updates from friends who are collecting nice paychecks, taking trips, and enjoying evenings out on a regular basis may exacerbate any doubts you have about your chosen path.

Doing some second-guessing is common among medical students, especially during the first two years when contact with patients is limited. If your school doesn't offer much patient contact prior to the third year, find out about opportunities to volunteer through school-sponsored or outside health clinics. Volunteering may help remind you why you wanted to do this job in the first place and keep you motivated until you get to your clinical rotations third year. Talk to your classmates as well. Sharing your feelings and finding out you're not alone may help you cope with them.

If you're seriously doubting your desire to continue pursuing medicine, talk to your advisor or another mentor to get help sorting things out. Keep in mind, though, that having doubts doesn't necessarily mean that you're not suited to this career. The journey to becoming a doctor is a long and difficult one, and wondering at times about the road not taken is natural.

You Can Be a Medical Student and Still Have a Life

Being a medical student doesn't mean that you have to forgo all leisure time, give up your hobbies completely, and put your relationships on hold for the next four years. You'll be busy in medical school, but maintaining your life outside of school is still possible (and highly advisable). Although it may not feel like it, taking an hour to go work out or spending an evening hanging out with friends won't put your grades in mortal jeopardy. In fact, downtime helps to prevent burnout and may allow you to be more productive when you get back to the books.

Make a point to have at least one outside interest or hobby during med school. That diversion gives you something to focus on outside of academics and can be a potential outlet for stress.

On the relationship front, it's possible to date, be in a relationship, or be married during medical school. Some students even start a family during medical school or are already parents when they matriculate. Being in a relationship or having a family as a med student takes some flexibility and understanding on the parts of everyone involved, but you can make time for both your studies and your family life.

It Goes By Quickly

Before you know it, you'll be marching across a stage to accept your medical degree. Medical school may seem to fly by because with all the information to learn, skills to master, and clinical rotations to adjust to, you're so focused on getting through the next challenge that you're barely aware of the time passing. After you're in residency, your med school days may already start to seem distant as you take on new responsibilities. In the midst of your intern year, you may even look back at med school with nostalgia and think about how easy you had it back then!

Chapter 21

Ten Terms You Won't Find in Your Medical School Textbooks

In This Chapter

▶ Understanding med school lingo

▶ Deciphering slang terms you hear in medicine

*I*n medical school, you hear so many unfamiliar terms flying around, especially on the hospital wards, that you may start to feel like medicine has its own language. In a way, you're right; however, though definitions for words such as *cholecystectomy* and *glioblastoma* are conveniently located in a medical dictionary and in your textbooks, you won't find translations for the many slang terms used by physicians in those sources. This chapter is a guide to some of the unofficial terminology in medicine so that you're in the know when the attending mentions a zebra on rounds, or a fourth-year med student complains to you about getting scutted by the resident that day.

Zebra

"When you hear hoofbeats, think horses, not zebras," is a common saying in medicine. The idea here is that the most common diagnosis that explains a set of findings in a patient is the one you should consider first. A *zebra* refers to a rare diagnosis, which med students are known to favor over more garden-variety ones. Make sure you don't overlook the rare entities entirely, though, because every once in a while the hoofbeats you hear actually *are* from a zebra.

Gunner

Gunner refers to a med student who is bent on getting the highest grade and looking good in front of faculty no matter what it takes. Gunners do all of the required *and* recommended reading. They blurt out answers to the attending's questions on rounds, even if the question was directed at another student. They make it their mission to dominate discussion sections and are either oblivious to or don't care about the fact that they're annoying their peers (and often the faculty). Every medical school has a few gunners, and you'll probably be able identify the ones in your class by the end of the first week.

Scut

Scut or *scutwork* is menial work that med students are assigned to do during clinical rotations. These duties usually don't involve patient contact and have little or no learning value. A few examples are tracking down lab results or radiographs, getting coffee for senior members of the team, and transporting specimens. The definition of scut varies; some students consider escorting patients down to radiology for imaging or doing blood draws to be scut; others say that any task that's part of patient care, no matter how basic, isn't scut.

Changes in attitude about medical education as well as electronic data storage have cut down on the amount of scut med students do. However, the tradition of scutting med students still lives on at some institutions.

Hit

A sentence such as "Last night was brutal; we had one hit after another" is likely to leave you baffled without proper translation. The key to understanding this statement is to know that a *hit* is an admission into the hospital. An admission requires taking a history and doing a physical examination, writing orders, checking test results, and performing the many other tasks it takes to get a new patient settled in. A night on the ward where you're slammed by hits means you may not get a minute of sleep, while a night with few or no admissions usually means at least a decent nap.

GI Rounds

Rounds involve discussing and visiting each patient on the service. During this time, the history, diagnosis, test results, and plan are mulled over and the attending or senior resident uses the cases as opportunities for teaching. Although rounds are a valuable part of the day, you may get tired of standing on your feet and being on constant alert in case you're asked a question by the attending. However, *GI rounds* are different. This term actually is a way of saying that the team is getting ready to head off to lunch or dinner.

Of course, if you're rotating on the gastroenterology service, "GI rounds" may mean the real thing, so check before you race to the cafeteria!

White Cloud

Good luck seems to follow some medical students and physicians. For these *white clouds,* admissions are light during call nights, diagnoses are straightforward, patients don't encounter complications, and discharges go off without a hitch. Some medical students seem to act as a white cloud for the entire team. The first day of his rotation coincides with a switch from nonstop activity to smooth sailing for everyone. The residents on the team may start to believe that the trend will hold up as long as the white cloud stays on the rotation, because even in a profession based on science, a bit of superstition still exists.

Black Cloud

In contrast to the white cloud in the preceding section, a *black cloud* is someone who seems to get constant admissions when he's on call, ends up with the most difficult and complex patients, and can't seem to catch a break. Don't despair if you're feeling like a black cloud, though, because your run of bad luck will eventually end and you may just be a white cloud on the next rotation.

404 Error

A *404 error* gets its name from the message that the server shows when a page can't be found on the Internet. This term has been co-opted by medicine: A physician who's digging for a lab result or a patient's medical record may say that he or she is "dealing with a 404 error" or "having a 404 moment." Now that many hospitals have switched to electronic medical records, information is much more easily accessible than in the days when charts were on paper, but data still goes missing sometimes. Not being able to locate the information you're looking for is especially frustrating if it's almost time for attending rounds!

Benign Rotation

A *benign rotation* is one in which the attending physician doesn't put students on the spot during rounds, the residents are friendly, and the overall environment is collegial. During a benign rotation, you may work hard, but finding time to grab a meal during your shift or get some rest on call isn't a major ordeal. Scutting is kept to a minimum. The residents remember what it's like to be a medical student, so they send you off to study or even to go home early if things are slow and there's nothing for you to help with.

The word *benign* isn't reserved for rotations; it also can be used to refer to residency programs that are known to treat their residents well.

Malignant Rotation

Every so often, you may end up on a *malignant rotation* that leaves you counting the days until you switch to the next service. The attending's idea of teaching is to ask medical students obscure questions in front of the rest of the team, and the residents seem perpetually cranky.

Sleep deprivation doesn't bring out the best in people, so you may be seeing the results of a program whose participants are overworked and stressed out. If you're interested in a specialty, don't let one malignant rotation dissuade you. Do an elective in the same field at another institution so that you have another experience to judge from. That same specialty may be enjoyable at another hospital with a different team.

Index

CME (continuing medical education), 28
COA (cost of attendance), 21–22, 298–299
COCA (Commission on Osteopathic College
    Accreditation), 251
college students. *See* premedical students
combined degree programs
    baccalaureate-MD program, 234–240
    MD-JD program, 248
    MD-MBA program, 248
    MD-MPH program, 248
    MD-PhD programs, 240–248
    osteopathic (DO) medical schools, 248
    overview, 18–19, 233
COMLEX-USA (Comprehensive Osteopathic
    Medical Licensing Examination), 29, 223
commercial letter service, 168–169
committee letters. *See* premedical committee
    letters
communication skills, 184
community clinics, 30
community college credit, policies about, 46
community hospitals, volunteering at, 54
community service, 60, 226
cost of medical school. *See also* financial aid
    budget, 299–301
    COA (cost of attendance), 298–299
    education expenses, 299–301
    international medical schools, 257
    living expenses, 300–301
    overview, 297–298
    researching schools by, 117–118
    sample budget for first year of medical
        school, 301
    working during medical school, 308
coursework
    for 2015 MCAT, 112
    overview, 12–13, 38
    planning your undergraduate, 44–47
    premedical coursework, completing or
        updating, 265–267
    recommended courses for medical school,
        46–47
    selecting smaller discussion-based courses,
        161
Critical Analysis and Reasoning Skills section
    (new section in 2015 MCAT), 111
critical thinking station in MMI, 182, 193

culture, school, 209
curriculum, researching medical schools by,
    118–119

• D •

difficulty of medical schools, 322
Direct Loans, 303–304
Direct Plus Loan, 304
Direct Unsubsidized Loan, 303–304
disabilities, applicants with, 21, 293–294
disadvantaged applicants, 21, 288–293
dual-degree programs. *See* combined degree
    programs

• E •

ECFMG (Educational Commission for Foreign
    Medical Graduates), 19, 259
EDP (early decision program), 80–81
education expenses as part of cost of medical
    school, 299–301
EFC (expected family contribution), 301–302
emotional well-being, 318
enrichment programs, 291–292
ethical scenarios station (MMI), 182, 193
evaluators, relationship with, 159–161
extracurriculars
    clinical experience, 53–57
    community service, 60
    DO medical school application, 231
    familiarity with medical field,
        demonstrating, 52–53
    joining clubs and organizations, 60–62
    not limiting your participation to one
        area, 64
    one position for extended time, choosing, 64
    outside interests, importance of, 53
    overview, 13
    paid employment as premedical student, 62
    prioritizing, 63–64
    research as, 57–60
    role in admissions process, 51–52
    shadowing physicians, 53, 55–56
    time management and, 62–64
    volunteering, 52–53